PRAISE FOR JONATHAN DAVIDSON, M.D., AND

THE ANXIETY BOOK

"Easy to read and filled with solutions ranging from spirituality to meditation to medication to a healthy diet. Authors Jonathan R. Davidson, M.D., and Henry Dreher explain the hows and whys of anxiety, how to recognize its components and how to treat it. It's peppered with real-life examples of people you may recognize in yourself and how they dealt with fear and anxiety."
—*The Dallas Morning News*

"A lay reader's guide on treating anxiety . . . Davidson successfully combines a self-help approach with his clinical experience, shining in his firm belief that within all anxiety sufferers lies the potential to control their disorder and regain an emotionally fulfilling life . . . a highly relevant choice."
—*Library Journal*

"There is no one better qualified than Jonathan Davidson to write such a book. Respected around the world, his work extends across the whole range of original research in psychiatry. He is a brilliant scholar and a true gentleman."
—*Randall D. Marshall, M.D., associate professor of clinical psychiatry, Columbia University College of Physicians and Surgeons, and director, Trauma Studies and Services, New York State Psychiatric Institute*

"Davidson sets a positive and compassionate tone throughout the text. . . . This is an excellent self-help resource."
—*Publishers Weekly*

"Dr. Davidson is unquestionably one of the foremost international leaders in the area of anxiety disorders and depression. What is most impressive in his body of work is its unmatched breadth, as it encompasses all anxiety and mood disorders."
—*Dr. Edna Foa, professor of clinical psychology in psychiatry, University of Pennsylvania, and director, Center for the Treatment and Study of Anxiety*

THE ANXIETY BOOK

Developing Strength in the Face of Fear

JONATHAN DAVIDSON, M.D.,
and Henry Dreher

RIVERHEAD BOOKS
NEW YORK

RIVERHEAD BOOKS
Published by The Berkley Publishing Group
A division of Penguin Group (USA) Inc.
375 Hudson Street
New York, New York 10014

Copyright © 2003 by Jonathan Davidson, M.D., and Henry Dreher
Cover photograph of the author © Duke University Medical Center,
Department of Photography
Cover design by Tom McKeveny
Book design by Victoria Kuskowski

First Riverhead hardcover edition: March 2003
First Riverhead trade paperback edition: February 2004
Riverhead trade paperback ISBN: 1-57322-376-X

The Library of Congress has catalogued the Riverhead hardcover edition as follows:

Davidson, Jonathan, date.
The anxiety book : developing strength in the face of fear / Jonathan Davidson
and Henry Dreher.
p.   cm.
Includes bibliographical references.
ISBN 1-57322-237-2
1. Anxiety.   2. Anxiety—Case studies.   I. Dreher, Henry.   II. Title.
BF575.A6D38   2003   2002031713
152.4'6—dc21

Printed in the United States of America

10   9   8   7   6   5   4   3   2

This book is dedicated to my family . . . especially to Julia Kathleen, in the hope that she and her generation will know more of peace and less of fear than we do in ours. —J.D.

For Sybil Leipow, Mike Dreher, and Jack and Deb Dreher. —H.D.

ACKNOWLEDGMENTS

"In contemplating our dangers with a disillusioned eye, I see great reason for intense vigilance and exertion, but not whatever for panic or despair."
—Winston Churchill, THEIR FINEST HOUR, 1941

The stories you will read in this book are stories of courage, drawn from people who have suffered devastating anxiety, and have learned to face, and gain control over, their all-consuming fears. Unappreciated by most of us, however, is the torment, isolation, shame, and stigma that go along with disordered anxiety. Mark Twain put it well when he said, "I have lived a terrible life, most of which has never happened." We can learn a great deal from the individual stories described in these pages; I know that I have been taught much by the many hundreds of patients whom I have been privileged to serve. *The Anxiety Book* is first and foremost a tribute to those who suffer from anxiety day in and day out, and to their courage in facing fear.

People follow their own pathways in coping with anxiety, but whichever one you choose, be sure that Winston Churchill said it right when he spoke of the "exertion" that is necessary to deal with danger, whether imagined or real. There is no "one size fits all" formula. Some create their own plans without professional input, some visit the clergy, others

Acknowledgments

see their family doctors, and so forth. Some hold to a biological view and seek medications. Others strive to develop heightened self-awareness, yet others make progress through cognitive therapy. My own bent and special interests have drawn me to examine the role played by medications, understanding that they have strengths and limitations. I hope *The Anxiety Book* will serve as a balanced, comprehensive, and helpful guide to the different approaches that are available.

Over the years, many have helped in my own professional growth and, in one way or another, this book owes them a debt. Important turning points include the wonderful opportunities given to me at the Durham Veterans Administration Medical Center and at Duke University Medical Center to establish treatment and research programs in posttraumatic stress and other anxiety disorders. Jesse Cavenar and Bernard Carroll are acknowledged for their critical support in this context. I am glad to acknowledge other colleagues, including Jerilyn Ross, James Ballenger, Edna Foa, Derek Gander, Elizabeth Robertson, David Raft, Michael Liebowitz, David Sheehan, Norman Rosenthal, David Spiegel (at Stanford), David Spiegel (in Boston), Peter Fisher, Steven Straus, David Reilly, Wayne Jonas, Nathalie Koether, Larry Dossey, and Jerry Cott. Closer to home are my colleagues at Duke, including Ranga Krishnan, Allen Frances, Robert Califf, John Fairbank, Kathryn Connor, Jill Compton, Frank Keefe, Tom Lynch, and Kishore Gadde. The accomplishments of our Anxiety and Traumatic Stress Program at Duke would have been much less had it not been for such a dedicated and skillful team of colleagues, including Rebecca Smith, Pat Segee, Rita Davison, Nabila Danish, and my administrative coordinator, Sharon Lloyd. This book owes much to them.

Jill Compton played a critical role and contributed generously in making it possible for us to represent and integrate psychotherapy as part of the overall management of anxiety. We especially acknowledge her sizable contribution. Should any blemishes be found in the picture we have painted, the responsibility is fully that of the authors.

At Penguin Putnam, the expert guiding hand of our editor, Amy Hertz, has greatly enhanced *The Anxiety Book*. Her assistant, Marc Haeringer, has been unfailingly helpful. I also thank Susan Petersen Kennedy for her enthusiasm for *The Anxiety Book*. And I am indebted to our agent, Janis Vallely, who helped make the project possible and who also contributed integrally to our book. My coauthor, Henry Dreher, has described far more skillfully, sensitively, and accurately than I could ever do the struggles, fears, and victories of those individuals who were kind enough to share with us what it meant for them to live with severe anxiety. I wish to express my profound gratitude to all those patients who were willing to give of their time and their hearts to make this book possible.

Especial thanks go to my wife, Meg, for her continuing encouragement and support throughout this project. She helps to keep me grounded, maintain my sense of priority, and thereby remind myself that some days at least, there is enough time before rushing to work, to take the dogs for a walk or go out together for a bagel.

—JONATHAN DAVIDSON, M.D.

I wish to join my coauthor in thanking Amy Hertz, our terrific editor, whose vision helped make this book possible, whose wise editorial guidance made it better, and whose support elevated the process. I, too, am indebted to our agent, Janis Vallely, whose shepherding of *The Anxiety Book* from conception to completion was as smart and sensitive as always, and whose friendship I value so greatly. I also thank Amy's assistant, Marc Haeringer, and our copy editor, Brenda Goldberg, for doing great jobs, and Susan Petersen Kennedy of Penguin Putnam for being an ardent supporter of this project. I'm grateful to my exceptional and always supportive transcriber, Terese Brown, and to Rachel Kranz for her invaluable assistance.

I wish to thank all of the patients from the Anxiety and Traumatic Stress Program at Duke University Medical Center who shared their stories with me, stories that were often harrowing and always moving. They inspired me both personally and in the writing of this book. I am also grateful to Jill Compton for brilliantly capturing the contribution of cognitive-behavioral therapies to helping people with severe anxiety.

My gratitude goes to my wife, Deborah Chiel, for her strong support and love throughout the writing of this book, and my daughter, Ava Rose Li Jia, for brightening my every day with her love and spirit. Finally, I thank Jonathan Davidson for being a wonderful partner in this process, and for his intellectual balance, perspicacity, and profound compassion for those suffering with anxiety.

—HENRY DREHER

CONTENTS

1

ANXIOUS? YOU'RE NOT ALONE

Do you have trouble focusing during the day or sleeping at night? Are you fraught with worry about your relationships, finances, work, and family life? Do you get little enjoyment out of life? Have a secret fear of being in groups of people? Can't get on a plane, do a presentation, or get through a thunderstorm? Are you irritable much of the time? Have you had a racing heart and fear that you'll die suddenly from a heart attack? Do you tremble, shake, have hot or cold sensations, get drenched in sweat when the pressure is on? Are you beset by other unexplained physical symptoms, such as dizziness, tingling, or muscle pains? Do minor physical symptoms trigger fears of deadly diseases? Do you constantly check the stove jets or the locks on your door before leaving the house? Has a traumatic event in your life left you raw-nerved, with frightening flashbacks or a feeling of numbness?

Perhaps you've complained to your physician, who implies that your symptoms are "all in your head." Maybe you've gone from doctor to doctor, searching for a physical explanation for your troubles. You may even have had an attack that propelled you to the emergency room, where doctors said there was nothing wrong and referred you to a cardiologist or neurologist. They were right if they told you it was a panic attack, but without further help you went home feeling just as anxious as you did when you arrived. You remain untreated, suffering in silence, feeling isolated and too fragile to handle life's ups and downs.

If you identify with any (or many) of these symptoms and scenarios, you're probably suffering from a startlingly common psychological condition—chronic anxiety. You're *not* a mutant, and you *don't* lack strength. Rather, you have an imbalance in your brain chemistry that leads to unhealthy forms of anxiety. If anxiety is the root of your problem, you're in good company: about one in every seven Americans is suffering from this disorder.

You don't have to live with chronic anxiety. And solving your problem doesn't require you to enter a drug-induced haze. I've been treating anxiety patients for over twenty-five years, and I've seen countless individuals metamorphose from paralysis to action, from isolation to engagement, from self-imposed home confinement to globe-trotting. I've learned that for people with crippling anxiety, anything is possible. You are not trapped; you are not alone; and you are not helpless. When you take charge of your healing, your exaggerated fears can gradually subside.

Why has anxiety struck you with such force? We can't say with absolute certainty. We do know that in some cases an overriding cause is childhood trauma. In others it's current stress, whereas in others it's a genetic inheritance. The vast majority of people with unhealthy anxiety, we believe, suffer from a brain chemistry imbalance. On the whole, chronic anxiety is due to a combination of factors, but the brain is always involved. Other influences, such as hormonal fluctuations (most common among women), and too much caffeine can make matters worse, causing further imbalances in brain chemistry. Ultimately, anxiety is probably caused by an interaction of psychological *and* biological factors, though which is primary remains a chicken-and-egg question. We do know one thing for certain: It's not your fault. Suffering from anxiety is like having high blood pressure or an injured leg: It's aggravating, but we now have the knowledge to successfully manage the problem.

THE RISING TIDE OF ANXIETY

Chronic anxiety is the most ubiquitous yet least recognized psychiatric condition in America today. At least 19 million Americans suffer from anxiety disorders—even more than those who suffer from depression. Research by the National Institute of Mental Health has shown that *anxiety is the number one mental health problem among American women and is second only to alcohol and drug abuse among men.* The most common forms of anxiety are: general anxiety, social anxiety (also called *social phobia*), posttraumatic stress, panic, specific phobias, and obsessive-compulsive disorder. Currently, more people visit doctors for anxiety than for colds.

Despite its widespread prevalence, anxiety disorders are among the least recognized and treated mental health conditions. Consider the statistics on social phobia: It afflicts over 10 million Americans, making it the most common anxiety disorder, yet it's woefully underdiagnosed. As a result of this "recognition gap," millions are left confused, hurting, and lacking proper treatment. One reason for the gap is that too many sufferers, ashamed of their symptoms, hide their anguish. But there are small signs of change, such as the "coming out" of celebrities with anxiety disorders, including Carly Simon, Chevy Chase, Oprah Winfrey, John Madden, Donny Osmond, Aretha Franklin, Ricky Williams, and Barbra Streisand.

Streisand, one of the great vocalists of recent times, was afflicted by such severe social anxiety that she stopped singing in public for twenty years. Football broadcaster John Madden was so phobic about flying that he took achingly long bus rides from game to game in far-flung cities across America. Phobias have vexed the famous and powerful across eras: Julius Caesar and Napoleon were both reportedly phobic about cats; Goethe treated his fear of heights with his own version of "exposure" therapy; while comedian Chevy Chase has admitted his abject fear of snakes.

Some authors have even labeled our time "the age of anxiety." In a December 2000 paper that analyzed pooled data on the severity of anxiety in population samples from the early 1950s to the early 1990s, the lead researcher found that anxiety levels have grown more severe over the past thirty to forty years. By the 1980s, otherwise normal children were scoring higher than child psychiatric patients from the 1950s.

Two major factors seem to explain this marked rise in anxiety. One is a loss of social connections, as our social fabric has become frayed by technological changes and the weakening of close-knit family and community ties. Another is the increase in "environmental threat"— violent crime and concerns about war, terrorism, and nuclear attack. Economic uncertainties, fueled by wild fluctuations on Wall Street and jitters on Main Street, must also contribute to the apparent epidemic of anxiety. Undeniably, the world in which we live plays a big part in whether or not we succumb to anxiety.

BAD TODAY, WORSE TOMORROW:
THE WAGES OF FEAR

Theresa was a worrier. She fretted constantly that she was doing badly in her job as creative consultant at an advertising firm. Everyone at the firm thought she was top-notch, but that didn't matter; she still worried that others viewed her as incompetent. For years, she got only three or four hours of sleep a night, because she'd awaken at 3:00 A.M. covered in perspiration and filled with dread. She couldn't get back to sleep, unable to turn off the movie in her mind, one that might have been titled *What Went Wrong Today . . . and What Will Go Wrong Tomorrow.* It ran every night with hourly screenings.

Theresa was an ultraperfectionist, so at work she worried that her projects weren't exceptional enough, and at home she worried that her housework was inferior. To make matters worse, one of her greatest anxieties was that she'd be discovered for what she was: a chronic worrier. So Theresa hid her fears, wanting to maintain a façade of competence and confidence, which caused her worrying self to feel trapped and isolated—even from her husband, Mark. On some level, Theresa knew that hiding her fears from the world didn't make them go away; it only made them worse.

Hiding her fearfulness intensified Theresa's inner tensions until she had trouble functioning. It got so bad that she left her job at the advertising agency. But quitting was only a stopgap solution for Theresa. Her stress levels eased for a while, but leaving her job only further damaged her self-esteem and soon she latched on to other worries.

When I first met her, Theresa had also become depressed. But it had taken courage for her to finally acknowledge her anxiety, because it cut against the grain of her need to appear strong. Theresa's shame and isolation in her own world of fear had prevented her from getting help and getting well.

Theresa is not alone. Generalized anxiety disorder, or GAD, is extremely common. People with GAD are prone to worrying about everything, hampering their ability to function and to feel joy. Theresa's anxiety was no sign of weakness on her part. It was not a failure of will, a character deficiency, or a punishment by God. While her anxiety was surely shaped by her upbringing and by current stresses, it was also influenced by two factors: her faulty thinking, which led her to see herself and her world through fear-tinted glasses, and an imbalance in her brain biochemistry. The good news was that both of these pivotal factors could be fundamentally changed.

I have devoted my career to understanding and helping people beset by anxiety, which includes the kind of global worrying that sullied Theresa's quality of life. I draw upon over two decades of research and clinical practice as a psychiatrist, and my experience as head of Duke's Anxiety and Traumatic Stress Disorders Program, to offer this message of hope to millions of sufferers: *You can treat and successfully manage anxiety. You no longer have to live in fear, shame, and isolation.*

Major leaps forward in treatment are the result of our deepening understanding of the biology of anxiety disorders—how the normal biochemistry of fear can go awry, and how we can correct the imbalances with medication and psychotherapy.

ANXIETY AND THE BRAIN: FEAR RUN AMOK

We all have a "fight or flight" stress response in which the *sympathetic* branch of our autonomic nervous system goes into high gear the moment our senses pick up danger in our nearby environment. Whether we encounter a raging animal in the wild or a mugger on a city street, our brain sends the "danger" signals spiraling through our system in a chemical cascade. Brain cells (neurons) start firing in a small cluster in the brain stem called the *locus ceruleus,* and in the almond-sized structure in the midbrain called the *amygdala.* The hypothalamus also sends hormonal messengers racing to the pituitary gland, which in turn signals the adrenal glands, shaped like three-cornered hats and sitting atop the kidneys, to pump out streams of stress hormones, including adrenaline and noradrenaline. These hormones cause our heart rate and blood pressure to spike, our breathing to quicken, and our blood to flow copiously to the muscles of our extremities—all so we can fight or flee the threat.

These evolutionary responses are entirely normal and healthy—as long as our systems return to a more quiescent state once the threat has passed. Fear and anxiety motivate us to protect ourselves and our loved ones from danger, solve our financial problems, take care of our health, better our relationships, and join with friends and neighbors to enhance the security and civility of our communities. Without a properly modulated sympathetic nervous system, we'd be rudderless in a world of risks and challenges.

Imagine what happens, though, when our internal security systems are so hypersensitive that they respond to all sorts of harmless stimuli as if they signaled danger. Our physiological alarm bells blare without surcease. With our systems on perpetual alert, our adrenal glands pulse out stress hormones, our hearts race all the time, and we're relentlessly fearful, jittery, and hypervigilant. Our indiscriminate and exceedingly touchy nervous systems leave us emotionally and physically exhausted. It's exactly like a home security system that's so hypersensitive it is set

7

off by mere gusts of wind. The police would arrive at the house ten times a day, and it wouldn't take long for them to become extremely testy and tired.

When you suffer from chronic anxiety, your internal police department, both biological and psychological, responds to false alarms every day, sometimes on an hourly basis. It's no wonder you become tired and irritable.

Why are your alarm bells so hair-trigger? The answer probably lies in other key brain structures, namely the *hippocampus* and the *amygdala,* which reside in the core of the limbic system ("the emotional brain") and which govern memory storage and emotions. Both the hippocampus and amygdala are hardwired to the hypothalamus, a command center of fight-or-flight responses. In other words, when you harbor fearful memories or associations, or for unknown reasons your limbic system is overreactive, then your emotional brain centers are trigger-happy—all too ready to dispatch fear messages to the brain's headquarters of your body's stress response. At the same time, your "thinking" brain (the cortex) is underactive and thereby unable to exert its normal checks and balances on the emotional brain.

But there's more. Just as your sympathetic nervous system is in overdrive, the brain chemicals responsible for modulating your emotional states are malfunctioning. These brain chemicals, called *neurotransmitters,* pass molecular information from one brain cell to another in the juncture known as the *synapse.* The messages relayed by the neurotransmitters from a brain cell to its next-door neighbor are the basic currency of emotional "information" in the brain. Brain scientists have identified three neurotransmitters as being critically involved in anxiety: serotonin, norepinephrine, and GABA (gamma-aminobutyric acid).

Broadly stated, norepinephrine mediates anxiety responses, while serotonin and GABA tend to quiet the stress response. Other neurotransmitters are involved in anxiety, but these three are pivotal.

In people with chronic anxiety, these three culprits may not be performing properly: They're overactive, deficient, or not making the right neuron-to-neuron connections. If neurotransmitters are the basic units of communication in the brain that keep our thoughts clear and moods stable, then what we have in chronic anxiety is clearly "a failure to communicate."

The failure of brain cells to properly communicate via the "language" of neurotransmitter molecules is a basic problem in both anxiety and depression. Psychiatric medications, psychotherapy, and other behavioral and cognitive modifications can restore the communication systems between brain cells that have become disordered. A highly choreographed dance that occurs in the synapse between brain cells determines whether cell-to-cell communication results in the proper transmission of GABA and serotonin. When there are enough GABA and serotonin "dancers" (neither too few nor too many of these molecular performers) and the dance is well choreographed, they connect with other dancers (receptor molecules on neighboring brain cells). These connections breed serenity and equilibrium in the whole mind-body system. With too few dancers (neurotransmitters) or lousy choreography (ineffective moves in the synapse), the connections are impoverished, and the result is unremitting fear, panic, phobias, or other anxiety disorders.

Our understanding of the biology of anxiety informs all our efforts to develop the best possible treatments, especially in the realm of medication. But there is increasing evidence that effective psychotherapy and the self-help strategies I set forth in this book may also balance and stabilize the sympathetic nervous system and neurotransmitters in ways that promote the healing of chronic anxiety.

PSYCHE AND SOUL IN THE ONSET OF ANXIETY

Let's not forget that we are more than the sum of our genes, brain cells, and neurotransmitters. The psyche (mind, soul) cannot simply be reduced to the actions of molecules in the gaps between our neurons. Our early life experiences, family relationships, and daily stresses play a role in whether we suffer from anxiety and how we suffer. The psychological contributors include early childhood experiences such as having parents who are overly critical, detached, and/or abusive or who "model" anxious behavior.

Parents are supposed to give children a realistic grasp of what to fear in their environment, how much to fear, and how to properly act on fear. But it's a fine-tuning job: Too little awareness of threats can leave kids vulnerable to trouble, but too much can leave them prone to anxiety disorders, many of which begin in early adolescence. A family that views the world as dramatically more unsafe than reality dictates is a breeding ground for anxiety. So is a family that insists on perfectionism (producing kids who are terrified of making mistakes), suppresses children's healthy expression of feelings, or quashes their ability to assert themselves.

We've learned that traumas can trigger disturbances in the brain that cause anxiety. In other words, every experience is both a psychological and biological event at one and the same time. A trauma, and its memory imprint in the brain, is an emotional *and* a chemical event. Why is it important to recognize this interconnection? The answer is pretty simple: When you suffer from anxiety, you often do well to address the biochemical imbalance with medication and the emotional imbalance with psychotherapy and the kinds of coping skills I offer in the healing program at the core of this book.

Your anxiety may not have clear-cut psychological causes, only biological ones. Is there a trauma or stressful conflict hidden in your subconscious that is causing your anxiety? You may never know. What matters most is that you can successfully transform your anxious worldview with the therapeutic methods I provide in this book, and you can rebalance your brain chemistry with medication. You can change both the beliefs and the biological dysfunction that ruin your quality of life. You can cultivate the strength to bounce back from stress and fear.

THE IMPACT OF SEPTEMBER 11

Recall the study that showed a marked rise in anxiety over recent decades, attributed to the gradual erosion of our social connections and an increase in environmental threats, violent crime, and the prospect or reality of war, among others. Since this study was completed in the mid-'90s, we've seen no obvious improvement in social connections, but there has been a significant drop in violent crime—a key marker of "environmental threat." This trend led the author of the paper, Jean Twenge of Case-Western Reserve University, to express optimism about the future of anxiety rates. However, more recently we've seen a whole new factor emerge in the anxiety equation: September 11, 2001.

In the months after the terrorist attacks in New York and Washington on 9/11, my colleagues and I have observed some worsening of symptoms among some people already diagnosed with anxiety. As a nation, our fragile collective feeling of invulnerability was shattered by these horrific events. They destroyed our illusion that we're immune on home turf or that massive terrorist attacks by foreign extremists only happen in other countries to other people. While anxiety was a fact of life before 9/11, those events, by piercing our shared sense of relative safety, have increased the prevalence of chronic fear and post-traumatic stress.

The role of September 11 in worsening anxiety was underscored in an illuminating study that was published in the *New England Journal of Medicine* in November 2001. Mark Schuster, M.D., and his colleagues at the Rand Corporation conducted a national survey of stress reactions after the terrorist attacks. Within three to five days of 9/11, the researchers interviewed a national sample of 560 adults about their reactions to the events. Close to half—44 percent—reported one or more "substantial symptoms of stress," while fully 90 percent reported some stress symptoms. Although people in New York had the highest rate of substantial stress reactions, others throughout the country, in communities large and small, reported high rates of significant stress.

"The psychological effects of the recent terrorism are unlikely to disappear soon," concluded the researchers. "Although studies of prior disasters suggest that stress reactions diminish over time in the vast majority of people who have had indirect exposure, the 9/11 attacks, the shocking televised images, and the profound ramifications are unprecedented . . . When people are anticipating disaster, their fears can worsen existing symptoms and cause new ones."

Like most Americans, I watched the television coverage of the 9/11 attacks and was horrified by the human devastation, shocked by the destruction of the World Trade towers. I recognized, as we all did, that our sense of safety and security had been undermined—perhaps forever. I wondered what this would mean for the psychological health of my patients and for the nation as a whole. Of course, our world has never been completely safe, but as Americans we've lived with the illusion that we are exempt from most external threats.

It's healthy to acknowledge that your world is not entirely safe. Yes, there are real dangers out there. But when you suffer from anxiety, you become preoccupied by imagined dangers, or you vastly overestimate the real ones. In other words, there are "outer" worlds of real danger and "inner" worlds of imagined danger. Those with chronic anxiety, consumed by inner worlds of imagined danger, see the world as dramatically more threatening than it really is.

If you've been fortunate enough to have been raised in a safe, secure environment and to have a balanced brain chemistry, then real events—terrorism, economic upheaval, the uncertainties of wartime—are less likely to throw you into a tailspin of perpetual anxiety. By contrast, if you grew up in an insecure environment and you have a biochemical susceptibility, you may be jolted by the realization that your world is not a thoroughly safe haven. This book's treatments and self-help strategies can help you manage your fears about an unstable world.

RECOGNIZING AND TREATING ANXIETY

What can you do if you're vulnerable to anxiety? Fortunately, hundreds of scientific studies have proven that you can manage anxiety by rebalancing your brain biochemistry and your perceptions of yourself and your world. In other words, you can feel safe again, even in an unsafe world.

Your goal is not to vanquish "normal" anxiety, an invaluable emotional signal that prepares you to face challenges in your environment.

When a coworker tries to undermine you at work so that he or she can get your job, anxiety keeps you on your feet, spurring you to action to protect yourself. When you walk down a dark side street in a big city late at night and you hear footsteps behind you, anxiety motivates you to head quickly toward the brightly lit and populated avenue.

Your goal should be to see your world truthfully, as a place that is mostly safe but that has its dangers. When you're beset by unhealthy anxiety, you see only danger lurking around every corner, so you spend countless waking hours ruminating, planning, hiding, or just plain suffering. With a healthy grasp of reality, you feel safe—unless or until you've perceived a clear and present danger. Then, with a real threat apparent—whether it's a drunk driver in the next lane, a potential mugger, a risky investment, a conniving friend, or a lump in your breast—you can take appropriate action. You're galvanized by appropriate fear rather than paralyzed by overwhelming terror.

There are many things we can worry about in the public arena: terrorist attacks, wars, violent crime, economic collapse. But most of us worry about everyday matters: money problems, illness, performing in public, personal rejection, professional failure, germs, driving over bridges, car accidents, plane crashes, snakes, spiders, or angry dogs. If your fears have a kernel of reality to them, pay attention to that kernel. When you have serious money problems, you must manage them. If you visit a patient with a communicable disease, you may need to wear a mask. And there's no good reason to pet an angry pit bull.

But when you suffer with anxiety, you're not taking sensible precautions; you're responding inappropriately to daily challenges. A job assignment becomes an opportunity for professional disaster. A yearly checkup at the doctor becomes a painfully tense confrontation with your own mortality. A party becomes an obstacle course in which your main goal is to avoid humiliation.

What if you're not sure whether you have unhealthy anxiety? I suggest that you consider that critical distinction between *healthy* and *unhealthy* anxiety. When I say "healthy anxiety," I do mean healthy. Anxiety does more than protect you from imminent danger; it motivates you to perform at peak levels. In the early part of the twentieth century, Dr. Robert Yerkes and graduate student John Dodson developed a law relating anxiety to better performance. They found that a certain amount of anxiety prepares you for situations that call upon peak performance. For instance, if you're about to take an exam or to give an oral presentation, a modest degree of anxiety spurs you to more thoroughly prepare. But if you're riddled with anxiety, it hampers your performance. Some anxiety and arousal improves performance; excess anxiety harms performance.

Among the telltale signs of unhealthy anxiety are chronic fearfulness, difficulty concentrating, irritability, sleeplessness, obsessive thoughts, ritual behaviors, avoidance of normal work challenges or social situations, and physical symptoms, including muscle tension, tingling sensations, excess sweating, hot and cold flashes, and a pounding heart.

I have developed a simple diagnostic screening tool to help you determine whether or not you suffer from unhealthy anxiety. Use this questionnaire before you implement the healing anxiety program in the chapters on the five solutions. Then use it again a month later, three months later, then at the six-month mark. See whether your signs and symptoms of unhealthy anxiety change significantly as you follow your healing path.

DO YOU HAVE UNHEALTHY ANXIETY?

Ten Screening Questions:

1. Is a fear of being the center of attention a problem in your life?
2. Are you afraid to speak in front of people? Do you panic when your boss calls or get nervous when you have to go to a party alone?
3. Do you experience sudden attacks of terror or panic?
4. Do you have a difficult time getting onto an airplane? Being in open spaces, with animals? Do you have a hard time being on a balcony more than a few feet off the ground? Are these situations that others are comfortable with but seem difficult for you to handle?
5. Do you feel that paying your bills, taking care of yourself and/or your family, getting through your work have become more than you can handle?
6. Do you find it difficult to control your worries?
7. Are you troubled by persistent senseless thoughts or impulses that you try hard to resist?
8. Does the need to check on things, wash, or clean make it difficult for you to go to sleep at night, or make you late for work or appointments?
9. Do you have repeated painful memories or nightmares about a terrible event that occurred to you, such as violent assault or abuse, injury, or the death of someone close to you?
10. Do you try hard to avoid any reminders of that event?

If the answer to any of these questions is yes, then it is possible that you have unhealthy anxiety.

If you have any doubts about your anxiety, if it's distressing or interferes with your life, see a psychiatrist or psychologist for a proper evaluation. You should certainly see a mental health professional if you believe you have unhealthy anxiety. While I encourage self-recognition, I strongly recommend that you have your diagnosis confirmed by a psychiatrist or psychologist.

Though you should seek professional guidance, the core of this book is a healing program you can initiate and maintain on your own. I offer this as your personal guide to healing anxiety, largely because both my research and clinical experience bear out this truth: When you take the helm of your own recovery while at the same time getting the professional help you need, you have the best chance, finally, of freeing yourself from overwhelming fear.

THE ANXIETY SOLUTION: FIVE LEVELS OF HEALING

The program includes five levels, but you'll probably discover that some components are more pivotal than others to your recovery. These pivotal components differ from person to person: For some, it will be psychiatric or herbal medication, whereas for others it will be cognitive-behavioral therapy, which involves changing your fearful beliefs. I find that a *combination of elements* often generates a deeper and more lasting freedom from chronic anxiety. This integrated approach includes these five solutions:

1. *Change your fearful beliefs:* Your fearful thoughts, perceptions, and beliefs are primary causes of your unhealthy anxiety. Using what we call the *rational response exercise,* you can systematically restructure the thoughts that trigger your anxiety, panic, phobias, rituals, or posttraumatic stress. Rational response, which comes from cognitive-behavioral therapy (CBT), is a four-step exercise that enables you to dismantle your negative thoughts. For instance, if you worry relentlessly about life-

threatening diseases, use rational response to question your assumptions of ill health. You can marshal evidence of past false alarms when your worst fears were never realized, and use your doctor's recent clean bill of health to replace your fearful beliefs with more rational—and reassuring—ideas about your health.

2. *Vaccinate your anxious mind—exposure therapy:* Another key psychological technique (also derived from cognitive-behavioral therapy) is *exposure therapy.* Using this approach, you gradually "expose" yourself to the very triggers of your anxiety. Exposure is particularly useful for phobias, which involve irrational fears (e.g., of flying, crossing bridges, snakes, dogs, spiders, etc.) and the avoidance that results. For instance, if you're terrified of being alone in an elevator, you would start by looking at elevators coming and going, then standing in a stationary elevator with a friend ("support person"), then traveling up one floor with your friend, then traveling one floor without your friend, and so forth, until you're able to ride the elevator many floors by yourself. Exposure techniques enable you to tolerate your anxiety until it finally abates, as you recognize through experience that nothing bad will happen.

3. *Develop serenity skills:* You will learn self-help strategies that can help ease your anxiety, panic, phobias, obsessions, compulsions, and posttraumatic stress. The most important serenity skills are progressive muscle relaxation, visualization, mindfulness, and breathing exercises. Spiritual pursuits, whether they be organized religious affiliation, prayer, or simply belief in something larger than yourself, can also shift the dynamics of anxiety. There is a growing body of evidence that religious observance, prayer, and other spiritual practices can promote both physical and psychological health.

Another key to developing serenity is social support. When beset by anxiety, you may feel that no one could possibly fathom your inner experience. You can overcome your isolation (which only worsens your anxiety) by joining a group comprised of others with similar conditions. Even if you can't join such a group, you can turn to friends and family for emotional and spiritual succor.

4. *Medications:* In the past decade, there has been a revolution in the medical treatment of anxiety disorders. I will provide you with the latest information on state-of-the-art antianxiety medications, including the *selective serotonin reuptake inhibitors* (SSRIs), which include Prozac (fluoxetine) and its chemical brethren. The other main class of antianxiety drugs is the *benzodiazepines,* including Xanax (alprazolam) and Klonopin (clonazepam). Because they are both more effective and cause fewer side effects than older drugs, these medicines have dramatically advanced the treatment of anxiety. You will benefit most from antianxiety medications when you are fully informed and engaged in the decision-making process with your psychiatrist or physician. In the final analysis, you'll be drawing upon your own inner resources to manage your life.

5. *Diet, exercise, and herbs:* Along with transforming your behavior and attitude, you can undertake simple lifestyle changes that offer large dividends in managing your anxiety. In terms of diet, the key is to lower your intake of unhealthy fat and refined sugars while you increase your intake of whole foods: fresh fruits, grains, vegetables, and lower-fat protein sources. It's often essential to reduce or eliminate anxiety triggers like caffeine. A relatively simple exercise program that involves walking, swimming, or some aerobic activity several times a week can also do wonders to calm the mind.

In my work with anxiety patients, I have researched and prescribed herbal antianxiety medicines, primarily St.-John's-wort and kava. In some cases, you may turn to these or other herbal alternatives, particularly if you have a mild anxiety disorder or if you've consistently had problems with psychiatric medications. While these herbal medicines have some side effects, both are believed to have fewer negative effects than psychiatric drugs but are also less potent. Indeed, I led a recent multicenter trial of St.-John's-wort for treating depression that suggested that it may not be effective for moderately severe depression. (It might still be useful for mild depression and anxiety.) Homeopathic remedies may at times be helpful, although in most cases they are less effective than psychotropic drugs or herbal alternatives. Despite their limitations, I offer guidance on how and when to try herbal medicines for anxiety.

In recent years, I have found, both in my experience with patients and in some revealing research, that people who overcome anxiety through various healing solutions, including state-of-the-art anxiety medications, actually change in fundamental ways. Most important, I believe, they become more *resilient*—able to bounce back from life's inevitable stresses, losses, and challenges.

Psychiatrists are awfully good at testing, quantifying, and labeling all of the mental health disorders, but they're not as adept at studying the *healthy* traits and states—like resilience. I am as interested in mental *health* as I am in mental *disorder,* so when I found that patients in some of my studies were becoming enduringly more resilient, I felt it was something to investigate and understand more deeply. My colleague Kathryn Connor and I developed a self-test for resilience, which I present in Chapter 8: "Resilience: Life Beyond Anxiety." Use the resilience test to find out whether you possess this positive ability to "get up off the mat" in the aftermath of stress, trauma, or hardship. Take it before starting your healing program and then again a few months later—when you feel you've made progress managing your anxiety. See if there's been an improvement in your resilience after you've applied the healing solutions in this book.

Don't be surprised if, at first, you don't score high in resilience—undoubtedly you are reading this book because you suffer from a form of anxiety, which usually means you have a hard time handling certain kinds of stress. Know, however, that with a commitment to the healing solutions in this book, you can become more resilient as well as calmer and happier.

Recovering from anxiety requires real commitment, but it is a liberating process that restores meaning and pleasure to your life. Explore the five levels of healing in this book, and look within each chapter for specific guidance on how to tailor the methods to your particular form of anxiety. You'll find the help you need in each chapter. Get guidance from a psychiatrist, therapist, or family doctor. Turn to close friends and family for counsel and support, and consider joining a group of people with similar anxiety problems so you can discover firsthand that you're not alone. Know that you can transform your life from a daily battle with anxious preoccupations, paralyzing fears, and compulsive behaviors to a state of greater peace, creativity, energy, and joy.

2

THE FIVE FACES OF ANXIETY:

WHICH ONE IS MINE?

There are five primary forms of anxiety: generalized anxiety, panic, social anxiety, posttraumatic stress, and obsessive-compulsive disorder. These forms are like five different faces, each with its own specific manifestations and symptoms. But they share one thing: a sense of apprehension so powerful that a person's everyday ability to function is substantially compromised.

You may see yourself in one or more of the descriptions that follow. In this way you will find it easier to determine which form of anxiety afflicts you. You may suffer from just one or from several of the major types of anxiety, and you may also be depressed, since 40 to 50 percent of those with anxiety also have major depression. (Remember, though, that anxiety is more than a symptom of depression—it is a state unto itself.) Use the following overview of the five forms of anxiety to solidify your "self-diagnosis." After I describe the signs, symptoms, and causes of each form, I offer simple tests you can take to further determine whether you may suffer from that particular type of anxiety. Of course, I urge you to seek professional help—a psychiatrist, psychotherapist, or both—to confirm the correct diagnosis and to guide your treatment plan.

HOW MUCH WORRY IS TOO MUCH WORRY?

For fifteen years, Anita was the social director of a seaside hotel and conference center in South Carolina. Everyone who knew Anita was drawn to her upbeat personality and disarmingly brash sense of humor. She was a devoted wife and the mother of two children—Harry, eleven, and Jennifer, who'd just turned sixteen. She loved her job and was the kind of woman who had a multitude of friends from different social circles. Anita's life changed dramatically, however, when her husband, Jim, grabbed an opportunity to head a paper goods company in North Carolina. The move was an upheaval for the family, and within a few months, their stress was compounded by the fact that Jim's company folded. Anita and Jim handled their adversity well. They decided to build their own paper goods business, and in time they were back on their feet.

Within a year of the move, however, Anita developed symptoms of severe anxiety. As stressful as her life changes had been, she wasn't fretting about leaving her old home, job, and network of friends in South Carolina or even the pressures of their new business. The focus of Anita's anguish was one event: her sixteen-year-old daughter's acquisition of a driver's permit.

What for most parents would be mildly nerve-racking was, for Anita, a terrifying prospect. Jennifer would be on the road, driving by herself, and anything could happen. "As soon as Jennifer got her permit, I was suddenly hit by a feeling of total lack of control. Soon my kid was going to be driving alone, without me there to supervise. I

23

know I'm a control freak, but to me this was intolerable, because it had to do with her safety."

Anita's fantasies covered every worst-case scenario: Jennifer would be on the road by herself, late at night, and she'd get into a horrible accident. The "wrong kids" would end up in her car. Someone would give her "bad directions," and she'd wind up in a dangerous neighborhood. A "maniac" would see this young girl driving alone and trail her down a side street. Anita would try unsuccessfully to block out images of her daughter "lying on a street somewhere." "Every time Jennifer's car pulled out of our driveway," recalls Anita, "it was just gloom and doom. It got so bad that I couldn't function normally."

Anita understood that she could handle most situations, including the radical changes surrounding her family's move to North Carolina, as long as she could exert some control. But she had no influence over her daughter in a car. Anita also valued her children more than anything else in her life, which is why most of her worrying involved her kids. "When we lost the business, all we lost was 'stuff,'" she commented. "That's only money; that's only a job. But I could never replace my kids or the relationship I've developed with them."

Anita recognized that she needed help. Her worries about Jennifer were getting worse, and she was also starting to worry about bad things happening to her son, Harry. She was becoming increasingly irritable, and suffering migraine headaches and insomnia along with her anxiety. Anita's worsening symptoms finally led her to our anxiety program at Duke.

Anita had generalized anxiety disorder (GAD). People with GAD tend to worry about many different matters, the most common among them being finances, family relationships, job security, romantic rejection, health, and the well-being of loved ones. While Anita worried most about her kids, she ruminated about any situation in which she felt out of control, including her husband's health, car accidents, and, from her days as a social director, events she planned but could not attend, so "anything could go wrong." Anita was relieved just to know that she had a common—and treatable—condition. "It was the first time anyone said to me 'You know, you're not crazy.'"

Since her late teens, Anita had believed intuitively that she had a biochemical vulnerability to anxiety, but there were no "experts" available then to explain or validate her feeling. Once we confirmed her instincts and explained the biology of GAD, Anita's mind-set shifted from one of confusion and helplessness to one of optimism and empowerment. Any shred of shame evaporated. "I don't have any problem with having chronic anxiety," she said recently. "I have a problem that *other* people have a problem with my anxiety. Some people have diabetes; some people have disorders in other organs. Everyone has a weak spot in their body. My weak spot is in my brain. I believe that and I accept it."

Do I Have Generalized Anxiety?

Unlike Anita, many people never recognize they have generalized anxiety. For a long time, GAD has been the poor stepchild of anxiety problems: ignored, pooh-poohed, underreported, and underdiagnosed. Generalized anxiety has been neglected not only by patients themselves, but by primary-care doctors, psychiatrists, psychologists, and research scientists. There are many reasons why general anxiety sufferers have not gotten the attention and care they deserve. When researchers first proposed the existence of generalized anxiety disorder, it was a diagnosis of last resort. If you were anxious but didn't have panic attacks, phobias, obsessions, compulsions, or posttraumatic stress, well, then, you had "generalized anxiety." GAD was little more than a grab-bag diagnosis.

In the late 1980s and early '90s, psychiatrists began to take GAD more seriously, establishing simpler criteria for its diagnosis, while beginning to research its psychological and biological underpinnings. It was no longer considered a diagnosis of last resort but a true clinical problem with its own specific symptoms and causes. While we understand this condition much better today, the medical profession and the public alike still need to know more about GAD, because it causes untold distress and still isn't sufficiently diagnosed or adequately treated.

Do you have GAD? Start with a simple question: Am I a chronic worrier, meaning that I worry incessantly, day in and day out? Then narrow it down a bit more. Consider these two key questions: Can I control my worrying? Do I worry about a number of issues and problems, not just one? From there, ask yourself whether you have any of the following six symptoms:

1. Am I usually restless, keyed up, or on edge?
2. Do I tire very easily?
3. Do I have trouble concentrating? Does my mind easily go blank?
4. Am I irritable much of the time?
5. Do I have a lot of muscular tension and aches or pains caused by this tension?
6. Do I have trouble falling and staying asleep? Is my sleep very restless?

Technically, you have GAD if you experience at least three of these six symptoms, if they are relatively persistent (they trouble you a lot of the time, not just occasionally); if they impair your ability to function or to feel good; and they've lasted six months or more.

This list can help you and your doctor determine whether or not you have GAD, but the most important inventory may be the one you take of what lies within. Only you know whether you spend mountains of time worrying, whether those worries are exaggerated, and whether anxiety affects your capacity for work, relationships, creativity, pleasure, and growth. Only you know whether your worries make you irritable, so much so that your family members or friends remark upon how irascible, jumpy, erratic, or moody you seem. Only you know if your relationships have become strained by your fearfulness or testiness. Only you know if chronic anxiety is causing you to avoid life's challenges and if this avoidance is hampering your success at work or in other creative pursuits.

For some of you, you'll be the last one to know you have such anxiety problems, so keep an open mind, as best you can, when asking yourself these hard questions. (It's in the nature of anxiety that you are often unaware of your anxious tendencies. You just know that you feel lousy and nervous much of the time.) Let's say, for instance, that whenever you take a school exam you're convinced you have failed. But if you've never before failed an exam, your anxiety is probably unfounded. Or perhaps you're a woman who worries that you have ovarian cancer whenever you experience low back pain, because you read in a magazine that it can be an early symptom. But if you have no family history of this dreaded disease and your back pain is nothing new, here again, your anxiety is probably unjustified.

To make this process of self-assessment more concrete, take the GAD test I provide at the end of this section. It will help you determine whether your chronic fears cross the line from "normal" worrying into a generalized anxiety condition that requires treatment.

Anxious Mind, Anxious Body

The odds that anyone will develop GAD in his or her lifetime is about 5 percent. (Translated, this means that up to 14 million Americans alive today either have or will develop GAD.) Recent statistics suggest that 4 million Americans currently suffer from generalized anxiety. By one estimate, GAD is the fifth most common diagnosis among patients who make visits to their primary-care doctor. The rate of GAD is about 60 percent higher among women than among men, and we don't understand the reasons for this gender discrepancy. Generalized anxiety disorder is a persistent condition that doesn't usually go away by itself. Some doctors and researchers view GAD as a chronic disease not unlike high blood pressure or diabetes. The good news is that it's a treatable, manageable condition—as long as you recognize it and pursue an established healing program.

If you have GAD, you may also have other related problems. As many as 90 percent of people who develop GAD also have another psychiatric condition. Over 40 percent will be clinically depressed at some time in their lives—often at the same time they suffer from anxiety. We often observe other psychiatric conditions among GAD patients, including social anxiety, specific phobias, and panic disorder. Alcoholism and drug abuse are more prevalent among people with GAD. Many of these addictions to alcohol and drugs stem from biochemical imbalances related to anxiety, possibly genetic factors, and misguided efforts to anesthetize anxious feelings and the depression often associated with them. And people with GAD sometimes have *hypochondriasis:* They worry that every physical symptom is the harbinger of life-threatening disease. Hypochondriasis is not uncommon among anxious people, especially considering the fact that they tend to experience many physical symptoms to begin with.

If you suffer from GAD, your body suffers with you. You're irritable or lethargic, restless or unfocused, jazzed up or run-down. Signs of an overactive sympathetic nervous system include profuse sweating, palpitations, and cold, clammy hands. You may experience chronic muscular tension and psychosomatic symptoms—real aches, pains, or other physical conditions caused or worsened by stress. Other common symptoms include headaches, low back pain, irritable bowel syndrome, stomach distress, muscle tenderness and joint pain. Many GAD patients get trapped in vicious cycles of physical conditions, which cause them to worry more and to make frequent and increasingly frustrating trips to the doctor. You don't have to experience all these signs or symptoms to have GAD, just some of them.

Insomnia is among the most prevalent of symptoms. You either have trouble getting to sleep because you're so keyed up, awaken in the middle of the night full of worry, or wake up too early and can't get back to sleep because you're drowning in a stream of negative thoughts.

Despite these symptoms, people with GAD are prone to ignore or deny their condition. You may say to yourself: "I'm just a nervous person"; "I have a lot to worry about"; "I'm not usually like this"; or "Look, I'm not hiding under the covers." Each of these statements may be partially true, but put your dismissals to the reality test. Everyone has worries, but you shouldn't spend a substantial part of your day worrying. In certain situations it's utterly normal to worry, but it's not normal to worry incessantly over things like vacation plans, routine work assignments, what others think about your accomplishments or looks, the ups and downs of your stock portfolio, your kids' well-being when they're in a reputable day-care program.

You may also worry too much about things worth worrying about: your family's health, your financial well-being, the safety of your family and fellow members of your community. These are real concerns, but you need not let them ruin your quality of life. Even if you're not huddled under the bedcovers, anxiety may still be eroding your ability to function and enjoy life. Telltale signs of excessive worry are those listed above: insomnia, restlessness, easy irritability or edginess, muscle tension, chronic pains or symptoms with no diagnosable cause, difficulty concentrating.

People with generalized anxiety usually come to our clinic when they're so distracted, edgy, forgetful, or grumpy that they simply aren't their "normal selves" anymore. They aren't getting their work done. Their colleagues or bosses aren't happy with their performance. Their spouses or partners have felt the brunt of their anxious irritability and have laid down the gauntlet: "You're impossible to live with; go do something about it." They are troubled by stubborn physical symptoms: the headaches, back pain, dizziness, fatigue, or stomach complaints that have plagued them for months or years. They usually come to our anxiety program out of desperation, seeking relief from their emotional and physical suffering. What they discover is that chronic anxiety is the root of their problem, one they've had for years or decades. Some studies indicate that people with generalized anxiety have had the condition, on average, *for at least seven years before they finally seek treatment.*

If you identify yourself with these symptoms and syndromes, don't wait seven years, or even one year, before you acknowledge your problem and get the support and treatment you need. Like every other established psychiatric condition, GAD is a biological disorder. You have no rational reason to be embarrassed or ashamed, and every rational reason to treat your condition, because the treatments work. Furthermore, when you combine several of the therapeutic strategies in this chapter, you stand an excellent chance of gaining mastery over your generalized anxiety.

THE PSYCHOLOGY AND BIOLOGY OF GAD

Theresa, the woman with general anxiety whose story I told in the last chapter, had a harsh religious upbringing that fueled her lifelong fearfulness. As a child, she was terrified that her parents would die, and she ruminated about the end of the world. As an adult, she worried about everything. No realm of Theresa's life—not her work, her friendships, her husband's health, her daughter's emotional state—was an anxiety-free zone. When I met Theresa, she strongly believed that her childhood experiences, which included ultrastrict parenting and ultraorthodox religious training, had directly contributed to her adult worrying. I'm sure she was right.

In many patients with GAD, it's impossible to deny the link between their anxiety and early life experiences, traumas, or recent stresses. While the evidence isn't overwhelming, it's very suggestive that psychological factors do play a causative role in GAD. Some studies indicate that people with GAD are more likely than others to have experienced loss or separation from a parent in early childhood. One large community sample demonstrated that people were at greater risk of developing GAD after stressful life events. A National Institute of Mental Health study of 2,900 subjects showed that men and women reporting one or more highly stressful or traumatic life events had a threefold risk of developing GAD.

Some psychological theorists believe that people with GAD have a hard time being assertive because of their internal conflicts and fear of rejection. Anxiety over rejection causes them to avoid others or become overly dependent upon others. Both avoidance and overdependence seriously hinder the chance for healthy relationships, which in turn makes them ever more anxious.

As with other anxiety conditions, there is some evidence that GAD is caused by genetic factors. GAD can run in families, but it's hard to say whether this increased risk can be explained by genes or by patterns of parental upbringing. One recent study of female twins raised in different homes did show genetics to be a greater risk factor than family upbringing. But these women were also at risk for depression, which suggests that in women, the genetic vulnerability for GAD and depression are united, and whether a woman goes on to develop one or the other probably depends on family environment and other social influences. The jury is still out, but if there's a genetic factor in GAD, it is probably quite modest.

What about the biology of GAD? We are learning more each year. In Chapter 1, we learned that people who suffer from anxiety frequently have an imbalance of three key neurotransmitters—GABA, noradrenaline, and serotonin—and that all three are involved in GAD. You may recall that the neurotransmitter GABA stimulates the so-called benzodiazepine receptors on brain cells. These receptors are "turned on" by Valium and Xanax (benzodiazepine drugs), which are both effective in treating anxiety. When these receptors are not sufficiently sensitive to our brain's natural calming chemicals, or when there is a lack of the receptors themselves, a person is vulnerable to anxiety. This appears to be a factor in people with generalized anxiety.

In people with GAD, the responses of receptors for noradrenaline, another neurotransmitter involved in anxiety, are blunted. Why? One theory is that chronic worriers have high levels of circulating stress hormones, including both adrenaline and noradrenaline, so their receptors for these hormones adjust downward, becoming less, well, receptive, a biological impairment that may contribute to chronic anxiety.

Serotonin is also relevant to GAD, though it has been less extensively studied. In people with GAD, some serotonin receptors may be overactive, whereas others may be diminished. GAD sufferers often require medications that restore equilibrium to an entire system that has spiraled out of whack, which may involve any or all of the three key neurotransmitters in anxiety.

TEST YOURSELF FOR GENERAL ANXIETY

Use this self-rating test to help determine whether or not you have GAD and, if so, whether your condition is mild, moderate, or severe. It's a simple but useful tool, one that can guide your decisions about treatment in tandem with a qualified professional.

GENERALIZED ANXIETY DISORDER (GAD) SELF-TEST

	NOT AT ALL	A LITTLE BIT	SOMEWHAT	VERY MUCH	EXTREMELY
I worry about things.	0	1	2	3	4
I feel restless or on edge.	0	1	2	3	4
It is difficult to control my worries.	0	1	2	3	4

	NOT AT ALL	A LITTLE BIT	SOMEWHAT	VERY MUCH	EXTREMELY
I am irritable or impatient.	0	1	2	3	4
I experience muscle tension in my back, neck, or shoulders.	0	1	2	3	4

SCORING KEY: 0–5   None–Minimal
6–10   Mild
11–15   Moderate
16–20   Severe

AFRAID OF PUBLIC SPEAKING?
NERVOUS IN SOCIAL SITUATIONS?

Isaiah, a software company executive, was just one year out of business school when he got his first corporate position. Six months into the job, his boss asked him to make a presentation to an important customer in front of a group of executives, mostly higher-ups in the company. Fourteen people were in the room when Isaiah got up to speak, and for the first time in his life, the fears he'd kept at bay throughout his college years emerged in him. (With a few rare exceptions, Isaiah had managed to avoid class presentations and other speaking situations.) Now there was no escape. He got up and tried to speak, started to shake and tremble, and was seized by embarrassment.

"I just stood there and tried to talk my way through it," recalls Isaiah. "I stumbled for ten minutes. I finally calmed down enough to wrap it up, but I think the people in the room were almost as embarrassed as I was." As his first social anxiety attack, the memory haunted

Isaiah for years to come. Whenever challenged to speak publicly, he would flash back on the physical sensations and punishing thoughts he experienced that first time as a twenty-three-year-old. Isaiah knew how everything could go wrong and how bad it would feel. He'd do anything to avoid the spotlight again.

Despite his obvious gifts—his business acumen and one-on-one skills with corporate clients—Isaiah was unable to make much headway in his career. His social anxiety has been an albatross he can't shake, causing him not only to sidestep speaking situations, but to shun opportunities to advance in the jobs he's held over the past twenty years.

"I was trying to progress, but I was also trying to avoid situations that would allow me to progress," said Isaiah, capturing the painful contradiction of living with social anxiety. Isaiah performed well as a consultant to software companies, but he managed to "turn down opportunities for promotion that would require me to be front and center." In one instance, Isaiah was offered a senior promotion at a large software company. "The one thing they wanted that I couldn't handle was to occasionally make presentations to the board of directors. I phoned them up and told them I didn't want the job. I just said it was for family reasons." It wasn't the first or last time Isaiah used the "family reasons" excuse.

Offered a solid position with a rising software firm, Isaiah moved from Nevada to the Raleigh/Durham area. But the same problems arose, and he knew he'd hit a wall. "I was fooling the system," said Isaiah, referring to the slippery way he managed to avoid speaking to groups. "But I was also fooling myself. I didn't want to run anymore. I decided I had had enough."

Isaiah suffered from social phobia, also known as social anxiety disorder, or SAD. He heard about our clinic, and when he consulted us, we recommended that he participate in one of our group therapy programs for people with social anxiety. His symptoms exemplify the problems encountered by those of you with social anxiety whose hopes and aspirations are often thwarted. Stories like Isaiah's lead me to suspect that the roots of social phobia often reach far back into your life, having originated in adolescence or early adulthood. Your symptoms undermine your ability to be whole and successful long before a full-blown condition ruins your ability to function.

Do You Have Social Anxiety?

We've all had nightmares of being in a social situation, usually at school, at work, at a party, or speaking in front of a large crowd, in which we utterly embarrass and humiliate ourselves. In these bad dreams, we stammer, sweat, make a monstrous mistake, say something silly, or look down to discover that we're wearing few if any clothes and that everyone is staring at us. We wake up, at first terrified by our humiliation, then relieved the moment we recognize it was just a dream. For some of you—one in six, to be exact—this experience is more than a nightmare; it's distressingly close to your waking reality.

Do you have an abiding fear of being humiliated or embarrassed in social circumstances? Do you become tremulous as you anticipate speaking or performing in front of groups? In these situations, are you desperately afraid of being judged as stupid, silly, awkward, or even crazy? Will you do anything to avoid crowds or public appearances? When you are in one of these dreaded situations, does your fear intensify to the point where you sweat, tremble, or stammer? Do you imagine that the people in your midst are judging you mercilessly?

If any of these descriptions hit home, you probably have social phobia, or SAD, an abject fear of one or more social situations, such as performing, speaking in public, making presentations at work, meeting new people, dating, attending parties or other social gatherings, eating in public, or using public restrooms. You may become especially anxious speaking to authority figures, or publicly disagreeing with others, say, in a work meeting. You don't have to be anxious in all these situations to have social phobia, just several of them. That said, some people have a more limited type of social phobia, often called *performance social anxiety,* in which their fears are limited to public performances or speeches. By contrast, those of you who fear a number of social situations are said to have "generalized" social anxiety. About two thirds of people with social phobia have the generalized type.

While it's considered a truism that anticipatory fear is worse than the actual feared circumstance, such is not the case when you have social phobia. When you're actually in the dreaded circumstance, it's every bit as terrifying as you imagined, if not more so. Your physical reactions are intense: In addition to shaking or stammering, you might feel pains in your gut, muscle tension, hot and cold flashes, or dry mouth.

Your anxiety is compounded by your fear of being "found out," and your physical symptoms make it more difficult to hide. The perspiration beads up on your forehead, and sweat stains that begin around your underarms spread across your shirt until it looks like you were caught in a rainstorm without an umbrella. Your social terror is further exacerbated by the thought: "They see how terrified I am, and they think I am _____." Fill in the blank with the word that best sums up your insecurities: incompetent, stupid, neurotic, wimpy, out of control, weak. The circuit of punishing thoughts and physical tensions rapidly heats up, until you either cool off or blow a fuse, in which case you retreat as fast as possible from the scene, whether it's a meeting, a date, a party, or a talk.

It's not widely known, but social phobia is the most prevalent form of chronic anxiety. People have roughly a 14 percent chance of developing social anxiety disorder during their lifetime, and 10 million Americans currently have this condition, making it our country's third most common psychiatric disorder. Roughly twice as many women as men develop SAD, which tends to show up in early adolescence. Still, people who seek treatment for this condition usually do so around age thirty—fully two decades after their symptoms first appear.

According to one study, the majority of people with social phobia never get *any* treatment. This is particularly tragic in view of the fact that so many people with social anxiety develop other psychiatric conditions, some of which could be prevented had they received early treatment—or treatment at all. In one community sample involving over thirteen thousand people, over half the people with SAD had other phobias. At some time in their lives, 17 percent suffered from major depression while another 12 percent had a milder form of depression called *dysthymia*. Fully one third reported alcohol or other substance abuse.

Social anxiety symptoms can range from mild to severe. On the mild side, you get anxious in a few defined situations, such as speaking to large groups. On the severe side, you experience disabling anxiety in a wide range of situations, from simple one-on-one encounters to public performances. Some people I treat for social anxiety can't make simple phone calls to meet basic needs. We see patients, for example, who are afraid to order pizza over the phone, fearing that they will make a verbal stumble and feel humiliated. Whether your SAD is severe or mild, it's worth treating, especially since the mild form can develop into a more devastating form.

Social anxiety disorder can decimate your hopes and dreams, but it doesn't have to. First, find out if you really have SAD. Determine whether you're simply shy or whether you have true social phobia. It's normal to feel some anxiety when you go on a first date, meet new employers or fellow workers, or present your work in classes or meetings. You won't need long-term therapy or medications for these common forms of trepidation. So how can you tell if you need help? Look for any one or several telltale signs:

1. Your anxiety is so intense that you're obsessively preoccupied with your fears.
2. You go to great lengths to avoid the social situations that trigger your anxiety.
3. Your work life and/or relationships suffer, because your avoidance leads to misunderstandings: Others may take your absences or quick exits to mean that you're disinterested, hostile, or unreliable, and some of your relationships may dwindle from sheer lack of tending. Many people with social phobia lose jobs or leave jobs because of their condition.

While these signs are good indicators of social phobia, take the social phobia test that follows to get an accurate read on whether your social fears cross the line from normal nervousness to chronic social anxiety that requires treatment.

THE PSYCHOLOGY AND BIOLOGY OF SAD

In his intriguing book, *Fears, Phobias, and Rituals,* British psychiatrist Isaac Marks looks to evolutionary theory and animal behavior to uncover the origins of social anxiety. People with SAD have a fear of being watched, an exaggeration of our normal sensitivity, present from infancy, to the eyes of others. It's why we feel discomfort when someone stares at us, a response apparent throughout the animal kingdom.

Staring evokes fear, and among animals of many species it's a tactic used to deter potential attackers. Marks describes the cuttlefish *(Sepia officinalis),* a species of squid that responds to the threat of attack by displaying on its back two black "eye" spots, which deter any would-be predator. Butterflies, birds, and mammals all respond to the image of two eyes with alarm, and many experiments have shown that paired circular designs resembling eyes provoke escape behavior in animals.

Of course, staring is not always frightening for humans, whether infants or adults. When we're an object of affection, we don't experience our loved one's gaze as a threat. It's all a matter of context: We shrink from the stare of a stranger in a strange environment, just as animals do, because our protective impulse kicks in. The fear of being watched is deeply ingrained in our biology, passed along via evolution because staring is one sign of dangerous intent. For reasons not fully understood, when we have social phobia our intrinsic discomfort when "being watched" is so out of proportion that we become overwhelmed whenever the social spotlight shines on us.

If Professor Marks's theory is right, other factors may trigger these exaggerated responses. Among the various possibilities is trauma, either in childhood or sometime prior to the onset of social anxiety symptoms. Psychiatrist Murray Stein and his colleagues at the University of California at San Diego found strong associations between childhood physical or sexual abuse and the development of unhealthy anxiety, including social phobia. People with these conditions were three times more likely to have suffered early abuse than others in a community sample. This association was strongest among women: 33 percent had experienced abuse, compared with only 8 percent in the community.

Sociologist W. J. Magee from the University of Toronto found that sexual abuse by a family member and verbal aggression between parents is a significant factor in the development of social anxiety. Sexual assault by a close relative was only a factor among women, and in these instances their SAD symptoms showed up before age twelve. Victims of incest are often (and wrongfully) blamed for their victimization and grow up with a heavy burden that transcends the pain and humiliation of the trauma itself. Having been conditioned to blame themselves for their own suffering, they become hypersensitive to blame, which is why they dread criticism in many social situations.

But trauma as extreme as sexual or physical abuse is not the only psychological contributor to social anxiety. Certain parenting styles favor the development of social phobia among children as they grow into adulthood. Australian researcher Gordon Parker compared the self-reports of patients with social phobia to those of controls, and found that the patients recalled their parents as more critical, less caring, and yet at the same time more overprotective.

The combination may seem unlikely: Would less caring parents also be overprotective? One Dutch researcher found that people with social phobia rated their mothers as less emotionally supportive and more overprotective than mothers from a normal control group, and likewise the fathers were considered less warm and more overprotective. In essence, his findings were identical to Parker's, suggesting that parents who are critical or cold but also smothering set up their children for social anxiety. Evidently, harsh judgment leaves its dark imprint on a child's consciousness, while parental overprotection conveys the message that the social world is a terribly unsafe place.

Do genes play a part in social anxiety? According to one study, generalized social anxiety (as opposed to performance anxiety) is approximately ten times more common among the close relatives of people already diagnosed with the condition. However, this research doesn't adequately tease out the contribution of genes versus social environment. Researchers from the Medical College of Virginia concluded from a study of over two thousand twins that there may be a modest genetic risk for social phobia, but that parenting, trauma, and other psychological factors are also critically involved. As with most psychiatric conditions, a complex interplay of genes and environment make an individual more or less susceptible.

Whether your social anxiety is caused by genes, upbringing, trauma, or a mix of all three, your condition has underpinnings in the brain. While these brain impairments are far from fully understood, mental health professionals are beginning to comprehend the abnormalities in people with social anxiety. As with several other types of anxiety, as well as depression, the causal signs point to an imbalance in how people process the neurotransmitter serotonin. Leading psychiatric researchers have found that patients with social anxiety have hypersensitive receptors for serotonin.

But the most intriguing research suggests that in people with social phobia the brain activity of the neurotransmitter dopamine is impaired. Using brain imaging techniques, researchers at Columbia University discovered that people with SAD have brain-cell receptors for dopamine that don't bind sufficiently to the neurotransmitter. (Proper connections between dopamine and its receptors are needed for balanced mood.) It's no accident that one of the most effective drugs for social anxiety is Nardil (phenelzine), a monoamine oxidase (MAO) inhibitor that boosts dopamine activity in the brain, restoring the neurotransmitter balance that prevents anxiety reactions.

In a study here at Duke, a team of researchers including Dr. Nicholas Potts and myself ran MRI scans of the brains of social phobia patients and compared them to those of control subjects with no psychiatric disorders. We found that a structure in the midbrain called the *putamen* shrank in size more rapidly with age in the people with social anxiety. What was the significance of our finding? The putamen is known to produce high levels of dopamine. Ours was the first brain imaging study to show that a dopamine-producing part of the brain could shrink in people with social phobia as they grow older.

We still have a great deal to learn about the biology of social anxiety. The fact that medications affecting serotonin—namely, the SSRIs—can be so effective in relieving symptoms suggests that serotonin is involved in SAD. Benzodiazepines can also relieve symptoms, which implies that the neurotransmitter GABA and its receptors are also disturbed in social anxiety. The biology of performance anxiety is a bit different from that of "generalized" social anxiety, because patients with performance anxiety respond somewhat better to beta-blockers, which quiet their hyperactive fight-or-flight response—the heart pounding, sweating, or trembling they experience when they perform. By contrast, beta-blockers are not usually effective for people with generalized social anxiety. Ultimately, we hope that the research on dopamine's role will lead to even better drug treatments, ones that correct the dopamine problem (and other imbalances) in people who suffer from social anxiety.

SELF-TEST FOR SOCIAL ANXIETY DISORDER (SAD)

Social Phobia Inventory

Please choose the answer that best describes how much the following problems have bothered you during the past week. Check only one box for each problem and be sure to answer all items. The SPIN Self-Test is intended for those who are 18 years of age or older.

	NOT AT ALL	A LITTLE BIT	SOMEWHAT	VERY MUCH	EXTREMELY
1. I am afraid of people in authority.	0	1	2	3	4
2. I am bothered by blushing in front of people.	0	1	2	3	4
3. Parties and social events scare me.	0	1	2	3	4
4. I avoid talking to people I don't know.	0	1	2	3	4
5. Being criticized scares me a lot.	0	1	2	3	4
6. Fear of embarrassment causes me to avoid doing things or speaking to people.	0	1	2	3	4
7. Sweating in front of people causes me distress.	0	1	2	3	4
8. I avoid going to parties.	0	1	2	3	4

	NOT AT ALL	A LITTLE BIT	SOMEWHAT	VERY MUCH	EXTREMELY
9. I avoid activities in which I am the center of attention.	0	1	2	3	4
10. Talking to strangers scares me.	0	1	2	3	4
11. I avoid having to give speeches.	0	1	2	3	4
12. I would do anything to avoid being criticized.	0	1	2	3	4
13. Heart palpitations bother me when I am around people.	0	1	2	3	4
14. I am afraid of doing things when people might be watching.	0	1	2	3	4
15. Being embarrassed or looking foolish are among my worst fears.	0	1	2	3	4
16. I avoid speaking to anyone in authority.	0	1	2	3	4
17. Trembling or shaking in front of others is distressing to me.	0	1	2	3	4

SCORING KEY: 0–17   None–Mild
18–34   Moderate
35–51   Severe
52–68   Extreme

FEAR AND TREMBLING:
PANIC ATTACKS

At age thirty-two, Martin seemed to have his life in good order. A former minister who'd been in the church for about five years, he'd spent the past year and a half working as a botanist, a challenging and satisfying career that to Martin represented the fulfillment of a childhood dream. Martin and his wife, Penny, had a four-year-old child and a new baby, whom they adored. And because Martin's new job was more lucrative than the ministry, Penny was able to stay home and be a full-time mother, an arrangement the couple had desired since Penny first became pregnant.

Yet Martin was also facing a number of stressful challenges that, taken together, proved to be overwhelming. Martin's father was suffering from advanced prostate cancer, and just as Martin was grappling with the latest bad news about his prognosis, he got a distressing call from his mother, who'd been diagnosed with cancer of the larynx and was about to have surgery. With two small children to care for, Martin couldn't even consider traveling cross-country to be with his mother, so that phone call would be the last time they ever spoke.

Both of Martin's parents died within the year. "I wanted my children to have healthy grandparents," he says as he remembers that time. But even before he lost his parents, he had to give up the vision he had cherished of himself, his parents, and his children all growing older together.

Besides the family losses, Martin was not as happy in his job as a botanist as he'd expected. Though it had been his childhood dream, he now realized that the ministry represented a more adult dream, an identity he'd grown into from his college days. Why, he wondered, should his wife be given the chance to fulfill herself as a stay-at-home mom at the cost of his own fulfillment in the ministry? And despite his sacrifice, there were still too many unpaid bills. So what was it all for?

Virtually without warning, Martin would feel overcome by intensifying bouts of anxiety, depression, and, eventually, panic. Over a six-week period, he went from feeling reasonably well to feeling completely overcome by unmanageable emotions. Once, playing golf, he became so disoriented that he felt weightless. Another time, as he shopped in the local grocery store, he felt wave after wave of discomfort flowing from his head down through his shoulders, back, and arms. And his skin began to flush and tingle, as though he were having a prickly hot flash. A month later, he experienced agonizing headaches, searing bouts of pain that descended on him without warning. He had aches and pains in his arms and legs, and severe cramps in his stomach. Martin began to suffer from insomnia, going virtually without sleep for four whole months.

Martin found all of his symptoms upsetting, not least because they came out of nowhere. But the most disturbing aspect of his new condition was the panic attacks, the sudden, intense buildup in tension that, while it lasted, seemed to promise that it would continue forever, followed by equally sudden and intense hot flashes that signified the tension's abrupt release.

Martin's self-concept was bound up in his idea of himself as a healthy person. After all, he'd been a minister for five years, a person charged with helping others to handle their emotional problems. But he gradually came to feel that he'd become an entirely different person. Once, he'd seen himself as being on an even keel. Of course, he felt anxious sometimes, but now he felt as though he'd become someone perpetually wired for anxiety and alarm. The smallest concern set him off like a hair trigger, and once he began to feel anxious, there seemed to be no end to his anxiety.

Martin found these bouts of panic so horrific that he began to dread them. Soon the panic itself was more upsetting than any of his real-life problems. The prospect of having a panic attack hung over him like a cloud of doom, and his fear of succumbing to panic would itself trigger a new panic attack. Within a few months, Martin felt utterly trapped by his own emotions—a state of affairs that lingered for over five years.

Recognizing that he needed help wasn't easy for Martin. He'd invested immense energy in hiding his condition from his wife and children, and in maintaining the semblance of normality with his colleagues. But no matter how hard he tried, everyone who knew him recognized that something was seriously wrong.

Finally, at the urging of his wife and friends, Martin began to research the various options for treatment in his local area. He discovered the anxiety program at Duke and contacted me. I diagnosed him with panic disorder, a form of anxiety in which a person is overcome by a terrifying array of physical and emotional symptoms. Among them are hot flashes or a freezing cold sensation, numbness or tingling in the extremities, shaking or trembling, a racing heart, sweating, nausea, and overwhelming feelings of dread, detachment, or unreality.

Martin had experienced most of these symptoms and learned that he was not alone: 2.4 million Americans currently suffer from panic disorder, and between 1.3 and 3.8 percent of the population will have this condition sometime during their lives. As with many other anxiety conditions, twice as many women as men are likely to have panic. Usually, people experience their first panic attacks in their early twenties. (It's rare for a true panic attack to occur in a child under the age of sixteen, or in an adult over the age of forty-five.)

People subject to severe panic may also experience chest pain, palpitations, shortness of breath, feelings of choking, nausea, and fear of losing control or losing their sanity. Nearly all panic sufferers experience the fear of dying in the midst of their attacks. Panic episodes begin abruptly, without warning, usually peaking within ten minutes and lasting for no longer than half an hour. People with panic interpret their immediate symptoms as sure signs that they are in danger of losing their lives, due to heart failure, choking, or a complete inability to breathe. People with panic tend to worry so much about potential attacks that they avoid any situation where they'd be unable to make a quick exit. This particular dread can lead to *agoraphobia,* the fear of being out in public.

Martin, at least, did not suffer from agoraphobia; yet he felt that his life had become severely constricted by his panic attacks. He came to feel so miserable that it was only through sheer force of will that he was able to survive. Only his commitment to his family, he felt, kept him from ending an existence that had become so oppressive.

As I took Martin's history, he realized that his panic attacks, apparently without origin, had in fact begun around age seven. Just as Martin's adult panic episodes came on without warning or apparent reason, so too had his childhood attacks. Martin recalled no specific circumstances that brought about his early panic attacks, only a pervasive feeling of terror. He raised the possibility that his condition was partly genetic, a suspicion I shared. He recalled that various family members were also prone to bouts of intense anxiety, a condition they masked with excessive drinking. Eventually, Martin recognized an arc from childhood through adolescence and young adulthood: seemingly minor bursts of anxiety that had mushroomed, over time, into unmanageable panic attacks.

When I educated Martin about panic disorder, he instantly felt relieved. I explained that once panic attacks begin, they become a cause and effect in themselves. While initially you may respond fearfully to a particular situation—the open spaces of a golf course, say, or the cramped quarters of a crowded convenience store—eventually the panic itself is your source of trepidation. Martin realized that he was suffering less from the fear of specific situations than from a free-floating anxiety about his own imminent panic attacks. "It feeds back on itself," was how he explained it. "Once these attacks become ingrained, you have a very difficult time not thinking about them. You get caught up in a vicious cycle, panicking about the panic."

Do You Have Panic Attacks?

Panic can be one of the most difficult anxiety disorders to self-diagnose. That's because the panic attacks that characterize the condition are triggered less by fears of specific situations or possibilities than by the fear of panic itself or, more precisely, by the fear of a panic attack.

This fear can take a number of forms. People who suffer from heart disease or asthma experience chest pains or shortness of breath brought on by their medical conditions. Whereas these medical conditions may indeed be life-threatening, panic attacks are not. In that sense, the self-perpetuating fear of a panic attack is irrational.

People with panic are usually terrified of losing control as well as being publicly humiliated. You might worry about being overcome by panic while driving, for example, causing a potentially fatal accident. It's not the driving itself you fear, but the possible loss of control. Or you might imagine having a panic attack in the middle of a crowded shopping center, terrified by the specter of losing control in front of hundreds of disapproving eyes.

Those of you with panic disorder may not be aware of the source of your panic. Like Martin, you may realize that you're frightened of your own fear, but you might also attribute your panic to surrounding circumstances. In fact, your real source of fear is panic itself and the prospect of humiliation or death in the midst of an attack. It's not driving, elevators, malls, or crowds of people that really frighten you.

Diagnosing panic is complicated by the fact that your condition is often associated with agoraphobia, the fear of situations you can't easily escape or of being stuck in places where it's difficult to obtain help. Settings likely to trigger an attack of agoraphobia include closed spaces such as elevators and tunnels, open spaces such as fields and bridges, crowded spaces such as stores and theaters, and vehicles such as trains, planes, automobiles, and buses. When you have panic disorder, you may experience panic and/or agoraphobia regardless of who is with you, or you feel safe only in the presence of a "safety person" who accompanies you.

Do you have true panic attacks? Take the panic test on page 56 to help make this determination. Also, simply ask yourself if you have regular or frequent episodes lasting up to a half hour that are characterized by intense fear accompanied by one or several of the following physical sensations and feelings: trembling, pain, nausea, dizziness, numbness, tingling, hot flashes, cold flashes, shortness of breath, a choking sensation, a sense of detachment or unreality, fears of losing sanity or losing control, or fears of dying.

Then, bearing in mind that many anxiety states may include panic, narrow it down a bit more. Ask yourself if you're basically *afraid of your own panic attacks*: Do you fear the sensations of panic itself? Do you worry that your attacks might lead to shame, humiliation, or even death? Or that your fear is related more to something outside yourself? Ask yourself, too, if you suffer from agoraphobia—the fear of being in spaces that you cannot control, spaces from which it's difficult to exit. To help clarify the contours of your fear, ask yourself:

1. Do I regularly avoid certain types of situations or places?
2. When I get a panic attack, do I fear I'm going to die?
3. Do I have a companion with whom I feel safe and without whom I refuse to visit certain places or engage in certain activities?
4. Do I sometimes wake up in the middle of the night in a panic?
5. Have I adapted to my fears by making accommodations such as living and working on a lower floor in order to avoid stairwells and elevators or shopping primarily by phone to avoid crowded stores?
6. Do I often use alcohol, drugs, or other medications to calm myself down?
7. Do I find ways to organize my life so as to avoid or to cope with my panic attacks?

If you answered yes to any of the above questions, you may have some version of panic disorder. Remember, just having panic attacks doesn't necessarily classify you as someone with a panic disorder. Many people have panic attacks a few times in their lives. And people with other types of anxiety may experience such attacks. The difference is that in other anxiety conditions, episodes are triggered by particular phobias, circumstances, or thoughts, rather than by panic itself. In true panic, the physical sensations of an impending attack—the familiar rapid breathing, tightening of the chest, pain around the heart, or sense of unreality—are your source of terror. You focus less on the perceived dangers of being in a wide-open space or being abandoned by a loved one than on your own out-of-control body.

Agoraphobia is most commonly associated with panic, although it occasionally occurs alone. People with agoraphobia can be afraid of open or unprotected spaces, because they occasion panic attacks and help may not be readily available. Likewise, a person with panic disorder may have no particular fear of being out in public. Often, though, people with panic come to fear the "outside world," because their attacks occur there. Whether the danger seems to be death itself (e.g., succumbing to a heart attack in a wide-open field with no way to phone a doctor) or the humiliation of publicly losing control (e.g., fainting in a crowded movie theater), fear of the panic attack becomes connected to fear of being away from home.

Because panic (with or without agoraphobia) can radically constrict your life, you have a high risk of also suffering from depression, as did Martin. Here, proper diagnosis is essential, because treating the depression alone, without treating the panic, and vice versa, is unlikely to be successful.

One striking symptom that plagues some people with panic is nighttime attacks that awaken them from a deep sleep in abject fear. These so-called nocturnal panics usually strike after 1:00 A.M. and between one and four hours from the time they go to sleep. Slightly more than half the people who have these attacks consider them more severe than the panic they experience during the day. Whereas daytime panic is brought on by subjective sensations of intensifying stress—the rapid breathing or familiar tightening of your chest—nighttime attacks occur suddenly while you're in a relaxed state, with lowered blood pressure, slower breathing, and a reduced heart rate.

Rate your panic disorder by taking the test on page 56, and if you believe you have genuine panic attacks, turn to the solutions chapters to learn how you can finally overcome your condition.

THE PSYCHOLOGY AND BIOLOGY OF PANIC

Martin, the minister turned botanist, had plenty of reasons to feel anxious. He was undergoing enormous stress from facing the loss of both parents, his dissatisfaction with his work life, and the difficulties of caring for two small children. Many patients with panic disorder report an overload of stressors piling up at about the time they begin to have attacks. Although they, like Martin, may have experienced panic before, it's only when the stress becomes unmanageable and the episodes more frequent that fear of the attacks triggers more attacks, creating a vicious cycle in which the person's own body and emotions feel like the enemy.

And, as with Martin, seeing themselves as the enemy is not a new feeling to those with panic disorder. The feelings of inadequacy, the inability to please others or to handle life's burdens, seem characteristic of those who suffer from panic, even though they are frequently viewed by others as supremely confident, helpful, and nurturing. As a minister, Martin was used to counseling others through their own stressful times, but it was difficult for him to acknowledge his own limits or his occasional need to lean on others. Martin's panic attacks may have partially been set off by the constraints of his own chosen roles. Martin recognized the ironic truth that he was a "super coper" who suffered from a disorder in which he'd temporarily "fall apart" and become increasingly terrified of the weakness and helplessness this revealed.

The psychological dimensions of panic, however, rest upon a strong biological foundation. There is a modest "genetic loading" for panic disorder and agoraphobia, so the condition may be partly explained by a genetic predisposition of the brain and body to respond in particular ways. People with panic also respond more sensitively than others to inhaling carbon dioxide, and may be particularly sensitive to sensations of suffocation.

But the most helpful biological explanation of panic disorder involves the body's means for regulating stress. As we've seen, when a person experiences high levels of stress, the noradrenaline and serotonin neuro-transmitter systems are engaged. One theory of panic disorder is that a range of trigger factors may overtax these systems, cuing our biochemical mechanisms to flood the body with stress hormones and neurotransmitters that carry the fight-or-flight message. The body becomes overly responsive to stress, and reacts in hair-trigger fashion to cues that would otherwise evoke only annoyance, mild dismay, or perhaps even idle curiosity.

Normally, for example, if someone feels slight chest pain, he may register the sensation and move on. The person with panic disorder, however, experiences the minor twinge of chest discomfort as if it were the disabling pain of a major heart attack. His nervous system reacts to a minor cue as though it were a major disaster. The body triggers itself to overreact, and the person whose body behaves in this manner learns to fear his or her own physical responses.

In some instances, people with panic do suffer from a cardiac condition known as mitral valve prolapse (MVP), a disorder of the heart's mitral valve that can produce dizziness and palpitations. If you have both MVP and panic disorder, you'll need to distinguish between genuine physical symptoms brought on by your cardiac condition and the similar symptoms induced by panic. You can also benefit by learning not to overanalyze your symptoms, recognizing that if MVP contributes to them—which some studies suggest—they are aggravating at worst but not potentially lethal. (It's exceedingly rare for MVP symptoms to herald a life-threatening condition.) But it's a hard task for those of you with panic, because an intrinsic part of your condition is profound fear of your own bodily sensations. Interestingly, in a 1992 study by researchers at Columbia University, medical treatment for panic disorder actually reduced the extent of the MVP abnormality as measured by echocardiograms. While this finding is not well understood, and has not yet been confirmed by other studies, it is another good reason to consider treating your panic if you also have mitral valve prolapse.

Certain psychiatric medications assist the body in resetting the brain's thermostat for stress reactions (see Chapter 6), thus restoring calmer physical responses to minor stressors. That's also why cognitive-behavioral therapy can be remarkably helpful, since it enables people to properly reframe their physical symptoms—the pounding heart or rapid breathing that triggers a full-blown attack—as relatively harmless.

TEST YOURSELF FOR PANIC

Use this self-rating test to help determine whether you have panic disorder and, if so, whether your condition is mild, moderate, or severe. Let the results guide your decisions about treatment, and have your diagnosis confirmed and treatment refined by a qualified professional.

PANIC DISORDER SELF-TEST

Have you been bothered by any of the following?:

	NOT AT ALL	A LITTLE BIT	SOMEWHAT	VERY MUCH	EXTREMELY
Sudden, unexpected attacks of panic	0	1	2	3	4
Dizzy spells	0	1	2	3	4
Feeling faint	0	1	2	3	4

	NOT AT ALL	A LITTLE BIT	SOMEWHAT	VERY MUCH	EXTREMELY
Trouble getting your breath	0	1	2	3	4
Avoiding places where you may feel panicky	0	1	2	3	4

SCORING KEY:
- 0–5 None–Minimal
- 6–10 Mild
- 11–15 Moderate
- 16–20 Severe

DO YOU SUFFER FROM POSTTRAUMATIC STRESS?

Tamara is thirty-five, and she's had nightmares for as long as she can remember. They were the kind of nightmares that startled her from sleep, forcing her out of bed to change because her pajamas were drenched in sweat. The lost hours of sleep left her exhausted during the day, disrupting her ability to work. Tamara's nightmares were always the same: They were snippets of events that occurred when she was a child between the ages of six and fifteen, when she witnessed constant, brutal beatings of her younger brother and sister by their stepfather. Tamara had been spared the physical abuse, but her emotional anguish was beyond measure, and it stayed with her for a quarter century.

Robert, forty-four, is a math teacher and high school basketball coach who, until recently, entertained fantasies of simply "disappearing" from his life. For the better part of two decades, he describes himself as having been "numb." His increasing disengagement only worsened until, he said, "it was an immense struggle just to get through the day." Robert had been divorced for twelve years and had a nine-year-old son, Ted, whom he dearly loved. But he stopped taking Ted on weekends because he was so ashamed of himself, so completely withdrawn from the stream of life. Robert traces his numbness and despair to a single event in college. He'd been a brilliant young basketball player on a scholarship when he was horribly injured in a freak accident. Robert collided with another player while jumping for a rebound, and his eye socket was crushed. The injury caused unsightly scars, badly compromised vision, and the death of his nearly lifelong dream of a professional basketball career.

Carolyn is twenty-one, and she can't concentrate on her college schoolwork. Worse still, she's irritable, jumpy, and reacts with extreme emotion to minor stresses and problems, responses that create a lot of problems in her relationships with friends and family. Carolyn finds herself avoiding certain circumstances, like being alone in a room with a teacher, or with any older male, for that matter. After she started psychotherapy for her symptoms, she traced them to sexual abuse by an uncle, which she endured from the ages of four to seven.

Tamara, Robert, and Carolyn suffer from posttraumatic stress disorder, or PTSD. At any given time, more than 13 million Americans suffer from PTSD, and the numbers may be greater due to underdiagnosis of the condition. An estimated 70 percent of adults in the United States have experienced a traumatic event at least once in their lives, and up to 20 percent of these people will go on to develop PTSD. Before September 11, 2001, national surveys showed that 5 percent of men and 10 percent of women had had PTSD at some time in their lives, making it the fourth most common psychiatric disorder in the

United States. Of all the searing traumas that can trigger the disorder, the one that appears to carry the highest risk of causing PTSD is rape.

The PTSD Diagnosis: Do I Really Have It?

In recent years, posttraumatic stress disorder (PTSD) has been in the news and in our national consciousness. We've finally developed a heightened awareness that traumatic events, such as rape, sexual or physical abuse in childhood, ongoing abusive relationships, physical assault, disasters, witnessing or being victimized by terrorist attacks, and wartime experiences, all have profound consequences for our psychological health and well-being.

Many of us never develop symptoms of PTSD, perhaps because we've had the social support and the coping resources to absorb and, ultimately, transcend the pain, grief, and anger of a trauma. Others, who have had fewer of these resources, or who have a genetic vulnerability, or who've been exposed to a particularly severe trauma, will develop posttraumatic stress. (Surely, the more horrific, life-threatening, or long-lasting the trauma, the greater the likelihood that any person will develop PTSD.) Often it arises in the immediate aftermath of a trauma, or more rarely, it develops years later, especially when our psychological defenses are strained by current stresses. An example of delayed-onset PTSD is that of the combat veteran who experiences symptoms later in life or when he or she retires, or following the death of a spouse or when facing declining physical health.

During the 1980s I spent five very fulfilling years working at the Durham Veterans Administration Medical Center, which is closely affiliated with Duke University Medical Center. Many of my patients were veterans of World War II, most of whom were in their sixties. A good number of my other clients, in their thirties or forties, had mostly seen action in Vietnam. I provided clinical care to many veterans who suffered from PTSD, men who had lived with the enduring feeling that the world around them was unsafe. Many had a chronic attitude of pessimism or even despair; they felt they had little control over their lives. They also had classic symptoms of PTSD: They often could not trust their feelings and impulses; they could be short-tempered, and they distanced themselves from others. These were often strong, tough men who were nevertheless strikingly fragile. They could be easily undone by the simplest reminders of their combat experiences. I'll always remember when President Ronald Reagan went to France for the fortieth anniversary of D-Day, because many of the World War II vets who watched the proceedings on television broke down in tears. They could barely cope with the memories and emotions that were so readily stirred up.

When the definition of PTSD was established by leading psychiatrists in 1980, the essential features had already been set out in literature going back to World War I. But in 1980, psychiatrists had in mind additional events such as the mass destruction of war, combat terrors, torture, atomic bombings, human-made disasters such as airplane crashes and auto accidents, and natural disasters, including earthquakes and hurricanes. More recently, our understanding of what constitutes a "traumatic stressor" has broadened to include the kinds of personal and family traumas that in previous decades were hardly discussed, such as sexual and physical abuse in childhood, incest, and rape. This cultural change has helped us all—the public as well as mental health professionals—to recognize that traumas are more common than we believed, and the long-term psychological damage they can cause is far greater than we'd ever imagined.

We've also come to realize that relatively "milder" traumas, such as long-term emotional abuse, the witnessing of a death or disaster, or the diagnosis of a serious illness, can lead to the same symptoms we observe in, say, a combat veteran. I believe that in most circumstances—even the aftermath of horrific traumas—we are "agents" who can choose to promote our own psychological healing processes. We can be remarkably resilient, even in the wake of an unspeakable catastrophe.

How do you know if you have PTSD? The disorder has three key sets of symptoms:

1. You constantly relive the trauma in the form of recurring memories, flashbacks, or nightmares (known as "reexperiencing" or "intrusive" symptoms);
2. You avoid feelings about the trauma, or situations that trigger those feelings, by becoming numb or detached (referred to as "avoidance" and "numbing" symptoms); and
3. You feel agitated, irritable, and quick off the trigger; have trouble concentrating or sleeping; are easily startled; and are on a state of "high alert" all the time (called "hyperarousal" symptoms).

Tamara, Robert, and Carolyn each exemplify these three-symptom complexes. Tamara's nightmares are an example of intrusive symptoms, in which a trauma survivor reexperiences traumatic events in the form of flashbacks, unwanted memories, or terrifying dreams. Such "reexperiencing" causes the person grave distress, often including physical symptoms such as palpitations, cold sweats, and shortness of breath. Robert's emotional withdrawal is an instance of avoidance and numbing. He took a virtual leave of absence from his life, finding little joy in his work while avoiding his young son. Looking back, Robert described his emotional state as "anesthetized." As you'd expect, avoidance and numbing make it extremely difficult for people to engage in meaningful relationships. Carolyn's irritability is an example of hyperarousal, the other common PTSD symptom. This set of symptoms involves emotional and physiological responses in which the person has trouble with irritability or anger, startles easily, has trouble sleeping, or is always "on watch."

Most PTSD patients possess all three types of symptoms to varying degrees. Tamara, Robert, and Carolyn were no exceptions; they evidenced each of these symptoms, though Tamara's most prominent problem was her intrusive nightmares, Robert's was his emotional anesthesia, and Carolyn's was her irritability. Most often, when you suffer from PTSD you live with the simultaneous presence of all three symptom complexes, moving back and forth between intrusive memories or dreams, avoidance and numbness, and a state of high anxiety or irritability. These symptoms are understandable: It's not easy to repress the memory of a painful, life-changing trauma, so it presses its way into your consciousness as a flashback or nightmare. At other times, you blot out the memory and the feelings it evokes by becoming numb. And sometimes, for some people, the sheer energy of bottled-up anger and fear makes you apprehensive, irascible, jumpy, or dazed.

When does PTSD appear? You may suffer acute stress in the days or weeks following a traumatic event, and in many instances, your stress reactions will resolve in time. PTSD occurs when your acute stress yields to chronic, persistent stress and the classic symptoms I have described. But PTSD can also have a "delayed onset" in about 5 percent of all cases, only appearing months or years after the trauma occurred.

PTSD is associated with a strikingly high prevalence of depression, substance abuse, panic, generalized anxiety, social phobia, suicidal tendencies, and even psychosis. Up to 50 percent of PTSD patients also have major depression, and many people with long-standing symptoms turn to alcohol, narcotics, or illegal drugs to deaden their psychological pain, a practice that leads to high rates of substance abuse and addiction. When you assess your own symptoms and consider your treatment options, I encourage you to acknowledge and seek help for all of your psychological and physical conditions.

PUBLIC EVENTS, PRIVATE TERRORS

Our society's increasing recognition of posttraumatic stress is a positive development. In many respects, the events of 9/11 enhanced our awareness of PTSD, and not only because we understood that the survivors, victims' families, and residents of Manhattan were directly or indirectly traumatized. Just watching the horrific events and feeling their tragic force was a source of stress, one that could leave a lasting mark. We now recognize that the 9/11 attacks caused a widespread rise of at least mild distress nationwide, and an increase in PTSD in downtown Manhattan and throughout New York City. As I mentioned in Chapter 1, the telephone survey of 560 adults throughout the United States that was conducted within a week of the tragedies found that 44 percent of all adults reported one or more "substantial symptoms of stress," while 90 percent had one or more symptoms to at least some degree. According to a survey of 1,008 Manhattan residents, published in the *New England Journal of Medicine,* 20 percent of those who lived downtown (near "ground zero") met the strict clinical criteria for PTSD.

An equally compelling survey was conducted in February and March of 2002 by public health researchers and psychologists, many from Columbia University, in conjunction with the U.S. Centers for Disease Control. About 8,300 of New York City's 1.1 million schoolchildren answered over one hundred survey questions about their reactions to the events of 9/11. The study found that 10.5 percent of children in the fourth through twelfth grades suffered from the classic symptoms of posttraumatic stress disorder. The researchers therefore estimated that 75,000 of the schoolchildren in these grades experienced PTSD symptoms after 9/11. Even more students—15 percent or well over 100,000—had agoraphobia, including fear of public places, especially riding in subways or other forms of public transportation. A summary of the study in the *New York Times* noted one finding that took researchers by surprise: ". . . the trauma wrought by September 11 appeared to be quite evenly dispersed through a large geographical area, not limited to the area near ground zero."

Given the massive media coverage and devastating TV images, it's no wonder that so many of us around the country, without personal knowledge of a single soul lost in the attacks, could feel profound loss for our fellow citizens who were killed, for the family members who lost loved ones, and even for ourselves, over the demise of our illusions that we life in a safe world.

The *New York Times* article on the schoolchildren study reported that people who had suffered previous trauma "were more likely to have mental health problems related to the terrorist attack." It's a phenomenon well known among PTSD researchers. For instance, a large group of Vietnam veterans first developed PTSD more than two decades after their traumas. What precipitated the onset of their symptoms? According to the veterans and their physicians, the answer was obvious: watching the Persian Gulf War on television. The war images triggered memories of their own searing combat experiences

The study of New York City schoolchildren also produced telling data on the prevalence of trauma. Among children in schools near ground zero, 51 percent said they had experienced a prior trauma.

Among children in schools in other neighborhoods, a stunning 64 percent reported at least one previous trauma.

Recognizing the prevalence of trauma moves us out of the realm of national catastrophe and into the realm of private terrors, the events we rarely disclose, the secrets we hold to our hearts because we're too ashamed, hurt, or frightened of the social or family repercussions to reveal them. Another national news story underscores this problem: the alleged sexual abuse by Catholic priests of children in their parishes—a story that broke in Boston in early 2002 and opened a Pandora's box of similar accounts from abuse victims in cities and towns across America.

The events in Boston, which began with the trial and conviction of one priest accused of abusing scores of boys, set off a firestorm of criticism of an institutional hierarchy that covered up the abuse. But coverage of these events also ripped away the veil of secrecy that surrounds sexual abuse and the trauma it inflicts on its young victims. (Before this scandal, open discussion of such traumas and their effects was still largely the province of daytime talk shows, not serious news programs.) Suddenly, we began to hear the anguished voices of adult men (most of the victims in this scandal were male) who came forward to reveal their traumas, probably because they sensed they would finally be taken seriously.

Many of these adult survivors reported, in heartbreaking detail, how the quality of their lives had been damaged if not destroyed by the early abuse and its consequences. Most victims undoubtedly experienced PTSD, at least to some extent. The crisis in the Catholic Church teaches us to be keenly, persistently aware of the short- and long-term effects of trauma on ourselves and others: the children we care for, the children down the street or down the hall, our friends and family members. When we ourselves have experienced trauma, we ought to bestow as much compassion on ourselves as we would on a trauma-tized loved one. One form of this self-compassion is to seek caring psychological, medical, and perhaps spiritual help.

PTSD can be successfully treated and sometimes even prevented. Our growing knowledge of the psychology and biology of PTSD is guiding the development of new medicines and therapeutic strategies. Among the most powerful approaches are imaginary exposure (see Chapter 4), a kind of "vaccination for the mind," and the new generation of anti-depressants (see Chapter 7). Whether your traumas are the result of private experiences or the impact of public events, including the on-going threat of terrorism, your PTSD symptoms are real, and you can treat them by engaging the five levels of healing I set forth in the solutions chapters of this book.

THE PSYCHOLOGY AND BIOLOGY OF PTSD

Of all the forms of anxiety, PTSD is the only one that by definition is caused by stressful life events. The diagnosis itself depends on a trauma having taken place. Not surprisingly, one of the challenges facing psychiatrists and psychologists is that patients with PTSD-like symptoms don't always remember the trauma, since they have often repressed the memory. Or if they do recall the trauma, they are too afraid or ashamed to disclose it to their doctors.

If you relate to these descriptions, ask yourself: Might I have experienced a trauma that I have banished from conscious memory? Have I had bad experience(s) that I've never thought of as "traumas" but that were so painful or scary they left an indelible mark on my psyche? If so, might they be related to my current symptoms or problems? Be willing to make this investigation.

The psychological contributors to PTSD might seem simple and self-evident: A trauma too painful to integrate makes its mark on your psyche and soul, causing changes in both the brain and body. The memory continues to reverberate, consciously or unconsciously, causing the spectrum of PTSD symptoms until it's either resolved or the chemical imbalance in the brain is remedied. While this is partly true, it leaves out one pivotal consideration: Many people who experience the same terrible traumas never develop PTSD. Thus, when we speak of "risk factors" for PTSD, the reality of having gone through a trauma and the severity of that trauma are not the only ones. Other elements—genetic, environmental, and psychological—determine whether you will develop PTSD in response to trauma.

We've begun to learn about the psychological factors that put a person at greater risk of PTSD. Among them are:

- A prior history of trauma, particularly of interpersonal violence
- Parents who also suffered from PTSD
- Other stresses occurring around the time of the trauma
- A history of sexual victimization
- A history of behavioral or psychological problems
- A family history of mental illness, especially anxiety, depression, psychosis, or antisocial behavior
- A lack of adequate social support

Consider whether you possess some or many of these risk factors. Your genes may also predispose you to particular psychobiological responses when you've been exposed to trauma. Just as people with a genetic predisposition to alcoholism do not respond to drinking the same way as others, those of you predisposed to PTSD are more likely to develop the classic symptoms than others. The research findings on genetic factors in PTSD are compelling but they aren't foolproof. These findings come from studies of twins, in which trauma survivors were shown to have a greater risk of PTSD when their twins also had PTSD, in comparison with people whose twin siblings never developed PTSD despite having experienced traumas.

The biology of PTSD is complex, but psychiatrists and neuroscientists are beginning to understand what happens in the brain (and body) during and after trauma. When we experience traumatic stress, our biological fear response involves multiple systems. "Fear central" in the brain, the almond-shaped amygdala, activates our circuitry of fear in response to a potential threat to life. Within milliseconds of a traumatic event, the amygdala stimulates the sympathetic nervous system as well as the HPA (hypothalamic–pituitary–adrenal) axis, which originates in the hypothalamus in the brain. These brain centers orchestrate surges of stress hormones, including adrenaline and noradrenaline, not to mention an entire cascade of neuropeptides and neurohormones that circulate through our brain–body systems. Our bodies are readied to fight or flee, with increased blood flow and blood sugar made available to our skeletal muscles so we can respond rapidly and vigorously to a threat.

While stress hormones prepare us for swift action, other systems suppress our stress responses so they don't spin out of control. In the aftermath of trauma, the time comes when we've either subdued or escaped the threat and our psychobiological systems must wind down, lest we become perpetually fearful, with a racing heart and suppressed immune system that can make us sick. A key nervous system hormone responsible for breaking our stress response is cortisol, which is also released during trauma. (Cortisol is a corticosteroid hormone with myriad effects on the body, including immune suppression.) Many studies have revealed that people with PTSD, including victims of rape or assault, have low levels of cortisol, and are unable to mount a sufficient cortisol response following stressful events.

According to one current theory, we need cortisol to keep our stress responses in check, to cool down the circuitry of fear long after the trauma is over. Thus the low cortisol levels of PTSD sufferers explain why their responses are out of proportion to minor events: It's as if they face the trauma all over again. They are easily startled, hypervigilant, and quick to anger. Simply said, they continue to react as if the original trauma is still occurring or about to occur.

What about the intrusive memories—the flashbacks and nightmares accompanied by physical symptoms such as sweating, heart palpitations, and panic? One theory is that the memory of the trauma has become associated with the raging release of stress hormones unchecked by cortisol. When stress hormones don't properly subside after the threat has passed, the memory of danger is exaggerated, because it's been "paired" in our systems with an overblown set of physiological responses. That's one reason the memory is easily triggered, repeatedly and for years afterward, with physical symptoms similar to those experienced when the trauma first occurred.

Research has also shown that in people with PTSD, the hippocampus—the brain's seat of memory—has actually shrunk in size. Scientists are studying this phenomenon, but it seems related to the memory impairments of PTSD: People either can't stop the intrusion of fragmented shards of memory, or they can't recover the memories at all. We also know many of the neurotransmitters implicated in anxiety malfunction in PTSD. These include serotonin, noradrenaline, and corticotropin releasing factor (CRF). These imbalances are undoubtedly involved in the spectrum of symptoms we observe in our PTSD patients.

Understanding the biology of PTSD is useful not only for psychiatrists and neuroscientists. It's just as important for those of you who suffer from PTSD, because you need to know that your condition does not reflect a character weakness or failing on your part. It results from a neurobiological impairment, one you neither wished nor willed into being. Genes, childhood events, and earlier stresses may contribute to your vulnerability, and none of these factors is your fault, either. Your symptoms result from a biological cascade of responses to terrible events in your life, and, with proper treatment, you can finally tone down the psychological and physical alarm bells set off months, years, or decades earlier.

TEST YOURSELF FOR PTSD

Now, take the following PTSD self-test, which covers the three primary types of symptoms. In addition to these symptoms the criteria for PTSD indicate that a trauma must have occurred and that your symptoms must persist for at least one month. If the test suggests that you have PTSD, the scoring key will help you determine if your symptoms are mild, moderate, or severe. Use your score to help guide your decisions about treatment, and have your diagnosis confirmed and treatment overseen by a qualified psychologist or psychiatrist.

POSTTRAUMATIC STRESS DISORDER SELF-TEST

In the past week . . .

	NOT AT ALL	A LITTLE BIT	MODERATELY	QUITE A LOT	VERY MUCH
How much have you been bothered by unwanted memories, nightmares, or reminders of the event?	0	1	2	3	4
How much effort have you made to avoid thinking about the event or doing things that remind you of what happened?	0	1	2	3	4
To what extent have you lost enjoyment for things, kept your distance from people, or found it difficult to experience feelings?	0	1	2	3	4
How much have you been bothered by poor sleep, poor concentration, jumpiness, irritability, or feeling watchful around you?	0	1	2	3	4

	NOT AT ALL	A LITTLE BIT	MODERATELY	QUITE A LOT	VERY MUCH
How much have the above symptoms interfered with your ability to work or carry out daily activities?	0	1	2	3	4
How much have the above symptoms interfered with your relationships with family or friends?	0	1	2	3	4

SCORING KEY: 0–6   None–Minimal
7–12   Mild
13–18 Moderate
19–24 Severe

HAMSTRUNG BY OBSESSIONS AND COMPULSIONS?

In the Academy Award–winning movie *As Good As It Gets,* the role of Melvin Udall is played by Jack Nicholson, whose performance is arguably popular culture's most famous attempt to depict obsessive-compulsive disorder, known both academically and colloquially as OCD. Nicholson brings plastic picnicware into his favorite coffee shop, where Helen Hunt is his (secretly beloved) waitress, because he's obsessive about the germs that might be present on silverware. He compulsively checks and rechecks the multiple locks on his New York City apartment door, and sways around the city's sidewalks to avoid cracks in the cement.

As Melvin, Nicholson gives a performance that is poignant, funny, and at times harrowing. In real life, for those who suffer with OCD, it's mostly harrowing. The obsessions and ritual compulsions that are its central symptoms are driven by an intense underlying fearfulness. OCD is so named because people who suffer from the condition either harbor obsessive thoughts, feel compelled to carry out certain rituals, or, most often, both. Indeed, in most cases, obsessive thoughts and compulsive behaviors go hand in hand. For instance, those of you who feel compelled to wash your hands thirty or forty times a day worry obsessively about germs—the thoughts drive the behaviors. When you check the stove endlessly, it's because you're frightened by images of the house burning down. In other words, your compulsions are efforts to reduce the anxiety generated by your obsessive worries. A minority of people with OCD suffer exclusively from obsessive thinking without the ritual behaviors.

If you have OCD, you are someone who may:

1. Ritualistically wash your hands, shower constantly, or clean and reclean your house or office on a daily basis because you have a dread of germs. These rituals represent an effort, albeit a misguided one, to gain control over threatening fears and feelings.
2. Repeatedly and obsessively check (e.g, the gas jets on a stove), count (e.g., the tiles on the ceiling), or repeat (e.g., various actions a certain number of times). This compulsive checking, counting, or repeating often makes it difficult if not impossible to leave home in a timely manner.
3. Compulsively maintain a specific order or pattern (e.g., Jack Nicholson's avoidance of cracks in the sidewalk), sometimes requiring symmetry (e.g., needing balance on both sides of a table setting) or the hoarding of objects.
4. Harbor private and perhaps terrifying obsessive fears of: germs or fires, losing control of your behavior, or catastrophic events such as sudden death, criminal or terrorist attacks, natural disasters, etc.

5. Feel hamstrung by pathological doubts, wondering constantly whether you said or did "the wrong thing," offended or hurt someone, remembered to check things (e.g., stove jets, door locks), or met various obligations.
6. Experience nagging fears that you'll lose control of your emotions, becoming aggressive, inappropriately sexual, or violent, even toward loved ones or family members.

Over 3 million Americans suffer from obsessions and ritual compulsions, or between 2 and 3 percent of the U.S. population, making it one of the top ten psychiatric problems in the country. Of course, OCD symptoms range from mild to extreme, and when you explore whether you have this condition, ask yourself whether you have a modest superstition, like checking the gas jets on your stove a few times before leaving the house, or a full-blown compulsion, like having to wash your hands forty times a day to ward off germs. The condition typically starts up when you're in your teens, but it can also begin in early adulthood. When severe, the ritual compulsions of OCD can completely disrupt your ability to function and cause a downward spiral of intense frustration and, often, depression.

When I met him, Lester, forty-one years old, had been suffering from OCD for twenty years. He traces his OCD to childhood fears about committing sins, but as an adult his anxieties took a different (but probably related) form. Lester traces his condition to one particular day in 1973, a time when he was under great pressure at work. He was changing the oil in his car, and when he pulled out the pan he found a dead mouse or two. As Lester got rid of the mice and cleaned the pan, he became convinced that he was now at risk for disease: His mind settled on plague, perhaps even bubonic plague. From that moment on, Lester felt he had to constantly wash everything—his hands, his body, his house, his office.

"I built up all of these rules about what it meant to be clean, and it's like building a castle," he said. The "rules" consisted of elaborate requirements for his washing rituals. Lester had to wash before doing anything and after doing anything. He had to wash any surface with which his hands came into contact—like his desk at work—if he hadn't washed his hands in the past ten minutes. "Once the structure is built, your anxiety might fluctuate, but the castle stays in place. You can't ever seem to knock it down. I'd spend three hours preparing to go to work, and once I got to work, I'd have to spend time washing my office: floors, office equipment, my desk, even my computer keyboard."

As with so many people beset by OCD, Lester's life was truly disrupted by his symptoms, and as you'll see in Chapter 4, he made a steadfast commitment to cognitive-behavioral methods in order to dismantle the structured rules and regulations (his "castle") behind his compulsive rituals. The rituals of OCD are difficult to break, because you come to believe that you can feel safe and secure only by keeping them up. The sheer complexity and tenacity of these rituals, the extent to which you may be willing to inconvenience yourself to maintain them, can make OCD difficult to treat.

One of my patients, Marcy, insisted that her husband change his clothes every time he came home, because he'd been out all day and who knew what contagion he'd been exposed to. Marcy ended up spending much of her time doing the laundry, sometimes redoing entire loads because she worried that the contamination had not been washed away. Another patient, Bernie, was a hoarder who never threw out any newspapers. A subscriber to both the *New York Times* and

Philadelphia Inquirer, he was afraid that he might lose some vital piece of information buried in an issue, so he piled them up in different corners of various rooms until the piles became like furniture—fixtures of his home. Bernie also hoarded aluminum cans for recycling, but he never managed to unload them, so they, too, piled up around the house. You might visualize Bernie as a dysfunctional loner in an urban tenement, but in fact he was a Hewlett-Packard executive, and his wife was none too happy about the state of their suburban home.

While OCD is sometimes quite difficult to treat, there is a body of research and clinical evidence to support the fact that you *can* heal your OCD and restore your sense of normalcy. One of the most helpful first steps you can take is to recognize that while you may *feel* crazy, you are *not* crazy. OCD is an anxiety disorder that sometimes involves bizarre thoughts and unusual behaviors, but it is not a form of mental breakdown. However, OCD can seriously hamper your quality of life, so it is therefore crucial that you get proper help and pursue your own healing. You can reclaim control of your life rather than be controlled by your obsessive thoughts and compulsive behaviors.

THE PSYCHOLOGY AND BIOLOGY OF OCD

Little is understood about the possible psychological causes of OCD, and it's often assumed that there are no psychological contributors, since the biological causes are far more apparent and better understood. However, some studies suggest that there is a greater occurrence of childhood trauma among sufferers of OCD than among nonsufferers. One recent study, conducted at a South African university and published in *Depression and Anxiety,* found that OCD patients reported significantly more childhood trauma and early emotional neglect than did a group of control subjects with no psychiatric disorders. This sort of evidence, in which patients look back and report on their childhoods, is not definitive, but it points to the possibility that early experiences may play a part in susceptibility to this form of chronic anxiety.

According to several twin studies, genes may also play a role. For instance, among 65 percent of identical twin pairs in which one has OCD, the other will also have OCD. This so-called concordance rate among fraternal twins, whose genes are not as similar, is only 15 percent. Overall, the research suggests that genes play a small but significant role in the risk of OCD. Also, some studies have shown that people suffering from head trauma have an increased risk of developing OCD.

We're beginning to ferret out the biology of OCD. We have mounting evidence that the metabolites of serotonin are abnormally altered in people with OCD, which probably explains why serotonin-active drugs, which enhance the neurotransmission of serotonin, can be quite effective in treating this condition. Indeed, one breakthrough in the treatment of OCD occurred when it became clear that the tricyclic antidepressant Anafranil (clomipramine) was effective in alleviating symptoms. Careful studies revealed that it was the drug's serotonin activity, and not its other neurotransmitter actions, that explained Anafranil's ability to bring about improvement in OCD patients.

Brain imaging studies have identified a specific circuit of brain structures that are overactive in people with OCD. These studies reveal increased metabolic activity in three interconnected portions of the brain—the *orbitofrontal cortex,* the *thalamus,* and the *caudate nuclei.* Interestingly, when OCD patients are successfully treated with SSRI drugs or behavior therapy, imaging studies document a reduction in blood flow and metabolic activity—in other words, a normalization—in these very brain structures, particularly the caudate nuclei. Most experts consider this strong evidence that overexcitement in these parts of the brain is partly responsible for the disorder.

TEST YOURSELF FOR OCD

Now, take the following obsessive-compulsive disorder (OCD) self-test, which covers the three primary types of symptoms. Use your score to help guide your decisions about treatment, and have your diagnosis confirmed and treatment overseen by a qualified psychologist or psychiatrist.

OBSESSIVE-COMPULSIVE DISORDER (OCD)—SELF-TEST

Troublesome thoughts keep bothering me about . . .

	NOT AT ALL	LESS THAN 1 HR/DAY	1–5 HRS/DAY	MORE THAN 5 HRS/DAY
1. dirt or contamination	0	1	2	3
2. harming others	0	1	2	3
3. sexual urges	0	1	2	3
4. hoarding things	0	1	2	3
5. blasphemy	0	1	2	3

I have to repeatedly perform certain actions concerned with . . .

1. cleaning or washing	0	1	2	3
2. tidying things	0	1	2	3
3. checking locks or appliances	0	1	2	3

	NOT AT ALL	LESS THAN 1 HR/DAY	1–5 HRS/DAY	MORE THAN 5 HRS/DAY
4. rereading	0	1	2	3
5. hoarding things	0	1	2	3

SCORING KEY: 0–10   None–Mild
                11–20   Moderate
                21–30   Severe

I've characterized the five faces of anxiety, describing the signs and symptoms, explaining the known causes, and giving you an opportunity to test yourself to find out, on a preliminary basis, what form(s) of anxiety you may suffer from. In the chapters that follow on five solutions, I explore the five levels of healing: changing your fearful beliefs; vaccination for the mind; serenity skills; medications and diet, exercise, and herbs. Based on what you've learned and discovered about yourself in this chapter, focus on the sections within each of these chapters that concern how you can apply that anxiety solution to your particular form, or forms, of anxiety. I offer tailored methods and medications clearly marked as subsections for each form of anxiety in each "Solutions" chapter.

You won't have to rigidly apply all five solutions to manage and overcome your anxiety. Frequently, one or two are crucial—say, changing your beliefs or taking medication—yet other methods also can be immensely important. Use the knowledge you gain from this book, combined with your deepest self-knowledge and intuition, in tandem with professional guidance, to get well and stay well. No matter which form of anxiety you suffer from, the healing solutions presented here are powerful ways to reclaim your capacity for inner calm, to end your sense of isolation and helplessness, and to feel whole again.

3

SOLUTION 1:

CHANGE YOUR FEARFUL BELIEFS

Paula sells commercial real estate for a living, and four years ago she came to a standstill in her work. She'd been quite successful over the years, but her creeping anxieties about failure began to stifle her advancement at work. Her agency was grooming her to be vice president, yet Paula did something seemingly incomprehensible: She tried to scuttle her own promotion. Why? Because she feared failure in the face of such high expectations and because she didn't want any more visibility with coworkers and clients than she already had. Paula would become so distressed while speaking to groups of more than two or three people that she'd sweat profusely and tremble inside. Around this time, the reality of her situation hit like a two-by-four: Despite her wish for success, she was ready to leave the real estate business rather than be thrust into the spotlight.

Paula suffered from social anxiety as well as generalized anxiety, and we recommended that she enter a group "cognitive-behavioral psychotherapy" program. Cognitive-behavioral therapy (CBT) is a mainstay in the treatment of anxiety, and the CBT therapist helps patients to reject and replace the negative, fear-reinforcing beliefs that cause so much of their chronic anxiety. (CBT can be effective either one-on-one or in a group setting.) Paula joined a group led by Jill Compton, Ph.D., and Thomas Lynch, Ph.D., clinical supervisors in Duke's Behavior Research and Therapy Program, which included several other patients with the same problem—social anxiety. Paula was both pleased and astonished to discover that the other group members mirrored her own problems: an intense fear of presenting their work or ideas, anxiety in large groups that went beyond simple shyness, shaking and sweating whenever called upon to speak in public. The sharing set her at ease and enabled her to open up about her condition.

The group members' first task was to catalogue the "automatic negative thoughts" that accompanied their anxiety. "I never realized how many negative thoughts I had until I wrote them down," said Paula. Paula's daily diary of negative thoughts included: "I'm certain to fail"; "I can't handle the pressure"; "People will see that I'm a fraud"; and "I don't deserve success." When she began to pay close attention, she realized how these thoughts directly caused her anxiety. The loud voices in her head bullied her into a state of fear, and one negative thought led directly to another, even more distressing one. "I finally realized how these thoughts would cascade out of control and grow into a total barrier to my success."

Paula's therapists encouraged her not only to catalogue her negative thoughts, but to go deeper, to peel the layers of negative thoughts piled one atop the other. Indeed, in a process her therapists called "peeling the onion," Paula would get to her core negative thoughts. In one exercise, Paula saw how "I'm certain to fail" led to "I'll get fired," which spurred "I'll never get another job," which triggered "I'll lose everything." Her core negative thought would invariably shred whatever sense of security she possessed.

"Peeling the onion" allowed Paula to see exactly how her negative thoughts caused her anxiety in real-life circumstances. Whenever she tried to sell a piece of property to a client, especially to a group of businessmen, she'd be terrified and start to tremble. In therapy, she was advised that whenever this happened, she should stop, breathe, and take stock of the thoughts threading through her mind. "I'd think, 'I'm going to embarrass myself'; 'I'm going to fail'; or usually both," Paula said. How would she fail? her therapist inquired. "I'd say or do something dumb, and they'd judge me, they'd be critical. I thought I would fail because they would judge me harshly."

Paula explored her conviction that she'd be judged, even ridiculed. Where did it come from? It didn't take a decade on a psychoanalyst's couch for her to find the answer. Her mother and father were farmers who had little time for their eight children. The kids, including Paula, got attention only when they failed to properly carry out tasks on the farm. In other words, the only attention Paula ever got from either parent was tough criticism. Paula's insight was very helpful, but such revelations were not the central goal of her treatment. Negative thoughts that trigger anxiety often have childhood roots, but the goal is to replace these thoughts with kinder, more realistic ones—to quiet those intimidating inner voices so they no longer have the power to create profound fear, self-loathing, or despair.

Paula learned to stop, breathe, and listen to her thoughts whenever she was pitching clients or talking to coworkers. Usually, she'd think, "I'll fail," and also, "They're judging me, they're judging me." After such events, her therapist advised her to ask herself: "*Am I* being judged?" "How do I know I'm being judged?" "Are these people *really* inclined to think ill of me?" Usually, the answers were no. If the answer to any question was yes or maybe, more questions would arise: "What difference does it make if (he, she, they) judge(s) me?" "If (he, she, they) judge(s) me, does it really mean I'm worthless? Or that my head is on the chopping block?" Taken to this deeper level, the answers would again be no.

When Paula put her core thoughts under the microscope of awareness, she found them baseless. For instance, Paula's constant fear that she would lose her job did not hold up under scrutiny. When she was able to replace her fear-ridden thought "They'll think I stink and I'll get fired" with the more rational "If I were being so harshly judged by clients or higher-ups at the agency, I'd have gotten the negative feedback by now. And no way would they offer me a vice presidency!"

Paula's group ran sixteen weeks, and halfway through—only two months into treatment—she felt an enormous difference. Her cognitive work was so effective that, to quote Paula, "the whole cascading negative thought structure collapsed." Her role-playing and, ultimately, her "exposure" experiences in real life (see the next chapter on exposure)—speaking to small groups at work and pitching real estate deals—enabled her to drastically diminish her social anxieties. By the end of the program, Paula had taken the position of vice president, and she knew she'd improve because she no longer soaked through her blouse after making presentations on the job.

CHANGE YOUR MIND, STOP YOUR ANXIETY: COGNITIVE REFRAMING

Negative thoughts breed negative emotional states. To quote from Corinthians in the New Testament, when we see the world "through a glass darkly," meaning that we always expect the worst, we're going to feel perennially anxious. Both depression and anxiety are deeply influenced by the negative thought constructs that badger us. When our worldview is grimly pessimistic and our thoughts about ourselves are denigrating, we're prone to depression. When our worldview is clouded by fear, we're prone to anxiety. And frequently there's overlap between these two phenomena: Pessimism and self-loathing can also cause anxiety, while mistrust and apprehension can cause depression. Indeed, anxiety and depression often coexist because negative thought patterns can breed both.

The simple but powerful idea behind Solution 1 is this: *Change the negative thoughts that breed anxiety, and you start the process of healing your anxiety.*

The most powerful approach to changing your fearful beliefs, drawn from the techniques of CBT, is the four-step "rational response" exercise, drawn from the pioneering work of Aaron Beck and David Burns, adapted by myself and my colleague, Jill Compton. Each "step" is a question you ask yourself.

The Four-Step "Rational Response" Exercise

1. *Finding the culprit* (identifying negative thoughts): When I'm in any situation that causes anxiety, what is my automatic negative thought or thoughts?
2. *Peeling the onion:* What is the core negative thought—the notion that goes to the heart of what makes me anxious?
3. *Reality check:* Is this core negative thought both logical and true?
4. *Rational response:* If the core negative thought is not logical or true, or mostly exaggerated, what is a more rational response? Can I construct a thought that is both more accurate and more compassionate toward myself and other people?

Here's how Paula carried out the four-step rational response exercise:

1. *Finding the culprit:* When I'm pitching clients or talking to agency honchos, I'm convinced that I'm saying or doing something stupid, that I'm acting strangely or speaking poorly, stumbling over my words.
2. *Peeling the onion:* Layer 1: They're going to judge me harshly, thinking that I'm dumb, incompetent, or both. Layer 2: They are going to share their negative judgments about me with each other. Layer 3: Clients will complain to agency heads or agency heads will decide that I'm worthless to the firm. Layer 4: The "core negative thought": I'll get fired and lose my income and self-respect.
3. *Reality check:* When I'm honest with myself, these thoughts are neither logical nor true. While I do occasionally stumble over words, I've never noticed anyone overtly reacting, and I've never heard any negative comments about my public appearance or presentation. I know rationally that my *core* fear of getting fired and losing my livelihood is unfounded, because the agency is offering me a promotion!
4. *Rational response:* While I'm not perfect on the job (who is?), and I can see room for improvement, the truth is that I'm doing well enough to be offered a promotion. My fear of judgment comes largely from my past, and I don't *really* believe that my clients or bosses think poorly of me. I'm a highly effective real estate saleswoman with employers who respect my abilities. I have every reason to feel that my future remains bright.

You can follow Paula's example by keeping a diary of your automatic negative thoughts, especially the ones that arise when your anxiety levels skyrocket. After doing this for one week, you'll swiftly see patterns—the same thought or cluster of thoughts occur again and again when you're anxious. Then use your diary to carry out steps two through four: peel the onion until you get to your "core" negative thought; ask whether there is any logic or truth to this thought; then restructure the negative thought into a "rational response." Pay heed to the following tips for carrying out each step (I don't include tips for the final step, rational response, since I'll be presenting many specific examples throughout this chapter):

Tips for Finding the Culprit: Identifying negative thoughts requires you to sharpen your awareness, since thoughts can pass fleetingly across your mental movie screen. How do you catch the culprit in your cognitive butterfly net? When you feel anxious, stop whatever you're doing, take a deep belly breath, and pay attention to your thoughts. The key to this process is fairly simple: Stop reacting, slow down, and pay attention. Say you have social phobia and you're anxious in a work meeting: Go inward for a moment, check into yourself, and say "Stop! What am I thinking right now?" Use the same process whether you're alone with general anxious thoughts about health, money, or relationship problems; you're having a flashback of a traumatic event; or you're in the midst of a panic attack while driving to work. In the latter case, you might pull off to the side of the road and try to uncover your semiconscious thoughts. The qualities you must cultivate to do this practice are patience, stillness, attentiveness, and focus.

Tips for Peeling the Onion: When you "peel the onion," engage in the Socratic method—with yourself. If you have children or if you've spent enough time with them, you know the routine: They ask a question, you give an answer, and they keep asking "why" until you hit some rock-bottom mystery about the nature of the universe. Peeling your cognitive onion is done in roughly the same way. Let's say your negative thought is "When I'm out on a date, I worry that I'm acting like a jerk." Question: What are you actually afraid of? Answer: He'll think I'm idiotic. Question: What would that mean? Answer: He'll never go out with me again. Question: What would that mean? Answer: My confidence will be bruised; I'll feel horrible about myself. Question: What would that mean? Answer: No man will ever want to be with me. Thus, your core negative thought about behaving awkwardly on one single date: *No man will ever want to be with me.*

Peel an onion, and you're usually left in tears. But you're also left with false assumptions. In this date example, the core thought is a made-up story. You couldn't possibly know that no man (or woman) will ever want to be with you. It's time to start uncovering your own made-up stories and the darkly negative assumptions they harbor.

Tips for Reality Check: Seriously question the rationality and veracity of your core negative thoughts. Be scrupulously honest with yourself, because there may be a scintilla of truth to your negative thought, but don't blow that up into rational support for your fears. In Paula's case, she had to acknowledge that she did occasionally stumble over her words. But she had *no* real evidence that (1) her clients or coworkers were mean-spirited enough to judge her for this insignificant imperfection; (2) it had any effect on her job status; or (3) it reflected on her worth as a real estate agent or as a person.

Once you've questioned the logic and truth of your negative thoughts, you can begin to understand that you are subject, on a daily basis, to cognitive distortions. In other words, such thoughts apprehend only one piece of reality and then distort it, until your perceptions are thoroughly clouded or downright mistaken.

————

Now that you have the basic "rational response" method for changing your fearful beliefs, I offer you custom-tailored approaches and tips for practicing this method for each form of anxiety. If need be, refer back to Chapter 2 to identify your form, or forms, of chronic anxiety, and use the specific rational response guidelines I provide in the pages that follow.

MIND SHIFTS: RATIONAL RESPONSE
FOR GENERAL ANXIETY

When Sean, a forty-year-old photojournalist, had a stubborn case of acid reflux, he knew he had stomach cancer. Whenever he was dead tired, he convinced himself it was the harbinger of chronic fatigue syndrome. When a urologist told him he had prostatitis, an infection of the prostate gland, he was sure the diagnosis was wrong: He really had prostate cancer. And Sean didn't worry only about his health. In most areas of his life, he was the perversely brilliant spinner of worst-case scenarios. He could dream up an unhappy ending for any event. A great photo assignment would end in failure because he'd bungle the one opportunity for a perfect shot. His financial problems would inevitably lead to bankruptcy. And his young son, just entering preschool, would become the victim of a random accident or premeditated attack. It was no wonder that Sean also suffered from insomnia.

To make matters worse, Sean was ashamed of his chronic worrying. Like many anxiety sufferers, he thought he lacked strength of character. (Men with anxiety disorders often think they're weak; women often think they're deficient, or crazy, or both.) He'd been in psychoanalysis for years, and it helped him develop greater insight and self-awareness, but it didn't stop him from worrying. When Sean came to our anxiety disorders clinic, we told him that he had generalized anxiety disorder (GAD), a diagnosis that in no way impugned his moral or psychological character. We referred him to one of our cognitive-behavioral therapists to help him overthrow the tyrannical thoughts that hounded his days and nights. Sean picked up on our optimism, and it motivated him to follow through with his treatment plan, which centered on the rational response technique.

In the following section, I'll use Sean's example to illustrate how you can apply rational response to your generalized anxiety. It can be the most effective way to awaken your innate courage—and resilience.

Step 1. Find the Culprit

Keep a diary of the negative thoughts associated with your worrying tendencies. Here is a sample of a chart you can use to record your negative thoughts.

NEGATIVE THOUGHT DIARY

TIME OF DAY	PRESENT CIRCUMSTANCES	WORRY	NEGATIVE THOUGHT

The purpose of the negative thought diary is to heighten awareness of your negative thoughts and to help you begin the process of rational response. You can't reframe the irrational negative thoughts that feed your anxiety unless you grab hold of these negative thoughts and consciously scrutinize them. This process is important because the negative thoughts that cause generalized anxiety (GAD) can be slippery, affecting you day in and day out just below your awareness. Indeed, you can think of these negative thoughts as hit-and-run fugitives: They damage your sense of security then slip away into the darkness of semi-consciousness. Use your thought diary as a tool to corral these thoughts, then apply the rational response technique.

Sean had been hounded by worries about his health (every symptom was a sign of cancer), finances (he was always headed for bankruptcy), career (he constantly imagined himself blowing opportunities), and the well-being of his four-year-old son (whom he visualized as the victim of an accident or violence). Here are two sample entries from Sean's diary:

Present Circumstances: Morning breakfast; a headache coming on

WORRY: Why have I had a headache every morning for a week? Perhaps it's a brain tumor.

NEGATIVE
THOUGHT: It's a brain tumor. I've finally got the cancer I have always feared, and it's going to kill me.

Present Circumstances: Taking my son to preschool

WORRY: Something bad will happen to him today.

NEGATIVE
THOUGHT: He'll be the victim of a terrorist attack, a fight with another kid, or perhaps some tainted meat. Whenever I leave him at the schoolhouse door, I can't stop thinking about his vulnerability.

Sean's diary entries illustrate two key elements of negative thought identification: First, your worries often arise in specific circumstances. Notice when your worries surface and how they are connected to the events of your day. (In some cases, you'll notice that they aren't connected to any event. They may arise seemingly spontaneously when nothing is going on and your mind is free to latch onto worries.) Second, your worry is often attached to an underlying negative thought. Sean's headache causes him to worry that he has brain cancer. His negative thought, however, runs deeper: He'll be diagnosed with a cancer that will kill him. Think of your worry as a surface anxiety and your negative thought as the deeper concern just below that surface.

Step 2: Peel the Onion

When you peel the onion of your negative thought, you search for a core negative thought—the idea at the heart of your anxiety. Let's take Sean's example again and show how he peeled the onion by asking himself questions about each thought.

WORRY: Something bad will happen to my son today.

NEGATIVE
THOUGHT:
LAYER 1: He'll be the victim of a terrorist attack, a fight with another kid, or perhaps some tainted meat. Whenever I leave him at the schoolhouse door, I can't stop thinking about his vulnerability

QUESTION: Why do I think he's vulnerable?

NEGATIVE
THOUGHT:
LAYER 2: Anything can happen inside that school.

QUESTION: Anything can happen to him anywhere. Why in school?

NEGATIVE
THOUGHT:
LAYER 3:   I guess because I'm not there. I worry about his vulnerability when I'm not around.

QUESTION: Why?

NEGATIVE
THOUGHT:
LAYER 4:   Because I have no control. I believe that my son is not safe when I'm not there to be in control.

Notice how each question prompts an answer, which in tern enables Sean to peel the onion further. For instance, when he asks himself why he's most frightened about his son's welfare when he's not around, the answer is "Because I have no control," which he then translated into his fundamental negative thought: "I believe that my son is not safe when I'm not there to be in control." Like Anita, the anxious mother who developed severe symptoms of GAD when her daughter Jennifer got her driver's permit, Sean had trouble tolerating the anxiety of being unable to micromanage his son's well-being. It's an understandable and universal anxiety among parents as their children become independent, but in Sean's and Anita's cases, their anxiety was both pervasive and extreme.

Of course, there is no set number of layers for you to peel; just keep peeling until you feel you've gotten to your core negative thought, your bottom-line fear. Practice peeling the onion, because it's your core negative thought that you need to question and replace with a rational response.

Step 3: Reality Check

Now put your negative thought to the test of reality. Is your thought logical? Is it realistic? How likely is it to be true? Sean put his brain tumor worries to the test by asking himself "How logical or realistic is it for me to have a brain tumor?" When Sean took the time to really consider this question, he realized that he's had chronic headaches since he was in his late teens. A few times a year, he'd have a headache that stayed with him for days at a time, and he'd often awaken in the morning with it. He took his inquiry further: Does the fact that I've had chronic headaches before mean that I don't have a brain tumor? When Sean stopped to consider this question, he had to remind himself that he'd had an MRI brain scan seven years earlier during one of his long-lasting headaches, and it showed no abnormality. But could it be a different story this time? This was Sean's pivotal question. His rational answer: It's not likely to be a brain tumor, because the headaches feel exactly the same as they did seven years ago, when I know that I did not have a brain tumor. Of course, Sean could not be 100 percent certain he was free of brain cancer unless he had another brain scan, but was it really necessary? No, not unless his headaches persisted for at least another week (in the past they'd always subsided after about a week), or they became noticeably more severe. Sean's brain tumor fear did not make it past his reality checkpoint.

Sean's brain tumor reality check illustrates an important principle of cognitive work for generalized anxiety: Use the past as a reference. Look back to see whether your future-oriented fears are way out of proportion. Whether you worry about brain tumors, natural disasters, terrorism, or abject failure on the job, ask yourself if your worst-case scenarios have ever occurred under similar circumstances.

Sean also ran a reality check on his core negative thought about his son: "I believe my son is not safe when I'm not there to be in control." Using the past as a reference, Sean realized that his son had had two accidents serious enough to require a few stitches: once when he was at preschool and once when Sean was taking care of him at a playground. His son was not immune from minor misfortune regardless of whether he was being overseen by Sean or by the excellent teachers at the preschool. By the same token, nothing terrible had befallen him when he was at the preschool or when he was being taken care of by babysitters or relatives. In sum, there was no logical basis for Sean's fear that his son was especially vulnerable when out of his sight.

Use "reality check" as your stepping-stone to a truly rational response. Ask yourself if your fear of failure at work has any basis and, if so, whether or not your fear is proportional. Ask whether your anxiety about money is justifiable, and, if you feel it is, take your inquiry to the next level. You may have money problems, but do your worst-case fantasies of being on the verge of homelessness have any realistic basis? And if you do find yourself in a financial rut, is there really no way out? Will you really lose your home? The key is not simply to find out if you have any rational basis for your worry, but to find out if your *level of worry* is justified. A wildly exaggerated worry about something real can be as irrational as a worry that is completely unfounded.

Step 4: Rational Response

Your final step is to devise a rational response to your anxiety-inducing negative thoughts. Try writing down your core negative thought on a piece of paper in a left-hand column, then on the right write your rational response. You've already found the logical weaknesses in your core negative thought. In most cases, you discovered that it's either completely false or out of proportion to the real dimensions of your problem. Now it's your job to develop a new thought—a rational response to live by. Let's return to Sean and see how he developed his rational response.

His core negative thought about his son was: "I believe that my son is not safe when I'm not there to be in control." In his reality check, Sean used the past as a reference to recognize that his son had never experienced a terrible mishap when he or his wife were not taking care of him and that a minor mishap was just as likely to occur when Sean was present. But Sean's anxious mind still had a ready retort for his reality check: "The fact that nothing horrible happened in the past doesn't mean it won't happen in the future." (This is one of the most common arguments a person with GAD uses to support his or her negative thinking.) He would need to develop a rational response that accounts for his "reality check" insights and also answers the persistent questions posed by his anxious mind:

CORE
NEGATIVE
THOUGHT: I believe that my son is not safe when I'm not there
                to be in control.

RATIONAL
RESPONSE: I realize that nothing terrible has happened to my
                son either in my care or in the care of others. And
                he's in good care at the preschool; I know all the
                teachers and they care about the kids as if they were
                their own children. No serious injury, illness, or
                violence has ever occurred to any child there. Can
                something terrible happen out of the blue? Sure, but
                it's extremely unlikely. And I must tolerate the anxi-
                ety that something bad could happen, whether or

not I'm with my son, because such uncertainty is a
part of life I can never extinguish. In fact, when I
learn to live with that small measure of uncertainty,
my anxiety level will abate.

Sean's rational response has two key elements: First, he's able to put
his worry about his son in proper perspective by developing an accurate read on the degree of risk. It wouldn't be truthful for him to say
"My son is one hundred percent safe when I leave him," but it is truthful for him to say "The risk of something happening is extremely
small." Moreover, he's able to recognize that this minute risk is probably no greater when he leaves his son with other caretakers. Thus, Sean
is able to develop a rational response that is proportional to the actual
risk involved, which in this case is minuscule. Finally, and just as important, part of Sean's rational response is the recognition that he can
never extinguish all uncertainty but rather that he can handle his uncertainty by learning to tolerate the anxiety it breeds. This involves a
skill called *distress tolerance*. When you learn to tolerate distress over
day-to-day risks and problems, your excess anxiety is reduced to manageable levels.

When you practice rational response, it's important to avoid
Pollyanna formulations to counter your negative thoughts. The reason
is simple: You won't believe in them. The key is to find the truth,
which is more often cast in shades of gray than in black and white, because only the truth will win over your conscious mind to a more rational position. If you create a rational response that's far too optimistic
or cheerful, you may only pretend to yourself that you believe in it.

Of course, there are times when your rational response ought to reject every shred of a negative thought. Let's say Sean continued to
worry that his headaches meant he had a brain tumor and went to the

doctor for an MRI scan. The MRI scan came back negative yet Sean continued to worry about brain cancer. He would then have had to use rational response to thoroughly reject this idea. (This is not a far-fetched example. People with GAD who obsess about life-threatening diseases sometimes don't believe the medical tests that give them a clean bill of health.)

As you work on your rational responses to alleviate your generalized anxiety, consider these six principles. Each one is a guide to replacing a particular cognitive distortion (drawn from the work of Aaron Beck and David Burns):

1. Question whether you engage in *all-or-nothing thinking*. Frequently, your core negative thoughts are based on the following kinds of polarized perception: either my child is totally safe or he's totally unsafe; either my work is brilliant or it stinks; either I'm financially comfortable or I'm about to plunge into poverty. If you suffer from generalized anxiety, you need to develop rational responses that recognize and embrace the middle ground between your fantasized heaven of hermetically sealed safety or surefire success and your feared hell of certain catastrophe. Most of your problems lie in that middle ground.

2. Watch out for *overgeneralization*. If you harbor negative thoughts such as "If I lose this man, I'll never have another relationship again," you're engaging in gross overgeneralization, something you need to correct in your rational response. When you suffer from GAD, you probably take one unhappy occurrence or trend and turn it into a template for your present and future. You can rectify your tendency to overgeneralize by deciding that a lousy date, mediocre performance, less-than-stellar job interview, or illness does not set in stone the pattern for your future dates, performances, job interviews, or health status.

3. *Proportionality* is a golden rule in creating rational responses. It's the opposite of magnification—the cognitive distortion in which you inflate the significance of any misstep or negative event. Where before your entire view of most situations was limited to a close-up on the one detail or possibility that spelled disaster, you now pull back the camera of your consciousness to get a wide shot, enabling you to see the whole picture, with all the details and possibilities. Now you can gauge reality with far greater depth, breadth, and accuracy. In Sean's case, leaving his son at preschool caused him to magnify the risk into a nightmare of dreaded outcomes. (He'd seen too many news stories of children being victims of accidents or violence at school.) The proportional response was "Yes, there is risk of something bad happening to my son, but it is minuscule, and I can handle that."

4. Avoid *emotional reasoning*. It can be summed up by the statement "I feel, therefore I think I know what will happen." In other words, you use your own feelings (fear, dread, anxiety) as evidence to buttress your belief in worst-case scenarios. For instance, Sean would be aware of butterflies in his stomach when he'd drop his son at preschool. The butterflies bolstered his belief that something bad would happen. Just below awareness, he was saying to himself "If my stomach is in a knot, there must be good reason." When you have GAD, often your feelings are poor barometers of present circumstances or future possibilities. After you've used rational response to straighten out your thought processes, your feelings will follow suit, and in time you'll be able to trust your gut again.

5. Have *compassion* for yourself and others. Rational responses should be not only more truthful than core negative thoughts, but also kinder. When you magnify your own weaknesses, your cognitions become skewed toward disaster because you don't believe in your ability

to handle stress or challenge. When you magnify the weaknesses (or dark sides) of other people, your relationships are characterized by mistrust, and you'll never feel safe in the world. You don't have to expunge awareness of your own imperfections, or whitewash the fact that people can be malevolent, in order to cultivate compassion. A compassionate worldview acknowledges all our multifaceted complexity but is purposely skewed toward the positive: You look for the good in yourself as well as in others.

6. Recognize how you *catastrophize*. Catastrophizing is as second nature to the person with GAD as pandering is to a politician. You can't seem to stop yourself from expecting the most disastrous outcome to any challenging circumstance. Whether in the realm of work, relationships, finances, or health, you turn a sun shower into a hurricane. Catastrophizing combines, in a creative splurge of wild imagining, elements of many of the cognitive distortions I've already mentioned: magnification, all-or-nothing thinking, and overgeneralization, to mention a few. You use these distortions to advance a "domino theory" of negative outcomes. One common example: My boss criticized my project, thus he thinks I stink; he wants me out; he's going to fire me; I'll never find another job; I'll have to spend my retirement savings; I'll end up jobless and broke. To create a rational response, use your intelligence to attack the false assumptions behind each successive link in your chain of ruin.

SCOTT'S STORY: RATIONAL RESPONSE FOR SOCIAL ANXIETY

When you have social anxiety, the thoughts that drive your fears and behaviors are punishing. These thoughts are largely irrational, and the more punishing they are, the more irrational they are. Your mind is filled with damning images and beliefs, mostly aimed at yourself. When you examine these thoughts further, you discover that they're aimed at others, too, because you assume that people are so narrow-minded or mean-spirited that they only think the worst of you. You don't mean to think poorly of others, only of yourself, but in so doing you cast unwitting aspersions on friends, family members, employers, and coworkers. Ultimately, as you try to overcome social anxiety you can learn to see yourself and others in a genuinely new light, neither a warm fuzzy one in which everyone (yourself included) has an aura of saintliness nor a cold harsh light in which you are worthless and they are nasty and judgmental. Most people in your midst, you will find, are not so merciless, even if they aren't exemplars of compassion. You'll discover that many (or most) are more flexible and caring than you imagined.

What's needed is a radical shift in your perspective of yourself (perceptions, beliefs, and self-image) and others, which you can bring about through the rational response method and through exposure, a technique I'll describe in the next chapter. These are the essential methods of cognitive-behavioral therapy (CBT), which has been proven effective in treating social anxiety. One recent analysis of over forty-two clinical trials proved that patients who received cognitive-behavioral treatment did significantly better than patients in control groups.

In other words, you *can* change your negative belief system with rational response. Consider the case of Scott, a retired navy pilot who'd always thought of himself as a fearless, take-charge guy. Scott tells the remarkable story of an international incident in the mid-1970s, when a plane he flew with a crew of a dozen was impounded after landing in a small city in Thailand. Thai officers brandishing guns entered the plane and essentially arrested the entire crew, who were forced to stay in a nearby compound.

It was a time of political instability in the country, and while the reasons for their detention weren't entirely clear, it was obvious that their captors were angry. Scott was second in command, and after twenty-four hours in quasi-custody, he led the crew in a bold action. At one point, the Thai officers were involved in frantic phone conversations with their superiors and U.S. officials, trying to figure out what to do with these American flyers. Scott seized the opportunity, instructing his crew, who were not behind bars, to simply leave the compound and head straight for the nearby tarmac, where their plane was sitting. The armed guards outside, who apparently assumed that the navy men had been released, stood by as they boarded the plane and started the engine. Scott and his men had expected a showdown, but their action was so audacious and carried out with such conviction, that no one challenged them. They flew safely into the skies and headed home.

Scott had always shone in pressure situations by spontaneously taking on the mantle of leadership. But even then, when he had to speak to groups and had any time to think ahead, he found himself stumbling over words, barely treading water in a sea of anxiety. On some level he always sensed this profound contradiction in himself, but it became painfully apparent as he grew older. In his late thirties, Scott became a consultant to companies that designed and marketed security systems. One of the companies he worked for, long the acknowledged leader in the security business, began to flounder and came to rely more and more upon Scott's strategic ideas. Scott developed a strong relationship with the CEO of the company, who finally invited him to come on-board as an executive to reorganize the creative teams within the company, teams that had communicated poorly with one another.

Scott found this new job very demanding; whenever he had to speak to large groups or the media he began to feel jittery. Then, all of a sudden, the CEO quit, leaving the company in a dangerous state of flux in the midst of its reorganization. The company's board of directors asked Scott to take over as interim CEO. "It was a huge jump," he remembered. "The idea of standing up there and talking to 1,200 people in the organization was something I thought I could never do. I went through pure agony just imagining it."

Scott was able to speak to the shareholders and lay out a strategic plan to restructure and rebuild the corporation. "I felt strongly that the strategy was right," he said. "I sold it to them hard, and they signed off on it. Only a month after getting started, the large shareholders stopped trusting each other and began doubting my strategy. I became the focus of controversy, which I couldn't handle." As Scott tells it, he politely informed the company's board of directors, "I'm out of here." He left in a matter of days.

While the circumstances were demanding and far from ideal, the CEO position had been Scott's most exciting career opportunity, yet he walked away from it. In need of other work, he and his wife decided to go into the retail jewelry business, which at first seemed far less daunting than his corporate jobs in terms of social interaction and speaking to large groups. But soon Scott realized that he'd have to attend trade association meetings and talk to big gatherings. Even more troubling, his social fears were getting worse, and now he had difficulty with phone conversations and one-on-one interactions, particularly if he felt put "on the spot." How could he be a salesperson and run several jewelry shops, he wondered, if he couldn't talk to customers and return their phone calls without significant distress?

One day during this tough period, he was channel surfing and came across a talk-show interview with Donny Osmond, who was speaking about his social anxiety disorder. "Donny Osmond is about the last person I would tune into," said Scott. "But I heard him say: 'I could sing on stage in front of thousands of people, but I couldn't return a shirt to a department store.' I stopped right there and started to listen. He talked about social phobia, and I realized that I had it and it was getting out of hand." The same month, Scott saw an ad in the newspaper for one of our research programs, and he promptly called and made an appointment.

Scott joined our group therapy program for social anxiety. We hoped that the group experience would help Scott get to the heart of his problem. He would come to understand how he could lead his flight crew out of danger but was now afraid to make business calls. Scott was asked to learn skills he believed would free him from severe social anxiety, enabling him to regain control of his work life and let go of years of shame.

Scott's first step was to restructure his thinking, to develop more rational responses to his ideas about himself and others in social situations. That can be your first step, too.

Step 1: Find the Culprit

Scott began examining his thought patterns whenever he felt social tension—speaking to a group, making a phone call, attending a business meeting where he was expected to talk. He quickly recognized that his overriding negative thoughts were: "I'll say something stupid" and "I won't be articulate," which quickly gave way to "They'll think I'm stupid" and "They won't like me." Scott's thoughts are among the most common in people with social anxiety.

First ask yourself which circumstances trigger your social phobias. Typical situations that bring on social anxiety are:

- Speaking to large groups
- Performing for an audience
- Meeting new people
- Attending parties
- Talking to a superior at work
- Disagreeing with someone, especially higher-ups on the job
- Starting conversations
- Asking someone for a date
- Making phone calls with something at stake—a job, loan, date, etc.
- Speaking up at a business meeting
- Interviewing for jobs or giving interviews to media representatives
- Making direct eye contact with others
- Using a public bathroom
- Eating or drinking with a group of people
- Dealing with any authority figures—teachers, employers, police, government officials, etc.

Once you've identified the situations that rouse your worst social fears, pay close attention to your automatic negative thoughts during these times. Here is a list of common "distorted automatic thoughts" among people with social anxiety disorder:

They think I'm stupid.
They're better/smarter/funnier than me.
They think I'm a fool.
No one liked me.
I blew it again.
Everybody is looking at me.
People know that I'm nervous.
I'm a loser.
I'll be tongue-tied.
I'll say something stupid.
I'll freeze up.
I'll be boring.

My face will turn red.
My hands are shaking.
I'm losing control.

Be honest with yourself—and as mindful as you can—when identifying your negative thoughts. Your automatic thoughts usually involve some form of severe judgment that you perceive to be in others' minds ("They'll *think* I'm stupid.") or that arises in your own mind ("I *am* stupid."). Don't try to develop a rational response *until* you feel that you've pinpointed the thoughts that tyrannize you during episodes of social phobia.

Step 2: Peeling the Onion

Now determine your core negative thought(s) by digging below the surface of your automatic negative thoughts. When you have social phobia, your core negative thought is frequently an assumption about a terrible outcome in a social situation. Other times, the bottom line is a global indictment of yourself in relation to others. Scott peeled the onion of his most frequent automatic thought: "I'll say something stupid." Then he used probing questions to go deeper. Here was Scott's dialogue:

AUTOMATIC NEGATIVE THOUGHT:	"I'll say something stupid."
QUESTION:	"What bad will come of that?"
NEGATIVE THOUGHT LAYER #2:	"They'll think I'm stupid."
QUESTION:	"So what if they think you are stupid?"

NEGATIVE
THOUGHT
LAYER #3:   "If I'm not perfect, they'll reject me as worthless."

Scott felt that one mistake in a work setting—whether it was a less-than inspired comment, ill-timed remark, or some pauses or stammers in his speech—would lead his listeners to think the worst of him. They'd view him as outright stupid or incompetent, which mattered to Scott because these were superiors, colleagues, clients, or potential customers. Scott's essential fear was that if he didn't perform flawlessly, he'd be dismissed by others as worthless.

Robert Leahy and Stephen Holland have provided a list of false assumptions common among people with social phobia. These common second- or third-layer thoughts, which reside just below your automatic negative thoughts, are distorted ideas about yourself in relation to other people.

False Assumptions
If I'm quiet, people will think I'm boring.
I have to have something intelligent or witty to say.
If I'm not perfect, they'll reject me.
If someone doesn't like me, it means there is something wrong with me.
If they see I'm anxious, they'll think I'm incompetent.
I have to make a good impression.
I must get everyone's approval.
I must not show any signs of weakness.
If I disagree with someone, they'll get mad or think I'm stupid.

Consider this list as you practice peeling the onion; it may help you identify your core negative thought. Often, there is an even deeper level underlying these assumptions, a level of painfully self-deprecating views. These are usually blunt, even crude self-assessments such as: "I'm weird"; "I'm dumb"; "I'm incompetent"; "I'm ugly"; "I don't have the right stuff"; "I'm a loser"; "I'm fat"; "I'm a nerd"; "I'll never make it"; "I'm not likeable"; and "I'm not lovable."

Are your negative thoughts driven by one or more of these merciless self-judgments? As you practice rational response, determine which of these you may hold, and question them. But as you devise rational responses, leave these negative self-assessments for last. They are often the toughest nuts to crack. Also, when you question and replace negative thoughts and false assumptions, these deeply held, negative self-images may simply recede. For instance, Scott's social anxieties at work made him feel incompetent, even worthless. But in his group he didn't directly attack this global self-image. (He probably wouldn't have succeeded if he had tried.) Rather, he attacked the core negative thought "If I'm not perfect, they'll reject me as worthless." As you'll see, this process enabled Scott to dismantle the negative thought structures that kept him feeling bad about himself as a worker and a person.

Step 3: Reality Check

As you move to the next step—putting your core negative thoughts about social situations through a reality check—I'm willing to predict that you will be astonished by how off base they are.

Scott ran a reality check on his core thought "If I'm not perfect, they'll reject me as worthless." Using the past as a reference, he recognized that in all his days in the navy and as a business executive, he'd never been "rejected as worthless" because of a mistake or verbal miscue on his part. Sure, he'd been criticized on occasion, but never seriously condemned or fired. Part of Scott's reality check was to look at his beliefs from other points of view. "Would these people really think of me that way?" For the first time Scott questioned the foundation of his fears. "I began to wonder why I had such dramatic beliefs—that people would think I was *stupid* or *worthless*." He realized that such strong words carried strong meanings, and he'd swallowed them without examining their validity.

When you do reality checks, these five questions can help you cut to the chase:

1. What would really happen if _____? (Fill in the blank. Examples: I said something dumb; I stammered; I wasn't perfect; I wasn't brilliant; I didn't get him or her to love me . . .)
2. Would *I* think such terrible thoughts (e.g., He's stupid; He's weird; He's a loser) about someone else in the same situation as me?
3. Would other people I know and admire (friends, family, personal heroes) make such harsh judgments?
4. Is there a bit of truth in my fear, but I'm blowing it way out of proportion?
5. Have I had a painful or traumatic social experience in the past (of rejection, humiliation, public embarrassment, etc.) that continues to distort my view of what will happen in the future?

Be on the lookout for certain cognitive distortions, the ones most prevalent in social anxiety disorder. Three of the most important are *mind reading, overgeneralization,* and *labeling:*

· *Mind reading.* You assume that people are reacting negatively to you, but you never question your beliefs. You imagine the most critical thoughts in people's minds, whether it's folks listening to you speak, the audience observing you perform, the object of your romantic affection, or even strangers you just met at a party. We all have intuitions about what others are thinking and feeling, and these hunches can be on target. But when you have social anxiety, your (always negative) intuitions are usually off base. Start paying attention to how you jump to unfounded conclusions about other peoples' thoughts about you.

· *Overgeneralization.* When you overgeneralize, you see a single negative event as part of a continual pattern. It's the bane of people with almost any anxiety problem, but it plays a special role in social anxiety. This can happen after you have a painful social experience of a particular kind, such as being callously rejected after asking for a date, dismissed by a teacher after an oral presentation, or roundly criticized for your new proposal at a business meeting. The memory cuts so deeply that you expect the worst whenever you're in the same situation. You're likely to overgeneralize this way if you're already susceptible, by dint of genes, biochemistry, or earlier traumas, to feeling hurt or shamed in social situations. Start being mindful of your tendency to overgeneralize.

· *Labeling.* Problems arise when you label others—or yourself—in what amounts to name calling. When you have social anxiety, you're likely to call yourself names whenever you make an error in judgment, a gaffe, or a minor *faux pas* in front of others. You'll tag yourself a "loser," "stupid," "inept," or "unlovable." First, thoughtfully take note of your name calling. Then, stop yourself by asking yourself: "Would I pin such nasty labels on a friend or colleague?" Cultivate more compassion for yourself.

Step 4: Rational Response

Write down your rational response, restructuring your core negative thought into one that is more realistic and positive. Build upon your reality check as you construct your rational response.

· Consider the likelihood that you'd really embarrass yourself in the social situation that frightens you.
· Consider the *actual* consequences if you did or said something you felt bad about. Would those consequences be so intolerable?
· Consider what *you* would think or feel if someone *else* did what you're afraid of (e.g., stammering, being quiet, misspeaking, showing weakness, disagreeing with an authority figure, etc.)

· Decide whether there is *any* truth to your negative thought. If so, be sure to tease it out from the distortions or exaggerations born of your own insecurities, early conditioning, past or recent traumas.

Using this approach, Scott developed this rational response to his core negative thought:

CORE
NEGATIVE
THOUGHT: If I'm not perfect, they'll reject me as worthless.

RATIONAL
RESPONSE: I have no real basis in my experience for believing that if I say or do something imperfect, I will be judged so severely. I get nervous when I think people aren't listening—*that's* when I repeat myself or stumble over words and become convinced that people think I'm stupid or worthless. But *I* never harbor such bad thoughts about people who are nervous while speaking. When I don't listen to a speaker, it's usually because I'm thinking about something else—often worrying about what *I'm* going to say, how *I'm* going to be received. Most people are probably like me—dwelling on their own anxieties, not focusing on my lapses.

    I'm learning that it's OK to be nervous; it's OK to be human; and it's OK if some people aren't listening to every word I say. Most people won't think such terrible thoughts about me, and if a few do, they're not people who should matter to me anyway. I don't have to be the world's most popular speaker; I just want to feel good about my leadership abilities, especially as I start up this new business.

Scott's rational response involved a variety of skills he learned in his group therapy. They included:

1. *Use the past as a reference:* "I have no real basis in my experience for believing that if I say or do something imperfect, I will be judged so severely."
2. *Discern the exact causes of your fear:* "I get nervous when I think people aren't listening—*that's* when I . . . become convinced that people think I'm stupid or worthless."
3. *Put yourself in the position of others to get a different perspective on their experience and behavior:* "Most people are probably like me—dwelling on their own anxieties, not focusing on my lapses."
4. *Cut yourself slack:* "I'm learning that it's OK to be nervous; it's OK to be human; . . ."
5. *Reshape your emotional needs and practical goals:* "I don't have to be the world's most popular speaker; I just want to feel good about my leadership abilities . . ."

Rely on these skills for your own rational response. Here are some sample "rational responses" for two prevalent core negative thoughts among people with social anxiety. Notice how you can apply the principles of rational response to the self-negating thoughts that fuel your social anxiety.

CORE
NEGATIVE
THOUGHT: "I must not show any signs of weakness."

RATIONAL
RESPONSE: "In my work life, on rare occasions, I've admitted problems to employers or coworkers—what some might consider "weakness"—yet I've never been criticized or rejected. Maybe I learned this message in childhood from my parents, but it doesn't apply anymore.

I feel anxious whenever I'm having trouble with a project. I'll hide the problem, afraid that my boss or colleagues will sense my tension and know what's going on. Then I get nervous, and the vicious cycle starts. They see my nervousness and, I'm sure, think poorly of me: She's not tough enough, strong enough, skilled enough. But I've seen colleagues have similar struggles. You can't tackle a tough assignment and never have moments of doubt or difficulty.

I'm finally realizing that I can share my concerns with coworkers and sometimes with my boss. I don't have to give them a moment-to-moment account of my anxieties, but it's fine to be up-front, especially when I can get help with problem solving. How can I get support when I can't admit I'm having difficulty? Plus, showing some nervousness may not be so bad. I've seen others do it, and it sometimes draws people closer to them because they can identify with them. I can show signs of weakness, and it might even do me some good!"

CORE
NEGATIVE
THOUGHT: "If someone doesn't like me, it means there is something wrong with me."

RATIONAL
RESPONSE: "Whenever I go out on a date or meet someone new at a party and sense that I haven't won her over, I feel that reflects terribly on me—my attractiveness, intelligence, and character. But I finally realize that's not logical. I've put it to the test: When I meet someone new on a date or at a party and I'm not drawn to her, how often do I think poorly of the person? Not often. Sure, once in a while I won't like the person. But mostly I feel that we don't click. It's not a bad reflection on her; our personalities simply don't mesh. I've met women whom I've liked and even admired but with whom I did not feel I wanted to pursue a relationship.

And what if a woman I meet really doesn't like me? Do I have to let that affect my feeling about myself? Must I allow my self-esteem to depend on how the last new person I meet seems to feel about me? When I do, I start to feel inhibited—like I have to watch myself to make sure everyone likes me. I'll feel a lot freer, more relaxed, and self-confident when I know that it's OK if someone I meet or date doesn't happen to like me."

FEAR OF FEAR ITSELF:
RATIONAL RESPONSE FOR PANIC

When you suffer with panic, one of your first challenges is to figure out what's triggering your attacks—thoughts about a particular situation or fear of the panic itself? As I emphasized in Chapter 2, when you suffer from panic disorder your fear is really centered on the attack, but you are not always consciously aware of it. You may seek a strictly physical explanation, such as epilepsy, hyperthyroidism, or heart disease. Or you may attribute your fears to a place, event, or circumstance, rather than to dread itself and the distressing physical symptoms it triggers.

To develop more rational responses, you need to educate yourself about your own physical reactions. If, say, you run quickly up the stairs on your way to an important meeting, you're likely to feel your heart pounding and your breathing accelerating. Even though you've brought on these symptoms by purely physical means, you might easily interpret them as anxiety. By the same token, if you're nervous and your heart starts beating, you might decide not that you're feeling anxious but that you're having a heart attack. Through the rational response method, you can learn to interpret your physical responses more accurately, which will help you to understand what they really signify and to view them as less significant—and dangerous—than you did before.

This last point is crucial, because when you suffer from panic, you interpret physical or emotional discomforts as indicators of genuine danger. You may choose to avoid any situation that makes you anxious, particularly if you worry that *any* anxiety will trigger a panic attack that you view as life-threatening.

Reinterpreting your own anxiety can be a difficult process. After all, our emotions are key to our survival. Nature has hardwired our fear responses into brain and body so that when danger looms, we'll either fight or flee. We need fear to protect us from danger, to ensure that we act immediately to save ourselves when truly necessary. But when you suffer from panic, you feel inordinately disturbed by even minor anxiety, because you misread its meaning. You misinterpret the real but essentially harmless anxiety associated with the sensations of a panic attack as life-threatening, as the ultimate humiliation, or as somehow inimical to your life or well-being.

What can you do? First, altering how you *perceive* anxiety can raise your tolerance for uncomfortable situations and the feelings they evoke. If, for example, you know that your heart is pounding because you just ran up the stairs, and not because there is any good reason to be terrified of your next meeting, the physical discomfort of your rapid heartbeat will not cause so much distress. And if you understand that routine stage fright before that meeting is a perfectly normal reaction rather than a sign that you're unfit for your job, the stage fright, while unpleasant, won't seem like such a big deal.

Second, changing your perception of your panic attacks makes them less terrifying, breaking the vicious cycle in which fear of a panic attack sets one off. Panic attacks are certainly not pleasant experiences, nor are they ordinary responses. But if you recognize that the attack won't kill you, the experience will be far less disturbing. If you can also stop viewing a panic attack in a public place as a humiliation from which you'll never recover, the attack becomes a far less threatening prospect. In time, these cognitive shifts can reduce the number and intensity of your panic attacks

Ultimately, rational response methods can help you reestablish a sense of your own humanity, which makes it easier to accept that none of us is in full control of our lives and our mortality, that a certain amount of confusion and helplessness is part of the human condition. Seeing yourself as one imperfect human among many, rather than as someone whose anxiety is a badge of failure, represents a major step toward overcoming panic disorder.

Many studies demonstrate that cognitive restructuring (along with exposure therapy) is enormously helpful to many people who suffer panic attacks. The following example demonstrates how you can apply the four steps of rational response to your panic attacks.

Step 1: Find the Culprit

In the case of panic, the negative thoughts that pass through your consciousness tend to be particularly fleeting and hard to pin down. That's just the nature of panic: You seem to be just reacting to the swirl of internal and external events, not thinking at all. But you are thinking; it's just that the thoughts are so quicksilver you don't even recognize them.

Suppose you've experienced a panic attack in a crowded shopping mall—an attack in which you feel dizzy and light-headed, experience a rapid heartbeat, and suspect that you might faint. When the attack passes, you're so upset about the prospect of a second attack that you leave the mall without completing any of your shopping.

Your first step is to find the culprit thoughts that flickered through your mind during and immediately after your panic attack. You might be able to pin down several such thoughts, but try to specify one. In this case, your most pressing thought might be "Oh, my God, I'm going to faint!" Now consider the layers of negativity just beneath your automatic thought.

Step 2: Peeling the Onion

Begin peeling the onion, getting at the thoughts that underlie this first negative cognition so that you can find out what's really disturbing you. "What's so bad about fainting?" you might ask yourself. "After all, fainting isn't dying. After you faint, you can usually get up and move on as if nothing had happened. So why am I so scared of fainting?"

As you consider your response, you might decide that for you, the most upsetting part of fainting is visualizing everyone in your midst staring at you with contempt. "Look at that foolish person!" you might imagine them saying. "She can't even control herself. She has no business coming to a store if she can't handle herself any better than that."

Then continue to peel away each layer of negative reasoning until you finally arrive at your core belief. In this case, ask yourself "What's so bad about people staring at me?" Your core belief may be that good people never lose control of themselves. In that case, fainting not only causes physical discomfort, it reveals some moral weakness or deficit of character. "I'm not just physically weak," you think, "I'm a bad person."

Frequently, you will discover that stinging judgments such as these are at the bottom of your fears associated with panic attacks: I'll be humiliated. I'm damaged goods. There's something horribly wrong with me. I can't function normally. I'm emotionally and physically out of control. All these thoughts merely serve to drive you deeper into panic.

Step 3: Reality Check

Proceed to step 3, reality check, by asking these questions: Is fainting really a moral weakness? Is a moral person always in control? Is a strong person always in control? Can you be a decent, capable person and still have moments of weakness, physical and emotional responses that you cannot completely control? What about other good, strong people you know—don't any of them ever lose control? What about, say, elderly people who become incontinent? Does their physical incontinence make them morally weak?

Essential to your practice of reality check for panic is your own understanding of panic as an anxiety disorder—one with clear symptoms, a particular brain malfunction, and causes that are beginning to be understood by neuroscientists. It's not an uncommon condition, and you can reframe your perceptions about your experience through this lens of understanding. Ask yourself "Am I the only one who has these awful feelings and experiences?" The answer is a resounding no. Are panic attacks a justifiable reason for a searing sense of shame? No. Can I always control the timing or intensity of these attacks? No. Am I going to die in the midst of a panic attack? No.

Step 4: Rational Response

Once you expose your core belief to reality, you'll finally be able to arrive at a rational response. In this case, the core negative thought beneath your fear of fainting in the midst of a panic attack is: "I'm morally weak, I'm a bad person." Here's your response:

RATIONAL
RESPONSE: My panic is driven by my fear of public humiliation. I'll faint dead in the middle of the mall or parking

117

lot, and people will think there is something terribly wrong with me—I'm weak, sick, or demented. First, I must question whether people witnessing me faint—if indeed I did faint—would think these things. But even if one or two did judge me, the truth is that sometimes people just can't control their bodies. This may not be pleasant, but it's hardly a sign of moral weakness. People with neuromuscular diseases or Parkinson's or Tourette's syndrome can't control their bodies, and it's not their fault, either. Panic is also a biological condition. Even if I had fainted, it wouldn't imply anything morally weak or inferior about me as a human being.

Cognitive therapists have identified a series of core negative thoughts that are common among people who suffer regular panic attacks. Consider this list and determine if any of these notions resonate with you. Then try to reframe these distortions to bring them more in line with reality:

· My attacks will cause me to die suddenly.
· There must be something wrong with me.
· Being this anxious is more than I can bear.
· This is going to drive me crazy, and I'll end up in an institution.
· Everyone can see how crazy I am.
· I'm always panicking—it's never any different.
· Everyone will hate me if they know how out of control I am.
· People will make fun of me for losing control.
· I'm the one everyone else leans on; this isn't supposed to happen to me!

Probably the single most common core negative thought is that you will die during a panic attack. Your rational response to this fear-based belief is simply this: "People don't die of panic attacks. But their fear of death drives them further into panic." Educating yourself about your condition—truly recognizing, even convincing yourself, that you have panic disorder, not some potentially fatal condition—can ease the very worst of your fears.

RECLAIMING TRUST:
RATIONAL RESPONSE FOR PTSD

When you have been traumatized, your negative thoughts about what happened contribute to your psychological symptoms. Some traumas—especially but not limited to sexual and physical abuse in childhood—can cause you to feel dreadfully guilty, as if you somehow caused your own victimization. The shame experienced by survivors results from distorted, self-blaming thoughts such as "I must be a horrible person to have this happen"; "It's all my fault"; or "How did I bring this on myself?" By helping you identify, reject, and transform these thoughts, rational response work can heal the shame.

Traumas can also decimate your view of the world as a safe place, where events unfold predictably and coherently, and where you have a substantial measure of control as well as a capacity to cope. When the trauma involves harm inflicted by someone else, especially one in whom you've placed your trust, you may come to see everyone as malevolent, unpredictable, and untrustworthy, and yourself as powerless and incompetent.

Rational response helps you recast this dark worldview, not only because it's inaccurate in its one-sidedness, but because it causes you immense suffering. Indeed, your negative worldview, unconsciously adopted in the advent of shattering trauma, not only contributes to your pain, but also keeps it going for years or decades. Your readiness to startle is a result of a nervous system wired for mistrust; your avoidance is a result of your abiding fear of people and places you view as unsafe; and your numbing is a defense against inner and outer reminders of just how unsafe the world feels.

Here are guidelines for applying the rational response method to your PTSD. While you can practice these exercises on your own, consider it an adjunct to professional treatment, since PTSD is not a condition you should try to handle entirely by yourself.

Step 1: Find the Culprit

Start by keeping a journal of your automatic negative thoughts that arise day to day, especially when you're feeling anxious or depressed, having physical symptoms, or engaging in substance abuse. Keep a record of any events that trigger flashbacks, intrusive memories or thoughts, or negative feelings linked to your traumatic event(s). Be particularly mindful of thoughts associated with guilt or shame arising from your traumas.

Consider the following list of distorted thoughts commonly held by those who suffer from PTSD, and ask yourself which one(s) you harbor:

I should have been able to prevent it.
I should be over this by now.
I brought this on myself.
I am a weak, bad person.
I'm in danger now.
Something terrible could happen at any minute.
I can't let my guard down.
No one will be there to help me if I need it.
I must always be on the alert.
I'll be overwhelmed if I think about what happened.

Step 2: Peeling the Onion

Peel the onion of your negative thoughts, getting down to the rock-bottom assumptions upon which they are based. In PTSD, there are some nearly universal core negative thoughts, although which ones you harbor will depend partly on the kind of trauma you suffered and partly on your personality. For instance, if you were traumatized by a car accident, you're afraid to drive again because you're flooded by thoughts such as "I'm in danger now" and "Something terrible could happen at any minute." Peel the onion, and your core negative thought is: "The world is inherently unpredictable and dangerous." However, if you were sexually abused as a child, your automatic negative thought in various relationships might be "Something terrible could happen at any minute." Peel the onion, and you uncover "I can't trust anyone."

When your trauma is sexual or physical abuse, whether it occurred in the distant or recent past or is still ongoing, you may struggle ceaselessly against negative thoughts such as "I'm weak"; "I'll be overwhelmed if I think about what happened"; and "I'm a terrible person." Your core negative thought, the one lurking below the surface of these floaters, often is: "What happened is my fault." Ask yourself whether you've been knowingly or unknowingly hanging onto this thought. If so, take special care as you do your reality check (step #3) and develop your rational response (step #4). When you believe that you're at fault for traumas of sexual or physical abuse, rape or interpersonal violence, you compound your own psychological and spiritual suffering. You must work hard to ferret out your self-blame, then examine it in the light of a compassionate awareness.

The universality of core negative thoughts in PTSD is quite apparent to therapists working closely with these patients. Here are some key examples:

What happened is my fault.
You can't trust anyone.
Bad things can happen at any time.
I am powerless to prevent catastrophe.
Life is pointless.
The future is bleak.
The world is basically unpredictable and dangerous.

Step 3: Reality Check

Carolyn, who suffered early sexual abuse, recognized her core negative thoughts as "What happened is my fault" and "You can't trust anyone." With the help of my cognitive-behavioral therapist colleague, Jill Compton, Ph.D., she ran them through reality check. These beliefs did not stand up to scrutiny.

Carolyn, whose story I will detail in the next chapter, used imaginary exposure (reliving her traumatic memories) and real-life exposure (confronting present-day situations that triggered her traumatic memories) to help herself get well. These exposure practices made it easier for her to restructure her erroneous beliefs. Specifically, as Carolyn consciously relived her memories of abuse, confronting the truth of what happened and her powerlessness as a young child, she rejected any shred of blame or responsibility. And when, in real life, she let herself be alone with male authority figures—a circumstance she'd always dreaded and avoided at all costs—she learned through experience that she was capable of trust. This learning process seemed to occur on a cellular level, because her bodily responses also changed. Alone with male figures, she no longer experienced the heart palpitations and trembling that had once plagued her. Carolyn's successful treatment is a wonderful illustration of how exposure and rational response can work hand in glove.

But questioning such deep assumptions may not come easily. For example, victims of early abuse often grow up with such self-loathing, guilt, and mistrust that they end up in adult relationships in which they are repeatedly victimized. If you re-create conditions in which you experience abuse, it only reaffirms your cynical worldview that people can't be trusted and the world is inhospitable. This pattern makes rational responses difficult, because you're likely to marshal examples, going back years or decades, to buttress your negative case. Here, a strong relationship with a therapist can be crucial. You learn through this relationship that others can be trusted, that you can handle your traumatic memories, and that the world is not nearly as unsafe as you'd come to believe.

On your own, you can steadfastly search for evidence that contradicts your deeply held views. You consciously shift from marshaling evidence for a negative worldview to a more benign and balanced view. (Remember, your purpose is not to whitewash the reality of bad people and evil intentions, but rather to stop piling evidence on the negative side of the scale, so you can attain some moral and psychological equilibrium.) One way is to record the experiences with friends, family, schoolmates, work colleagues, or authority figures in which you've felt safe. Alternately, or in addition, create a list of people in your life, whether past or present, whom you've found to be genuinely trustworthy.

Step 4: Rational Response

From your reality check process, you now have "alternative evidence" of people and the world, the raw material with which you can develop rational responses.

Make a concerted effort to turn to this alternative evidence whenever you become mired in insecurity, trepidation, depression, or anger. No matter what kind of trauma you've experienced—whether it be abuse, violent attack, combat experiences, or man-made or natural disasters—don't allow your inner case against people or the world to go unchallenged indefinitely.

When you've been traumatized, there's little risk that you'll embrace a gullible, Pollyanna view of the world. The only exception is the victim of early abuse who, as an adult, unwittingly and repeatedly enters into abusive relationships with his or her eyes closed. Even here, the cycle of trust and mistreatment only serves to fuel a subconscious view of people (e.g., men, women, authority figures, . . . depending on the characteristics of the abuser) as untrustworthy. As you develop rational responses, your purpose is to embrace the complexity of people and the world, finding oases of trust and safety to counterbalance your long-held recognition of the dark side.

Based upon her trauma of early sexual abuse, Carolyn developed the following rational response to one of her core negative thoughts:

CORE
NEGATIVE
THOUGHT: "I cannot trust any man in a position of power."

RATIONAL
RESPONSE: "I'm now aware that my deep mistrust and even my
             physical reactions to men in positions of power are
             the direct result of the years of sexual abuse I experi-
             enced at the hands of my uncle. I can, indeed I must,
             be mindful that when these feelings arise, they come
             from my past. Now, I can put myself in the presence
             of men in positions of power—professors, advisors,
             or physicians—and recognize what I am feeling and
             why I am feeling it. I can tolerate these emotions

better, because I know that the person I am with is not the cause. I can also keep my eyes wide open, just in case I find myself with an individual who is, in fact, untrustworthy. But this has not happened since I've acquired my newfound awareness. I now see my faculty advisors, professors, and male doctors as well-intentioned decent men. I can be with them and experience trust, and I can be myself without feeling that they will cruelly take advantage of me."

Here's another rational response, drawn from our clinical experience with veterans with PTSD:

TRAUMA: Combat stress; witnessing the death of fellow soldiers on the battlefield.

SYMPTOMS: Intense startle reactions, trepidation in situations that involve minimal risk (e.g., driving), hot temper, cynical about others' motives, survivor guilt, alcohol abuse, moderate depression.

CORE
NEGATIVE
THOUGHT: "The world is inherently unpredictable and dangerous."

RATIONAL
RESPONSE: "Having confronted my memories of death and destruction on the battlefield, I now realize just how traumatized I was by these experiences. I denied the real impact of these events because I thought, 'I'm alive, and my body wasn't destroyed.' But I can see now how witnessing the horrible deaths of comrades, a few of whom were close friends, and living in constant danger of death affected my mind and body.

So my belief that the world is basically dangerous and unpredictable comes from these awful experiences. Now I can separate the past from the present, because I know exactly where all my fear and jumpiness comes from. I can see that other people are not out to destroy me; that if you're a careful driver, then driving on highways is not that unsafe; that terrorists are not lurking around every corner. I can let myself relax because that's the only way I can be productive and enjoy my life. I can also feel proud of my contributions to defending our country."

OVERTURN YOUR OBSESSIONS: RATIONAL RESPONSE FOR OCD

When you suffer from OCD, you're hounded by obsessive thoughts that are always fear-based. In most cases, your worst-case scenarios are so terrifying that you are literally driven to perform ritual behaviors to fend off the anxiety your thoughts arouse. If you wash your hands forty times a day, it's because you believe, on some level, that a normal hand-washing routine—a few times a day—would never be sufficient to counter the threat of virulent germs getting on your skin. When you check the stove for ten minutes before leaving for work, it's because you're convinced the house might burn down otherwise. Other obsessions are even more unrealistic, and the rituals employed in a vain effort to fend off fear rarely make sense from an objective point of view. If you suffer from this syndrome, you may well be aware that your obsessions and compulsions aren't rational, but you *still* can't stop yourself.

That is why changing your fearful beliefs is only one strategy for overcoming OCD, and not the central one. If you only tried to question your fears of germs, fires, or other lethal threats, it's not too likely that you would succeed in your efforts to heal. Based on a body of clinical research, it's clear that exposure to the very sources of your fear—the "vaccination of the mind"—is the most powerful treatment for OCD. Because exposure is experiential, you learn in the most immediate way that your fears are unfounded. But changing your beliefs is an effective adjunct to exposure—a secondary but often extremely helpful strategy.

You can apply the rational response method to the kind of thoughts that typically arise, including:

Germs are everywhere and they can infect me at any time.
I've definitely been *contaminated*.
I have to clean this right now or germs will spread.
I just know that the house will burn down.
I forgot to lock the door and the house will be invaded.
I know I have cancer.
The house is in disorder, and if it's not perfect I'll go crazy.
If I throw away ____, I'll need it in the future and it won't be there.
Everything has to be just right, or else I'll be struck down by
    bad luck.
I'd better check ____, or everything will be in disarray.
Something awful will happen to someone I love, and it will be my
    fault unless I ____.
If I don't keep myself under control, I could do something terrible.
I'm a horrible person for having such thoughts.

My colleague and collaborator, Edna B. Foa, Ph.D., of the University of Pennsylvania School of Medicine, a great pioneer in the treatment of anxiety disorders, including OCD, catalogued the errors apparent in this kind of obsessive thinking. Among them are:

1. You view the world as dangerous until proven safe rather than safe until proven dangerous.
2. Your ideas about probability are substantially off base. Example: You wildly overestimate the chances that your house will burn down, even if you were to leave the gas jets on.

3. You judge events on the basis of limited information immediately at hand rather than complete information. Example: You hear sensational news stories about people murdered by burglars and you blow out of proportion the risk of this happening to you.

4. You focus so exclusively on trying to reduce the risk of harm that you ignore the losses you suffer because of your avoidance and ritualistic behavior. Example: You hoard hundreds of old newspapers in piles all over your apartment, trying to reduce the risk that you'll lose some vital piece of information, but meanwhile you've created a fire hazard and alienated your spouse to the brink of divorce.

When you apply rational response, use Dr. Foa's list of common errors in thinking to find the culprit, peel the onion, and perform a reality check. Ask yourself whether your fears are based on a reasonable grasp of probability. Are your fears based on limited information, like media reports that spotlight incredibly rare events and make them seem commonplace? (Examples: terrorist attacks, hamburgers contaminated by *E. coli,* serial murders, etc.) Are you so gripped by fear that you neglect to recognize the risks and losses associated with your compulsive rituals? (Example: Your checking behavior makes you late to work so often that you are in danger of losing your job.)

In Chapter 2, I told you about Lester, who combined medications with psychotherapy to unravel his obsessive-compulsive behavior. Lester was so terrified of catching an infectious "plague" that he repeatedly washed not only his hands, but the rest of his body, his desk at work, his car, and other objects with which he came into regular contact. Here is an example of one of Lester's rational response practices:

Step 1: Finding the Culprit

Finding the culprit is often a simpler process for OCD sufferers than it is for people with other forms of anxiety. Lester was fully aware of his automatic negative thoughts, because they relentlessly invaded his consciousness every day and they were basically the same all the time: "Because I came into contact with X, Y, or Z, I may have become contaminated with germs that will cause me to become infected with a deadly disease—possibly the plague." You may recall that Lester's obsessions about germs and compulsive washing started twenty years earlier, after he had removed a dead mouse from the oil pan in his car. He now believes that the onset of his OCD was related to the intense stress he was experiencing at work during that time in his life.

Step 2: Peeling the Onion

When you have OCD, the "onion" of your negative thoughts has few layers. Two or three peels, and you usually get to the bottom line: "Something horrible, life-threatening, or damaging will happen to me, my loved one(s), or my home." Depending on your particular obsessive thought, the focus will probably be on harm to yourself, your family members, or your abode. Lester feared for himself and his family: He would catch bubonic plague, get deathly ill, and pass on the infection to his wife and children.

Sometimes the core negative thoughts are not about death or the destruction of one's home and security. Some OCD patients obsess about acting out sexually, becoming violent, or losing control. Their fundamental fear may be of humiliation, punishment, or ostracism.

It's important to realize, though, that when you have OCD, you are not only afraid for your life, you're also afraid that you can't tolerate your own fear and anxiety, and that they will overtake you until you're emotionally shattered. As I will show, a combination of exposure and serenity skills can enable you to tolerate your fears and anxieties. This approach, sometimes called *distress tolerance,* enables you to move beyond fear.

Step 3: Reality Check

When you perform a reality check to question your obsessive assumptions, it's best to have the help of a therapist—an objective mind who can expose the logical inconsistencies and holes in your core negative beliefs. But on your own, make your best effort to marshal facts on the side of safety. Think of it this way: You may have spent years, perhaps most of your life, with a debate going on in your head between assumptions of safety and assumptions of threat. If each side of the debate is a team, the threat team has been loaded with loud, strong-willed debaters whereas the safety team has one lone voice only capable of a whisper. Now it's time, finally, to give the safety side of the debate a real chance. Strengthen the voices on this team and procure lots of information—at least make your own internal version of *Crossfire* more balanced and fair.

In the case of Lester, his therapist helped him to question the extraordinary illogic of some of his fear-based beliefs. For instance, if Lester even touched a newspaper before leaving his house in the morning, he would either have to wash his hands again (often for the fifth or sixth time—and it was only 8:00 A.M.), or he'd have to avoid touching anything whatsoever, on himself or in the house. During a reality check, his therapist had Lester take apart this belief, part of his "castle" of fears and regulations. He worried about "contamination" from the newspaper, but the real problem was that the black ink "looked dirty" if any got on his hands. Ink is not dirt, his therapist pointed out, and even if it was, contact with dirt does not cause infection in someone with a healthy immune system. Then his therapist asked pointed questions: Had Lester ever read that newspaper ink is potentially lethal or infectious? To his knowledge, has anyone ever gotten sick or died from newspaper ink or from dirt on a newspaper? Lester had to admit that he had no hard information to back up his fears about newspaper contamination.

Step 4: Rational Response

Construct a rational response to your obsessive fears, particularly the ones that drive any compulsive behaviors on your part. Here is a sample from Lester:

CORE
NEGATIVE
THOUGHT: If I don't wash the germs from my hands after I touch newspapers, I risk getting seriously sick with an infectious disease.

RATIONAL
RESPONSE: I've learned that anxiety rises up in me when I fear being contaminated from any source, like a newspaper or a dead mouse. First, I can question the assumption that I might get infected. I've consciously decided to explore whether newspaper ink can make me seriously sick, and the answer is it can't. If I swallowed several gulps of ink from an ink bottle it would be toxic, but I get no such exposure from small smudges of ink on my fingers. I've never heard of anyone getting sick from touching newspapers. People work in newspaper printing rooms for decades, and they don't die of toxicity or infection.

> But I have my belief that if I don't wash my
> hands, I will become so riddled with anxiety that I
> will not be able to function. I've learned through
> experience that I can handle some anxiety and that it
> may get temporarily worse, but if I don't try to drive
> it away by washing my hands, it will begin to subside.

Toward the end of *The Wizard of Oz,* you may recall, the Wizard is caught behind his curtain and exposed as an ordinary man from Kansas, albeit a particularly clever and wily character. In one of the movie's most poignant scenes, he tells Dorothy and her compatriots that they already possess the traits they've been seeking; they merely need some form of affirmation. To the Cowardly Lion, who's been searching for his courage, the Wizard says, "As for you, my fine friend, you're a victim of disorganized thinking. You are under the unfortunate delusion that just because you run from danger you have no courage."

When you suffer from any form of anxiety, you are precisely a victim of erroneous thinking. And the fact that your anxiety causes you to avoid stressful situations—to "run from danger"—does not mean you lack courage. You lack only the means to awaken your native courage. To rouse that inner strength, it helps immeasurably to overturn your fearful beliefs through the rational response method. Your next step in this sequential approach to healing is to actively confront your fears through a compassionate but challenging method called *exposure.*

4

SOLUTION 2: VACCINATE YOUR ANXIOUS MIND—EXPOSURE THERAPY

Vaccines present the body with small amounts of a disease agent—bacteria, viruses, other microbes—so that our immune systems mount a proper defense against them. Since childhood, we've understood this basic principle of *inoculation*: Exposed to bits of a bug that have been rendered harmless, our systems are armed and ready.

Exposure, a psychotherapy method, is like psychological inoculation. If you have anxiety—say, a phobia—your whole psychological "system" is thrown into chaos when confronted by a specific stimulus. (In phobias, the stimulus is usually an object—say, a snake, spider, or dog—or an experience—flying on a plane, being in a crowd, speaking before a large group.) During exercises of exposure, you confront those very objects or experiences a bit at a time, until you build up psychological immunity. Just as the immune system has memory and defenses, so does the brain. As you're gently and gradually exposed to the triggers of your darkest fears, you gently and gradually learn that they are no real sources of danger or that they're a source of danger you can effectively manage. You build up your mental defenses until your terror subsides and you no longer expend so much psychic energy in torment or in hiding.

When you practice exposure, you enter real-world situations where you face the things, people, or situations that make you anxious. (These anxiety triggers are called *cues*.) Ideally, you practice this form of exposure with the help of a "support person"—a friend or therapist—who accompanies you as you fly on a plane, pet a dog, or ride an elevator. In time, you can confront these objects or situations without your support person.

Each form of anxiety involves different kinds of cues, which require different kinds of exposure therapy. For a specific phobia, the cue is the feared object or experience. For social phobia, the cue is the social situation—presenting your work, speaking to a group, going to a party. For generalized anxiety, the cues are life circumstances (e.g., a visit to your doctor or accountant) or mental reveries on a subject that makes you worry ceaselessly. For panic disorder, the cues are the physical sensations you experience in the midst of a panic attack—the shaking, sweating, and palpitations that make you feel out of control. For obsessive-compulsive disorder, the cues are situations that spur obsessive fears or the mental images or thoughts that corral you into ritual behavior.

Exposure can be used for all forms of anxiety, but some require a different sort of approach. For instance, if you suffer from posttraumatic stress, you might have symptoms (e.g., flashbacks, irritability, numbness, hypervigilance) that are set off by certain life circumstances. But your real cues are not the circumstances themselves. They lie within, in your mind. What frightens you most, the ultimate trigger of your condition, is the *memory* of the trauma (or traumas) that caused your condition in the first place.

Can you "expose" yourself to a memory? The answer is yes. You can inoculate yourself against the harmful effects of traumatic memories by reexperiencing them, a little bit at a time. Using your own imagination, in an exercise I will call *imaginary exposure,** you can retrieve and reexperience a traumatic memory. Think about exactly what happened and what you felt at the time. The purpose is to let in the shock, anger, terror, or heartbreak—emotions that were too threatening to experience at the time of the trauma or since. The goal is to keep reliving the memory in your imagination until your emotional distress peaks, then finally subsides. Having confronted the memory and discovered that you can handle the pain it evokes, you can finally live with that memory. It no longer threatens you like the monstrous murderer who lurks around every corner in a serial horror movie, because you've looked that monster straight in the eye and survived. You've not only survived, but you've become more whole, and you've effectively freed yourself from the clutches of a traumatic memory.

It's most helpful to perform exposure exercises with the help of a therapist and the assistance of a support person. If you can't find or afford a therapist, ask a highly trusted individual to be your support person. This individual should be the friend or family member to whom you feel most comfortable admitting your anxiety symptoms, the one least likely to judge you for your condition. With that person's help, you can follow the basic guidelines here on practicing exposure on your own. After I provide these guidelines, I'll demonstrate how you can tailor exposure to your specific form of anxiety.

Here are essential guidelines for *real-life exposure*:

---

* Cognitive-behavioral therapists usually refer to this practice as "imaginal exposure" or "prolonged imaginal exposure."

1. *Prepare and set goals.* Exposure is a challenging process for which you need to prepare in two key ways. First, understand that an intrinsic part of the process involves *learning to tolerate your anxiety.* Perhaps it seems contradictory that a treatment designed to reduce anxiety has you learning to tolerate it, but that's exactly the point. By learning to directly face and handle your anxieties, rather than run from them, you gain mastery over them. For instance, if you have a spider phobia, you're never going to feel safe in your house, because a spider could turn up around any corner. But if you're able to be in the same room as a spider, then get closer and closer, feeling and tolerating your anxiety while learning firsthand that the spider can't hurt you, your anxiety will slowly subside. You've gained mastery over your spider phobia. So be prepared to feel some anxiety, and reassure yourself that it doesn't have to overwhelm you. Know that countless others have gone through the same procedure, with the same intense fears, and have not only survived but thrived.

Set clear goals: If you have a driving phobia, specify that you want to drive on a highway. If you're phobic about public speaking, decide that you are going to give an important talk at work. If you have a dog phobia, make it your goal to pet a dog. Decide exactly what you want to do, and give yourself a time frame for reaching your goal. For instance, if you have social anxiety that has made you shy away from all parties, decide that within three months you'll attend a party of friends or coworkers.

2. *Create an exposure hierarchy.* Since exposure is based on the principle of "a little bit at a time," it's important that you develop a hierarchy of steps, from least anxiety-provoking to most, in which you "expose" yourself to your anxiety triggers. If you're afraid of flying, exposure does not mean that you buy a ticket, go to the airport, and board the plane. Rather, you create a hierarchy of steps like the following:

1. Take your support person with you to an airport and walk inside the terminal.
2. Join with your support person at a departure gate and look out the window, watching planes take off and land. (You may need to request a security pass to do this!)
3. Repeat steps 1 and 2, but this time go by yourself.
4. Book a ticket for a short (half-hour) flight for yourself and your support person.
5. Take the flight with your support person.
6. Schedule and take a longer flight with your support person.
7. Schedule and take a short (half-hour) flight by yourself.
8. Schedule and take a longer flight by yourself.

In our post-9/11 world, step 2 of this procedure may be hard to pull off, given the new security measures. But the exercise is one good model of an exposure hierarchy; there are other kinds that fit other forms of anxiety. For instance, let's say you're a woman with severe social anxiety, and a variety of circumstances trigger your fear of being judged. You might construct a hierarchy like this:

1. Call a friend to make plans.
2. Meet that friend for lunch.
3. Speak up at a small work meeting of several colleagues.
4. Speak up at a work meeting of many colleagues and your boss.
5. Go to a party of strangers accompanied by your support person.
6. Go to a party of strangers by yourself.
7. Strike up a conversation with a male coworker to whom you are attracted.
8. Call the man and ask him for a date.
9. Go on the date.

3. *Practice exposure, recover, and repeat.* Once you've created your hierarchy, it's time to follow through with your "exposure" plan. To help you gauge this delicate process, you can use a simple anxiety scale. Ba-

sically, it's a ten-point scale in which zero represents no anxiety, and ten represents the most anxiety you've ever felt. Use this tool to assess your own anxiety levels as you move through your hierarchy. It will help you tune into yourself, so that you can learn to tolerate gradually increasing levels of distress without getting overwhelmed or flooding yourself with distress.

Let's return to the airplane example. You go into an airport terminal with your support person and walk around. Every five minutes or so, you check into yourself and rate your anxiety from zero to ten. You allow your anxiety level to rise to a four or five—when it seems increasingly hard to manage—then give yourself a break by, say, stepping outside the terminal or browsing in a bookstore. Then return to the terminal, and make the same rounds, going to the ticket counter and toward the departure gates, all "cues" bringing you closer to the experience of getting on an airplane. You let your anxiety level rise again and then continue . . . until you notice a drop-off by a few points. The whole process could take longer than an hour, but remember your purpose: You *want* to experience difficult levels of anxiety *until you gradually become used to the experience and your anxiety starts to abate.*

The best analogy for the start-stop-start technique of exposure is swimming in cold ocean waters. You start by getting your feet wet. Then you wade in until the seawater laps at your legs, then step back and then forward again, letting parts of your body adjust to the bracing cold. The hardest part is often your back and belly: You may need to move in and out a few times before finally jumping headlong into the waves and breaking into a breast stroke. In those first moments after whole-body immersion you'll experience the waters as freezing; five or ten minutes later, your body will have adjusted to the chilly temperatures.

For exposure, your adjustment process to the cold waters of anxiety is called *habituation* or *desensitization.* You move back a little, then move forward again (also called *recover and repeat*), but for any one step in your anxiety hierarchy, do your best to stay the course. In other words, when the waters get too cold, step back, but try not to run out of the ocean to dry land and a warm towel. Use your zero-to-ten scale to gauge your progress, knowing that once you've "habituated"—learned that you can tolerate your anxiety and nothing terrible will happen—you'll notice a drop in your anxiety levels. That's your sign that exposure is working.

Here are the basic guidelines for *imaginary exposure:* Turn to imaginary exposure whenever real-life exposure is impossible or impractical: when your anxiety cues are not readily available, when it isn't realistically possible to evoke them, or when, as in PTSD, your anxiety cues are thought clusters or memories that only reside in your mind.

Let's say you have a snake phobia and you're about to go camping. How do you expose yourself to a snake so you don't have a complete anxiety meltdown if you happen to encounter this creature in the wild? The answer is: You expose yourself beforehand to snakes *in your imagination.* First, you construct the same sort of hierarchy as you would for real-life exposure: You and your support person see a snake behind a glass cage; you see the snake without your support person; you and your support person see a snake at a distance in the wild; you're by yourself when you see the snake in the wild, etc. But you accomplish all this in your imagination. Either with the help of a therapist or on your own, go into a quiet introspective state by closing your eyes and taking several slow, deep breaths. Then allow these scenes to unfold in your mind's eye. Imaginary exposure can enable you to tolerate and ultimately reduce your distress levels in exactly the same manner as real-life exposure.

Let's say you suffer from generalized anxiety and you worry obses-

sively about the death of a parent or spouse. You can only expose yourself to this "cue" in your imagination. Or you're dreadfully afraid of
public performance. You can't arrange to give a performance specifically for your exposure practice, and you certainly can't rig a real-life
hierarchy of performance situations that range from mildly to very distressing. But you can *imagine* yourself giving progressively more anxiety-
provoking performances in front of larger and larger groups of people.

When you have PTSD, your real anxiety cue is a traumatic memory.
In these cases, it's usually best to practice imaginary exposure with a
therapist, because the memories that surface can be very painful, even
shattering. You'll need the support and professional guidance that only
a therapist can provide. That doesn't mean you can never be alone
when you practice imaginary exposure for traumatic memories, rather
that it's safer and more effective to work with a therapist, e*specially*
when you first try this technique.

In the following sections, I provide more detailed guidance on how to
employ exposure therapy for your specific form of anxiety. The methods I have outlined thus far are well suited for generalized anxiety
(GAD). Anyone with generalized anxiety will benefit from rational response, and some (though perhaps not all) will benefit from exposure.
If you have generalized anxiety, how do you know whether or not to
practice exposure? The answer is clear: When worry causes you to
avoid all sorts of real-life situations, such as conversations that make
you anxious, people you fear or admire, challenging jobs, parties or
other gatherings, vacations that require means of transportation that
make you nervous or take you places that give you jitters.

If you suffer from GAD, use the guidelines I've provided thus far to
engage in real-life exposure in circumstances you usually avoid, and use

imaginary exposure when you worry obsessively about future circumstances you find threatening. You can imagine yourself in these situations, exposing yourself repeatedly to these events in your imagination until you can handle your feelings more effectively and the anxiety begins to subside.

In the remainder of this chapter, I'll offer more specialized guidelines for using exposure to treat your social anxieties, panic, phobias, PTSD, obsessions, and compulsions.

STAND AND DELIVER:
EXPOSURE FOR SOCIAL ANXIETY

Treating your social anxiety (with medication, rational response, etc.) without using exposure would be like treating a broken leg without taking off the cast. Using rational response for social fears is akin to correcting the break in a limb by treating the wound and applying the cast. Rational response sets your thinking straight, giving your mind and emotions a chance to heal themselves from psychic wounds and biochemical imbalances. To continue the analogy, the next phase of healing a broken leg is just as essential. The doctor removes the cast and sends you to rehab, where physical therapists help you exercise the leg to tone your muscles, which have atrophied from disuse. Finally, you get out into the world and walk, to further restore muscle tone and regain your full strength and flexibility.

Likewise, after you've begun to heal wounds inflicted by relentless negative thinking, you need to start "exercising" your social abilities. That's the purpose of exposure for social phobia. First, you "practice" meeting people or public speaking in a group with the help of a therapist and support person. (It's the psychological equivalent of going to a rehab center for your broken leg.) If you join a group, you participate in role-play exercises with other members in a safe and supportive environment. Finally, you get out into the real world and do the very things that have made you anxious, whether it's dating, attending social events, performing, or talking in meetings. Your purpose is twofold: You're "testing out" your newly rational thinking in relation to others, and you're rebuilding your social muscles, which may have atrophied after years of disuse. As with physical rehab, which wouldn't have you jog the first day out, you don't instantly dive into the toughest social situations. You progress a bit at a time, starting with mildly difficult circumstances and moving gradually to the most distressing.

While I encourage you to find a cognitive-behavioral group for anxiety, if you can't, follow the guidelines here for real-life exposure. But without a group or an individual therapist, proceed gradually. If you push too hard or fast, you might retreat back into your protective armor. Exposure requires you to sustain a delicate balance: You want to challenge yourself, but you don't want to pressure yourself to the point where you suffer a backlash of fear. You can also practice imaginary exposure—putting yourself in feared social situations in your imagination so you experience the resulting anxiety, repeatedly, until you can tolerate the feeling. It's a way to prepare yourself for real-life exposure, and it's useful when your dreaded social situations occur rarely—e.g., a musical performance—and the only way to re-create them is in your imagination.

Whenever you practice exposure—in your imagination, in therapy, or in real life—monitor your anxiety from beginning to end. Use the zero-to-ten rating system to gauge your anxiety levels, noting how much they increase when you first "expose" yourself to social stress. Then see whether the levels drop off as you continue. The more you repeat the exposure exercise, the more your anxiety should subside.

Recall from the last chapter the story of Scott, the retired navy pilot who showed great valor during his time in the service. Later in life, Scott struggled with severe social anxiety, first in his corporate job, then as he tried to start up a retail jewelry business. Scott's progress was cemented during the exposure phase of his therapy, initially in group, then in real life. In his group, he participated in role-play exercises that re-created his anxiety-provoking work situations. First, he wrote down his five most feared situations, from the least to the most anxiety-inducing. (This is a standard practice of exposure; the list is called a *fear hierarchy*.) Then he acted out these mini dramas with a therapist or fellow group member.

One of Scott's less fearful situations was to return a shirt to a cranky department store clerk. One of his most distressing circumstances was speaking in front of a large group of people. After testing the waters by role-playing these situations in his group, Scott's "assignment" was to do the same thing, this time in real life.

Scott set himself a specific goal from the top tier of his fear hierarchy. A jewelry trade association was having its annual meeting, and Scott knew there would be a gathering of three hundred people in which everyone would have a chance to address the whole group. Scott wanted to introduce himself, a plum opportunity to give his new business a higher profile. His plan was to stand up and tell the whole audience about himself and his business. The meeting occurred toward the end of Scott's sixteen-week course of therapy, so he was able to attend the meeting and report back to the group. Here's how Scott described what happened:

> The night before, I thought about the coping tools I would use in this situation. I studied my notes from the role plays in group that had put me in exactly this situation. Then, the next day, the CEO changed the game plan. Originally he had planned on having people come up and

speak, but instead a mike was going to be passed around for everyone to voice their opinion.

You can imagine me in this group of three hundred, and the mike is coming around the room to me. I was one of the last people to get it, so I had a long time to think. It couldn't have been a better-designed scenario. I remember having the usual feelings, the usual anxiety, the same "I'll do anything to avoid this." In the group I learned that my anxiety took over when I had time to think ahead. But when I was thrust into a leadership role—like in the navy, when our plane was impounded—I was great. So I tried to put myself into that leadership frame of mind, even though I had so much time to think.

I must have been the 150th person to speak. When the mike finally came, I stood up and introduced my wife. Then I took a risk and cracked a little joke, and people laughed. I was bound and determined not to see their reactions, but I did it anyway. I saw them in a kind of different way. I wasn't looking for the person shaking his head and being bored. I was looking for the person who had a positive response, because they're out there, too. I locked onto one of them. Then I made a suggestion for the trade association.

I sat down, and my wife whispered, "That was great!" At the end, the CEO said, "Well we've gotten a lot of good suggestions, I especially like the idea I heard . . ." He was talking about mine. When I went back to our [social anxiety] group, I told everyone: "It can be done!"

I used the skills I learned from the group, including rational response. During my talk I thought, probably 299 of these 300 people are being more critical of themselves—what they're going to say or what they already said—than of me. And why would they judge me? I've got every reason to stand up and be a leader here. And I have my lovely wife with me. I focused on her contributions [to their business], and praising her kept me from focusing too much on myself. I remember doing that in the service when I was in a leadership role—focusing on my crew's contributions. When I sat down, I looked at all these people, and I thought, "Maybe I've got more friends than enemies here."

Scott's experience exemplifies the value of exposure. On paper, exposure sounds like a cold shower, but in practice it can be a warm revelation. He remembered how in the navy his leadership instincts took over when he had little time to ponder the circumstances. The memory of taking charge when his flight crew was taken into custody by Thai policemen with guns reminded Scott of his capabilities. He also knew that it would be folly to try to extinguish his anxiety. By definition exposure involves discomfort—Scott admits having been "a nervous wreck" at the trade meeting. Indeed, exposure is like physical exercise: no pain, no gain. Yet as Scott's story illustrates, learning to tolerate some distress in social situations is only one aspect of exposure. Another key is to see others in a less fear-based, more positive light, so that when you bring this recognition with you into a room of people, your anxiety abates.

By confronting rather than running from your fears, you break the cycle in which avoidance and anxiety feed upon each other. Emerging from the shadows of evasion, you recognize that your worst fears almost never materialize. When you break your addiction to avoidance, you discover that your recurring images of social disaster were off base, and you reenter the stream of life with increasing comfort. You also discover that when you do feel embarrassed, the consequences are not catastrophic. *Living with some anxiety is better than living in constant dread of anxiety.* In the former, you stay in the present, and your experiences and feelings change dynamically as you interact with people. In the latter, you live in the past or the future, shunning certain kinds of social contact and remaining frozen in a state of anticipatory fear. When you're diligent in your practice of exposure, your social anxieties abate over time, and the anxiety you do feel is just the inescapable result of being alive in the world.

PANIC INJECTIONS: NORA'S STORY

Exposure has proved to be extremely useful in treating panic disorder. As with other forms of anxiety, exposure for panic involves gradual contact with the object, thoughts, or sensations that trigger the anxiety attack, until finally it becomes possible to confront that which has always seemed utterly overwhelming.

Someone for whom exposure proved particularly helpful was Nora, an emergency room nurse. Nora had two small children and a reputation among her friends and family for being the person that everyone could lean on. She loved her children so much that she felt she could deny them nothing. At work, she was consistently given the toughest assignments, including breaking the news to families of patients who had just died in the ER. Nora thought of herself as someone who couldn't say no, or "I'm not up to that right now." No matter what it took, she would always reach inside and wrest the emotional resources to do whatever had to be done.

One day Nora was driving along the highway when she suddenly felt light-headed. Her heart was palpitating, her hands were sweaty, and she thought she was going to faint. Although Nora was shaken by the experience, she didn't think much of it at first. But when she started having similar panic attacks, she began to avoid driving in general and highways in particular.

Her panic attacks spread to other settings. Nora began avoiding circumstances where she had to stand in line, like at the grocery store. She was unable to go shopping by herself. She limited herself in one situation after another, but the attacks didn't go away. Instead, they took over even more areas of Nora's life. Her case is a prime example of how avoidance as a way to cope with anxiety attacks doesn't work; it only makes matters worse.

The emotions grew worse, too, expanding from mild panic episodes to full-blown panic attacks. Perhaps most disturbing to Nora was her inability to comprehend why this was happening to her. Although her racing heart and dizziness made her suspect a heart condition, she knew she had no medical basis for such a diagnosis. She got tested for allergies, thyroid problems, and hyperglycemia, desperate to find a physical syndrome that would explain her symptoms. For a while, she thought she was suffering from severe PMS. Then she thought perhaps she had a systemic yeast infection. Though she went from doctor to doctor in search of an answer, Nora never got one, and she was never able to stop the attacks.

"I always thought of myself as being in control," Nora says now. "I think that feeling so out of control was the most difficult part."

When Nora finally came to see me, she was at the end of her tether. However, the moment she heard my diagnosis and description of panic disorder, she felt enormous relief. We discussed the prevalence of panic, the fact that many decent, strong, and sensitive people are prone to this disorder. "I was so relieved to hear that I wasn't going crazy," Nora says now. "And to hear that it's not something wrong with me, that I'm not bad, and that it doesn't mean I'm not a strong person." I told Nora that coming to see me proved she possessed strength of character. "That was the best thing you could tell me," she later confided.

I worked with Nora to find the right medication, but I also believed she would benefit from exposure. We began with imaginary exposure exercises. I asked her to visualize her worst-case scenario, which for her was having a panic attack on the highway. Gradually, Nora came to realize that the worst that could happen was that she'd have to pull over and get out of the car. "All right, I'm going to look stupid, I'm going to feel out of control, but am I really going to drop dead?" Nora says now. "Then I had to think about why I was so afraid of dying."

When Nora felt relatively comfortable with imaginary exposure, we moved on to real-life exposure. Eventually, Nora recalls, "I went right back out onto the highway. Of course, I didn't go very far, but even that little trip took a lot of work. A lot of my concern was about how I looked to other people. Then I said to myself, 'If I have to pull off the road, so what? There's always a way out of the situation. I'm not confined to the car. There's always something I can do.'"

Nora challenged herself to drive farther and farther. I suggested that she progress gradually from super-short trips on the highway—getting off after one exit—to increasingly longer trips, waiting longer before exiting the highway. Initially, she took her husband with her, finding a sense of safety in his familiar presence. Finally, she began driving alone. Each time, she'd ask herself, "What's the worst that could happen?" And the answer was always surprisingly simple: that other people would see her lose control.

With the combination of medication and her exposure exercises, Nora was finally able to reduce her panic attacks. But the things she'd learned about herself in the process extended far beyond her ability to drive. "It forced me to look at other issues," she says. Nora came to realize that sometimes she had to say no, she had to take care of her own needs even as she cared for others. "A lot of nurses have this problem," she says now. "We nurture everyone but ourselves." Today Nora continues to work as a nurse, though she's left her stressful position in the ER. She's better able to set limits with her husband, children, and friends, which has made her personal life less draining and more gratifying. In fact, the transformations in Nora's life have been so profound that today she says, "I don't even regret going through the panic and its treatment. It helped me in ways I would never have imagined."

Exposure is a highly effective method for panic as well as for specific phobias—say, to spiders, snakes, dogs, or flying. Since one of the strongest triggers of panic attacks is the physical sensations themselves—the fast-beating heart and hyperventilation—some exposure therapists will have patients re-create these sensations until they gradually become accustomed to them. (This can be accomplished by fast breathing, running in place, or other physical exercises.) In essence, this is an experiential learning method: The person learns that panic-associated physical sensations do *not* mean that he or she is going to die. I don't recommend that you induce these sensations on your own, because you need a knowledgeable, supportive therapist to guide you through such an exercise. If you think you'd benefit from this form of exposure, see the Resources section to help you find a CBT therapist who uses exposure for panic.

A PSYCHOLOGICAL VACCINE FOR PTSD?

I've told you about Carolyn, the twenty-one-year-old college student who couldn't concentrate on her work and whose over-the-top emotional reactions to minor events caused strain in her friendships and family relationships. Carolyn had trouble sleeping, mostly because of nightmares, so she was always fluctuating between edginess and exhaustion. When she came to see us at Duke, she was aware that the sexual abuse by her uncle between the ages of four and seven was causing her nightmares, which were terrifying variations of her real memories. Carolyn also knew that the trauma caused her to avoid circumstances such as family reunions, driving through the town where her uncle lived, and other reminders of him. Sexual violence on TV made her physically sick, and whenever it appeared she'd have to leave the room.

But Carolyn wasn't aware that her other symptoms—her day-to-day irritability and high-strung emotionality—were symptoms of PTSD. She first met with my colleague, Dr. Kathryn Connor, who connected the dots for Carolyn, explaining that her entire complex of symptoms were the result of posttraumatic stress. Carolyn was immensely reassured by Dr. Connor's explanation that her symptoms were normal features of PTSD, problems she'd seen in scores of patients who got better with treatment. Dr. Connor's prescription was a combination of medication and cognitive therapy with exposure. She put Carolyn on the SSRI drug Zoloft (sertraline), which has been shown to be effective in treating PTSD, and referred her to our colleague, psychotherapist Dr. Jill Compton, for CBT with exposure.

Within a month of starting Zoloft, Carolyn noticed improvement in two areas: She had fewer nightmares and therefore slept more soundly, and her ability to concentrate improved. As she began to feel better, she started therapy with Jill Compton. Her treatment involved the three key elements I've discussed: imaginary exposure, real-life exposure, and cognitive restructuring. The central and most powerful part of Carolyn's therapy was the imaginary exposure. During five weeks of lengthy twice-weekly sessions, Jill guided Carolyn as she reexperienced, repeatedly in her imagination, the worst trauma of sexual abuse that she could remember.

Jill prepared Carolyn for the experience by explaining its purpose—to enable her to confront the memory and tolerate the painful feelings it brought forth. Hiding from the memory, Jill explained, had kept her psychologically "on the run," causing most of her symptoms. By facing the memory, she would finally be resolving the very source of her avoidance, anger, hyperarousal, and intrusive thoughts and nightmares. Carolyn was reassured to learn from Jill that the exposure process had helped so many PTSD sufferers to free themselves from their ceaseless suffering. Still, she was nervous when, during their second session, the exposure process began.

After relaxing in a chair and moving into her imagination, Carolyn was gently led by Jill back to a specific scene of sexual abuse by her uncle. While she'd been victimized many times, this single event had come to symbolize the terror, helplessness, and humiliation of the entire four-year period of abuse, which occasionally involved violence. At first, Jill had Carolyn share her thoughts and feelings about the memory, then prompted her to reveal specifics of the event. "She'd have me talk about [the trauma] in more and more detail as the sessions progressed," says Carolyn.

Carolyn had never told anyone such details about the trauma; she could hardly bear to think about them herself. As she shared the truth with Jill, she often spoke through tears, weeping and sometimes raging over the abuse her uncle had subjected her to. She had felt utterly trapped, having been left alone to visit him at his house many times during those years. As commonly happens in sexual abuse, her uncle threatened her harm if she told anyone. Carolyn's anger and her grief over her loss of innocence and power welled up as she reconstructed the story of her victimization.

This process, sometimes called *prolonged imaginary exposure*, was certainly cathartic, but it was more than that. Over many sessions Jill had Carolyn tell the narrative again and again, long after she'd released strong emotions during the early retelling. As she recounted the same terrible event, the emotion gradually drained out of her storytelling.

The purpose was clear: to help Carolyn learn, through direct experience, that she could possess this terrible memory without it continuing to haunt her.

The strategy worked. After the ten sessions, Carolyn no longer lived in fear of her own memories. "They used to come into my mind all the time," she said. "I'd be overwhelmed by them and push them out of my head. Now, when a memory comes up, I think, 'OK, there it is. I've dealt with this. I understand it.' I could finally handle it instead of being scared by it or forcing myself to ignore it." After repeated reexperiencing with Jill Compton, Carolyn's memory had lost its emotional intensity—and its power over her mind and spirit.

Carolyn's imaginary exposure also enabled her to make connections between her traumas of abuse and many of her current difficulties. She finally understood why she was so uncomfortable whenever she was alone in a room with male authority figures. (When she had private meetings with teachers or doctors, she could barely catch her breath, and her heart would pound in her chest.) Carolyn began to recognize the reverberations of the trauma in so many areas—her social relationships, work, and family life. The exposure process taught her more about herself in a matter of weeks than she'd gained since the traumas ended when she was seven.

Exposure also helped free her from self-blame. Carolyn had long lived with a deep-seated belief that somehow her uncle's sexual abuse was partly her fault. As she worked her way painfully through the specifics of the abuse, she discovered, with Jill Compton's sensitive guidance, that her assumption had been dead wrong. (During the exposure sessions, as Carolyn began to reflect on her experiences, Jill brought cognitive restructuring into the process, helping Carolyn to question and supplant her self-blaming beliefs.) Carolyn had used her imagination to rediscover the paralyzing terror and powerlessness she experienced as a little girl, and she recognized for the first time, in her gut, that the abuse wasn't her fault—in any way, shape, or form.

What happened to Carolyn in her therapy bears out the wisdom of the insights described by my colleagues, Elizabeth Hambree, M.D., and Edna Foa, M.D., that the three factors critical to successful processing of trauma are:

1. emotional engagement with the memory of the event
2. organizing the story of what happened
3. connecting the erroneous cognitions that are attached to the traumatic experience

While imaginary exposure was the core of Carolyn's therapy, you saw how she also used cognitive restructuring—the rational response method—to change her self-blaming beliefs. Also, based on Dr. Compton's precise suggestions, she carried out "homework" exercises in real-life exposure, in which she confronted situations that she'd previously avoided because they were linked in her mind with the abuse. (Shortly, I'll explain this approach and Carolyn's experiences with it.) After completing treatment, Carolyn felt strongly that she'd healed the wounds of her abuse, and her PTSD symptoms virtually disappeared. Today, her nightmares are almost gone. She no longer dreads being alone with men. She's less irritable and doesn't alienate friends and family. She no longer has long, inexplicable crying jags. Her relationships (and her dating experiences) are more satisfying, and her concentration is vastly improved, which she feels is responsible for the big jump in her grade-point average.

Carolyn attributes her remarkable improvement to both her medication (Zoloft) and psychotherapy, though she parses out the credit. "I definitely needed them both," she reflects. "But my work with Jill was probably most important, especially in how it changed my relationships. However, I started Zoloft a while before I began therapy, and I'm not sure I could have done therapy without it. I was calmer and more able to focus. In the past, I might have gone into therapy with an attitude, like 'This isn't going to work. I haven't seen any hope in the past.' I had more faith in the whole process because the medication was working."

Before Exposure: Softening Denial

Before considering imaginary exposure, it will help you to find out whether you've experienced a trauma that has caused PTSD. As I mentioned in Chapter 2, you may have used strategies of repression or denial to keep traumatic memories at bay. Remember that denial is a natural and understandable response to trauma—nothing to be ashamed about. If you've used denial to cope with a trauma and its imprint on your mind and heart, recognize it as a coping mechanism that served its purpose long ago—to keep you from psychologically falling apart. But denial may no longer serve your best psychological interests.

The value of moving beyond denial was captured in a recent, fascinating interview on CNN's *Larry King Live* with Marla Hanson, the New York City model whose face was slashed (and modeling career ended) by two men in 1986, in an attack coordinated by her landlord. Hanson told Larry King how she'd only recently recognized that her long-term irritability, depression, and other classic symptoms were a result of PTSD. Despite fifteen years of intense suffering, she never came to grips with the causes of her condition, until one day a few years earlier. Hanson was riding a train out of New York when she began chatting with the man sitting next to her. The media coverage of her slashing had been widespread, and the man recognized her. He said bluntly, "You must have PTSD." Hanson knew little about the condition but the man did. He was a Vietnam combat veteran with PTSD, and when he described his symptoms, she felt she was hearing a recitation of her own. Hanson felt a flash of recognition that she described as a moment that changed her life. She read up on PTSD and sought treatment, including medication, that she says has restored her ability to function creatively and experience joy in life. Hanson has also become committed to educating the public about PTSD, its treatment, and prevention.

One note of caution: On occasion, a psychotherapist, in his or her conviction that psychological conditions are always traceable to certain types of trauma, may press you to dig for events (usually in childhood) that may not have caused PTSD or that may never even have occurred. In the 1990s, much media coverage was devoted to the problem of "false memory syndrome," in which unwitting patients were so subtly and effectively pressured to concoct traumatic memories that they actually came to believe in them.

While it's uncertain whether "false memory syndrome" was extremely rare or widespread, it certainly did occur, and may still occur when unscrupulous or overzealous practitioners are paired with highly vulnerable patients. One warning sign of such zealotry is the therapist's stated belief that certain (PTSD-like) symptoms indicate, beyond a shadow of a doubt, a certain type of early trauma. It's a thorny problem, because when some patients with PTSD first visit a psychiatrist or therapist, they may have all the classic symptoms but no clear memory or recognition of a past trauma. If you suspect this in yourself, it's important that you work with a reputable therapist or psychiatrist, preferably one affiliated with a recognized mental health facility. With great care and compassion, such a mental health professional can help you explore these issues without undue pressure or preconceived notions of the traumas you may have experienced.

Imaginary Exposure for PTSD: Ten Guidelines

Those who engage in imaginary exposure to treat their PTSD, in particular, need to work with a psychotherapist experienced in this technique. This therapeutic approach requires skillful administration. If you tried this form of exposure on your own, you might be flooded with intense emotions you could not handle. Indeed, in the midst of imaginary exposure some patients, especially those who suffered early childhood abuse, may "dissociate" from the memory. In other words, they "space out" in a desperate attempt to shut off overwhelming feelings.

An experienced therapist can help you gauge how much memory and emotion you can tolerate in a given session, walking that fine line between prompting you to go deeper and preventing you from going too far, too fast. Also, as you practice imaginary exposure, you need a therapist to challenge the often distorted thoughts that arise—the self-blame, denigration, guilt, or shame. It's too much to expect yourself to sort through these agonizing thoughts and feelings. With a therapist's knowledge and support, you can complete the exposure process with far greater clarity and emotional freedom than you had beforehand.

Consult the Resources section for organizations that can refer you to CBT therapists who practice exposure for PTSD. Due to the intense nature of imaginary exposure, patients like Carolyn are often frightened of the prospect. But once the process is underway, you begin to experience it as liberating, even if at times painful. As Carolyn said, "Anticipating what would happen was much scarier than doing the exposure itself. The practice taught me that I could handle the memory and the feelings."

So you can know what to expect from imaginary exposure, I'll relate ten of the guidelines used by exposure therapists, as conveyed by Jill Compton and other experts in the field:

1. Begin imaginary exposure by relaxing, closing your eyes, and giving yourself and your imagination time to orient yourself in the past.
2. The session, which can run from ninety minutes to two hours, is tape-recorded for you to listen to later.
3. Begin to tell the story of your trauma, using your imagination to visualize it as accurately as you can.
4. Be as detailed as possible in your remembrance and telling of the trauma. As you speak aloud about the event(s), don't discuss it as a memory. Speak in the present tense, as if it were happening now. For instance, don't say "I was walking down the street, and I remember the mugger coming up behind me . . ." but rather "I am walking down the street holding an umbrella, thinking about what happened today at school. All of a sudden, this mugger comes right up behind me . . ."
5. Rely on your senses as you describe details of the event(s): what you saw, heard, smelled, and felt physically.
6. If and when emotions arise, including sorrow, anger, fear, or grief, let them come. Don't make a strenuous effort either to force emotions or to inhibit them.
7. During pauses in the story, or between retellings, rate your level of emotional distress on the zero to ten scale, with zero being the least distressed and ten being the most. This heightens your awareness of changes in the "emotional charge" of the memory and of whether or not it continues to cause severe distress.
8. The therapist should end sessions at a point when you are not highly distressed. It's important for you to recognize that the memory does not *have* to be associated with intolerable negative feelings.

9. Remember that the purpose is to fully reexperience the trauma with emotion, but that with repeated retellings these emotions will change. Indeed, the strongest negative emotions will begin to subside.

10. As homework, listen to the tape recording once a day until your next session, and rate your distress levels each time.

Jill Compton relates a recent case of a professional tennis player who was walking down an isolated city street when confronted by a man with a gun. The man evidently mistook him for a drug connection and shot him in the stomach. The tennis player fully recovered from his wound, but he developed clear-cut symptoms of PTSD: He was constantly angry, agitated, and depressed. "He went through exposure and repeatedly relived the shooting," says Jill. "At our most recent session, he said, 'Oh, do we have to do that again? It's so boring.' I said, 'That's great! That's what we want.' In the early sessions he felt the terror and anger associated with the event. Now he tells the story with no strong emotion. We want the patient to tell a traumatic memory the same way they tell us what they did on Thanksgiving. We want it to be like any other memory."

Difficult though exposure may be, rest assured that its purpose is to free you from trauma's grip. As Jill Compton summed up the process, "You learn to take control of the memory so it doesn't have control over you."

Moving Through Pain: Real-Life Exposure for PTSD

In practicing real-life exposure, you deliberately place yourself in situations that trigger your anxieties so you learn that your worst fears are unfounded and that you can handle the feelings that come up. Since the main anxiety "cue" in posttraumatic stress disorder is the memory of the trauma, imaginary exposure is the best strategy for confronting—and defusing—that memory. But real-life exposure has an important place, too, because you may avoid life situations that remind you of the trauma and that trigger a raft of associated feelings.

The examples are legion: The man who has survived a horrific car accident is terrified of driving again, so his real-life exposure involves small, incremental steps toward driving again. The war veteran is overwhelmed by TV images of war, so his exposure involves watching war films, starting with the least graphic and moving gradually to the most. The survivor of early physical and verbal abuse who lived in a violent household flinches at loud noises, so her exposure involves going to increasingly loud venues—sports stadiums, action movies, rock concerts.

Carolyn, the patient at our anxiety clinic who is a survivor of early sexual abuse by her uncle, not only did intensive imaginary exposure, she also practiced real-life exposure. Recall from Chapter 2 that Carolyn was afraid of being alone with male authority figures. Therefore, one of her "homework" assignments was to set up a meeting with her faculty advisor. A distressing incident with her abusive uncle, in which he purposely spilled hot coffee on her when she was seven years old, left her with a hatred for the taste and smell of coffee. Her exposure therapist instructed her to spend time at coffee bars. Carolyn had a painful memory of visiting her uncle in a VA hospital, and she felt sick whenever she passed that hospital on the highway. One day, she purposely entered the hospital and spent an hour walking around. The uncle, whom she never confronted about the abuse, had passed away several years earlier, but Carolyn continued to avoid her aunt, a living reminder of the years of abuse. Her therapist recommended that she get in touch with her aunt, toward whom she harbored no ill will. Carolyn chose to write her a warm letter.

These exercises enabled Carolyn to conquer her patterns of avoidance, an important part of her healing process. Kelly, thirty-two, was another patient in our program who was referred to our therapist, Dr. Compton, for psychotherapy. At the age of sixteen, Kelly was invited by a group of five high-school boys to a party. Excited at the prospect, she joined them as they drove to a neighborhood house, but when they entered, there was no party. All five boys proceeded to rape Kelly.

As horrific as this trauma was, her victimization didn't stop there. Word about the event spread, yet none of her fellow students believed her version. Instead, they blamed her, and for the remainder of her time in high school she was tagged a "slut." Whenever she entered the school cafeteria, she was the object of tittering, teasing, or name-calling, so she starting skipping lunch. When Kelly couldn't stand the humiliation anymore, she dropped out of school. Yet Kelly couldn't escape them, because she internalized some of the blame, wondering if she had somehow "asked for it." She should have known better than to go with those boys, she thought. One of the most tragic ironies, considering the nature of her trauma and the accusations hurled at her, was that the gang rape had been Kelly's first sexual encounter.

When she came to Duke, Kelly was suffering from exceedingly painful memories of the rape, an inability to form intimate and sexual relationships, severe bouts of depression, and a tendency to cut herself. (Self-mutilation is not uncommon in people with PTSD and borderline personality disorder.) To cope with the pain, Kelly took drugs such as marijuana and narcotics, and she had become addicted. Dr. Compton explained to Kelly how the treatment would proceed, obtaining her full commitment to the process. Compton guided Kelly through many sessions of imaginary exposure to help her grapple with the memory of this ghastly trauma. But she also encouraged Kelly to try real-life exposure. One of her most difficult assignments was to return to the high-school building where she'd endured so much humiliation fifteen years ago.

Kelly got permission from the principal to roam around the school building. (She claimed to be doing research on high-school education for a college class.) She went into classrooms, observing the kids and soaking in the feel of the building. It was difficult at first, but she gradually got used to it. She noticed how young the kids were, and how small the rooms were compared to her memories of them. The hardest moment was walking into the cafeteria, the scene of her worst social humiliation. But the longer she stayed, the better she felt. In her imagination the school had been a huge castle of horrors. Now, in reality, she saw it as a small building filled with kids who looked much younger than she expected. That vision spurred Kelly's healing insight. She recognized just how young and impressionable she'd been in high school: too young and naïve to have known what those five boys were up to. Too vulnerable to be able to protect herself from the cruelty of her high-school classmates. So young that the rape and subsequent humiliation would, of course, wound her to the core. Kelly strode out of the school building lighter than air, a monumental weight of shame, self-blame, and sorrow having been lifted from her spirit.

You can practice real-life exposure using the guidelines at the start of this chapter. If you avoid many situations or places because they conjure up the memory and feelings associated with your trauma(s), then create your own "fear hierarchy," a list of these situations or places ranked by the degree to which they cause anxiety. Move sequentially from the least to the most anxiety-provoking as you take on each challenge, and find a support person, if you feel you need one, to accompany you. If at first you go with a support person, revisit the place or circumstance again without him or her.

As with imaginary exposure, these real-life sojourns are not meant to be masochistic exercises in which you force yourself to feel more and more pain. On the contrary, you progressively challenge yourself to access the pain that already resides within, so you can finally transcend it. In the end, you find a place of safety within yourself, and by so doing, you feel safer in the world, as well.

EXPOSURE AND RESPONSE PREVENTION FOR OCD

Lester, the patient with OCD who washed ceaselessly because of his fears of an infectious "plague" used medication (an SSRI antidepressant and a benzodiazepine antianxiety drug) as well as cognitive-behavioral therapy to get well. But the exposure part of his therapy was central to his recovery. His therapist helped Lester use rational response to question his fear-riddled assumptions, but the core of his treatment was exposure plus a related technique called *response prevention*.

Basically, Lester would be "exposed" to something he believed was contaminated and then be prevented (through encouraging words from his therapist, not forceful intimidation) from engaging in the ritual washing he used to try to relieve his anxiety. This specific combination—exposure and response prevention—has one of the best success rates of any psychotherapeutic approach to OCD. The combination seems to work because it helps people learn that: (1) they *can* handle the anxiety that arises when exposed to the object(s) of their fears without resorting to compulsive rituals, and (2) they will *not* suffer the awful consequences that they dread day and night. Germs will not make them sick; fires will not consume the house; they will not act out sexual or aggressive impulses; natural disasters will not befall them and their loved ones.

Guided by his therapist, Lester would stop one of his washing rituals at a time, enabling him to internalize the fact that no germs present would cause an illness, infection, or "plague." For instance, Lester would wash his hands whenever he touched a newspaper, so we gave him instructions and moral support to achieve one simple goal: to resist this powerful impulse. Once he accomplished this—and learned, experientially, that he'd be fine—we moved to the next goal and then the next. Lester called this process "taking apart the castle"—his own apt metaphor for the elaborate construction of rules and rituals he'd built up around his obsessive fear of germs and illnesses.

It would be a "brick-by-brick" demolition. If we'd taken a wrecking ball to Lester's castle, he might have crumbled along with his own intricate structure of ritual behaviors. Although it took two years to conclude, by the end of our work together, Lester's OCD was in full retreat. In essence, on a deep level Lester had finally been disabused of the irrational fears that had long ago taken root, because he experienced no catastrophic or even mild infection, or any other untoward effects, as he stopped his washing and cleaning rituals.

All Lester had to do was learn to tolerate his anxiety each time he let go of a compulsive ritual, and in time his anxiety level began to abate. This represents the wonderful paradox of cognitive-behavioral approaches: When you try to escape anxiety, it will never stop hounding you; when you learn to tolerate anxiety, it begins to melt away. Exposure was the vaccination against fear that Lester needed to finally recover from two decades of tenacious obsessions and compulsions.

As you practice exposure, treat yourself the way you would a beloved child who is troubled: firmly *and* tenderly. Without firmness, you won't challenge yourself to confront feared people or circumstances; it's always easier to fall back on quick exits, endless ruminations, addictions, escapism, or ritual behaviors. Without tenderness, you'll only perpetuate your guilt and shame about your patterns of anxiety and avoidance. To practice exposure—getting out into the world or sometimes into the recesses of your fearful mind—you need both courage and compassion, especially for yourself. Your mantras ought to be: "I can handle this" and "Yes, I'm vulnerable, but my humanness is also my strength."

5

SOLUTION 3:

DEVELOPING SERENITY SKILLS

When you suffer from anxiety, your mind and body, which are inextricably bound together, overreact to certain events, people, or mental associations. While you participate in this exaggerated response, you don't consciously choose to respond in such an inappropriate way. Due to a biochemical imbalance, early conditioning, trauma, or all three, your nervous system has its wires crossed—you react to stimuli as if they represent threats when they're actually rather benign. Likewise, you may respond to real "normal" stresses—pressures on the job, financial disappointments, quarrels with a spouse—as though they were life-or-death confrontations.

As I explained in Chapter 1, the hallmark of unhealthy anxiety is a fight-or-flight stress response that is exaggerated, turned on inappropriately, or both. Our brains, starting in the almond-sized amygdala, misinterpret benign or mildly stressful events as major catastrophes in the making. As a result, fear messages are relayed from the amygdala to the hypothalmus and other parts of the brain, which in turn signals the pituitary adrenal glands to pump out the stress hormones ACHT, adrenaline, and noradrenaline. Thus begins the hormonal cascade known as the fight-or-flight response, which also involves the parallel actions of neurotransmitters and other brain chemicals.

The hallmark of unhealthy anxiety—as opposed to the necessary and useful *healthy* anxiety that spurs us to self-protective action—is a sympathetic nervous system in overdrive, which leads to irritability, exhaustion, and chronic states of fear. When we're always readying ourselves to fight or flee, whether from tough bosses, crowds of people, terrifying memories, or neighborhood dogs, our lives become dramas in which we are constantly shadowboxing—ducking, dodging, or battling our worst fears. Both our minds and bodies suffer almost continuously.

THE IMPORTANCE OF RELAXATION

We all have a built-in counter to the ravages of excessive fight-or-flight responses. When we sit and quiet our minds, our bodies change gears: Our sympathetic nervous systems, the branch responsible for fight-or-flight, are finally becalmed. At the same time, our parasympathetic nervous systems, responsible for slowing down our cardiovascular and endocrine systems, are bolstered. Our stress hormone output dissipates; our heart rate and breathing slows; our blood pressure eases up, and our muscles slacken.

Anxiety is an emotional component of the fight-or-flight response. In the case of *healthy* anxiety, we have this experience whenever real threats or stressors call upon our minds and bodies to take swift action. In the case of *unhealthy* anxiety, our sympathetic nervous systems go into overdrive even when no real dangers or stressors challenge us. We shadowbox with remembered or imagined threats, seeing hazards everywhere, spinning stories in our heads about the dire trouble lurking within everyday challenges. We react to these stories as if they were pure objective truth, and by so doing we tax our cardiovascular, nervous, endocrine, immune, and musculoskeletal systems. Those of us with unhealthy anxiety tend to be shallow breathers with tense muscles, tremulous hearts, and racing minds.

You might think about a relaxation or meditation practice as *an opportunity to regularly find a safe place within*. Many people dealing with stress, depression, anxiety, or illness say that such practices enable them to tune out the pressures, confusions, even the sheer pandemonium of their hectic lives. In an era of multitasking, information overload, and threats to our security, most of us need some pathway to inner peace.

Relaxation techniques, which I refer to as *serenity skills*, are a tremendously helpful component of their treatments, and have proved to be effective in treating people with panic attacks, agoraphobia, and other phobias. Indeed, these skills are clinically useful for virtually any form of anxiety. Among the most successful are deep-breathing procedures (especially for panic), progressive muscle relaxation (in which you tighten and release muscle groups from head to toe), and mindfulness meditation. But other relaxation techniques can also take you to a safe place within, whenever your inner and outer worlds feel chaotic, impossibly demanding, or even dangerous.

In the pages that follow, I will present step-wise exercises for the practices of simple meditation, abdominal breathing, mini relaxation exercises, progressive muscle relaxation, mindfulness meditation, guided imagery, and the body scan meditation. They have been drawn from a variety of sources, including leading teachers of meditation and relaxation, such as Herbert Benson, M.D.; Alice Domar, Ph.D.; and Joan Borysenko, Ph.D. (all of whom developed their clinical practices at the

Harvard Medical School's Division of Behavioral Medicine); as well as Edmund Jacobson, M.D.; Martin Rossman, M.D.; Jon Kabat-Zinn, Ph.D.; and Stephen Levine (all of whom are leaders in mind-body medicine).

All of the serenity skills are useful for virtually every form of anxiety. However, some are more helpful for particular anxiety disorders. Let's begin with two essential exercises that you can use for any form of anxiety—simple meditation and basic visualization. Then, as I discuss different serenity skills for different forms of anxiety, I will offer exercises for the other serenity skills.

Simple Meditation

1. Find a comfortable, quiet place where you won't be disturbed.
2. Sit in a chair in a comfortable position with your legs uncrossed or cross-legged on a mat or cushion. Close your eyes.
3. Become aware of your breathing, observing how your breath goes in and out. Don't try to control it in any way. You might notice that your breathing begins to slow and deepen as you focus on it.
4. Choose a focus word or phrase that has some meaning for you. If you can't think of such a phrase, try two-word phrases such as Let Go, Let Be, My Time, Be Well. Say the first word silently to yourself as you inhale, then say the second word to yourself as you exhale. Do this for several moments; if your mind wanders, gently bring it back to the first word as you breathe in, and the second word as you breathe out. You can also use a religious phrase or spiritual mantra if that has meaning: Examples include Hail Mary or Our Father (Christian), Shalom (Jewish), Allah (Islamic), Shantih or Om (Eastern).
5. As you continue to focus on your breathing and your focus word or phrase, remember the following: Don't judge how you are doing. The purpose of meditation is not to "do it right" or even "do it well." The purpose, simply, is to do it. If thoughts or feelings

intrude, know that that is normal; it's part of the process. Don't encourage these intruding thoughts or feelings, but don't push them away, either. Simply notice that they have emerged, and gently return your focus to your breathing and your repetitive phrase.

6. As your meditation time comes to a close, stay aware of your breathing, while beginning, gradually, to return your awareness to your outer environment, opening your eyes, perhaps stretching. Take your time emerging from meditation.

7. Practice meditation at least once a day for fifteen to twenty minutes, or longer if you wish. Try to practice at the same time every day so that you have a meditation routine. If you feel you will benefit, practice twice a day, in the morning and again in the late afternoon or evening.

Visualization

Visualization has a unique power in the repertoire of mind-body medicine. The imagery we conjure in our minds is both an expression and a shaper of our moods and bodily states. Guided imagery was first popularized in the 1970s as an adjunctive therapy for cancer patients, who would visualize their cancer cells being eaten up by immune cells or destroyed by chemotherapy drugs. While this approach remains controversial as a cancer treatment, there *has* been evidence that visualization can alleviate pain and reduce anxiety and depression in people with psychological conditions and chronic and life-threatening illnesses.

One way visualization alleviates anxiety is by eliciting your relaxation response. Imagining yourself taking a hot bath, strolling a beach, or sitting in a quiet meadow can markedly shift both your mind state and physiology toward stillness and tranquility.

The following basic exercise in visualization, also called guided imagery, is from the book *Self-Nurture,* coauthored by Alice Domar,

Ph.D., a health psychologist at Harvard Medical School and senior researcher at the Mind/Body Medical Institute, and Henry Dreher:

1. Find a quiet place where you can sit in a comfortable position. Close your eyes and take several slow, deep, cleansing breaths.

2. Now go to a special place in your mind that you love, a place where you have felt relaxed or know you would feel relaxed. It can be a favorite vacation spot, your parents' or grandparents' backyard, a place you have seen in the movies. It does not matter what environment you choose, as long as it makes you feel at peace.

3. Now spend time in this peaceful place, seeing yourself sitting or standing in one spot, or moving along. Take in the sounds, smells, and views all around you.

4. Focus on colors and shapes: If you are out of doors, note the color of the sky and the shapes of the clouds. See the whole expanse of sky, or sand, or grass, or forest, or stream. If you're in your grandmother's backyard, see the scene in its entirety. What does the lawn or terrace look like? Visualize the trees, shrubbery, fences, or outdoor chairs that were part of the environment you remember.

5. Focus on smells: If you're on a beach, smell the ocean or the suntan lotion. If you're in your best friend's house, conjure up the aromas that were present in the living room, the cooking odors from the kitchen, the fragrance of grass and trees in the yard. Savor the fresh air smells deep in the forest, by your favorite babbling brook.

6. Focus on sounds: Listen to the ocean waves breaking, the sound of your grandmother's voice, the gurgling of water across rocks in the brook.

7. Focus on movement: Watch the movement of clouds, or water, or seagulls, or cars. If you wish, see yourself moving: walking on the sand inspecting seashells, traipsing through high grass in the backyard, bouncing from rock to rock in the babbling brook.

8. Focus on sensations: Enjoy the feeling of salty ocean air on your skin, the grass tickling your naked feet, the slippery surfaces of the rocks as you step along in that brook.
9. Allow yourself to become totally absorbed in the sensual aspects of these images, all in a place where you feel comfortable, at home, at peace.
10. If your sense of peace is interrupted by anxious or disturbing thoughts or images, observe them. Then gently return to the specific sights, smells, and sensations that surround you.

SPIRITUAL GROWTH AND PRAYER

From my experience as a clinician working with people beset by fear, and from my reading of a number of published studies, I have come to believe that spiritual beliefs and practices can add a potent dimension to treatment for anxiety—in some instances, a pivotal one. Certainly a hallmark of religious faith is that it enables us to find strength and serenity in the face of fear. And recent research attests to the psychological and physical health benefits of spiritual practices, including prayer. The late Dr. David Larson of the National Institute for Healthcare Research catalogued scores of studies that suggest that spiritual practices, including prayer, have genuine clinical value in the treatment and prevention of mental health conditions, including anxiety. In some of these studies, therapies for depression and anxiety that incorporate religious beliefs in treatment result in faster recovery from illness than do traditional therapies.

Consider whether your own religious faith or spiritual beliefs could be a source of serenity, then ask yourself: Would a more consistent practice of my beliefs—whether in the form of attending religious services, joining a spiritual community, praying regularly, or making a deeper commitment to a spiritual life—help me to heal my chronic anxiety? If your answer is yes, take concrete actions in which you make time every week, if not every day, for religious or spiritual serenity skills.

I've treated anxiety patients for whom the importance of religious or spiritual practice to their recovery was unquestionable. In many cases, medication and/or psychotherapy helped stabilize them enough to give them hope. As a result, they were able to rediscover their spiritual selves, and began to more regularly attend services or pray. Some relied on a brief daily prayer or mantra to cope with their anxieties, and found this method enormously effective.

The hopelessness people feel when they are beset by relentless anxiety becomes an impenetrable obstacle to the very spiritual growth that can create an enduring basis for healing that anxiety. So it's a psychological catch-22, but medication and therapy can break the vicious cycle. When patients pursue spiritual practice at the same time, as their functionality and hope are gradually revived through appropriate treatments, their faith becomes a foundation for their recovery.

This sort of synergy was exemplified by one of my patients, Frederick, a businessman from Los Angeles who suffered from posttraumatic stress. Frederick had been viciously assaulted one evening on a street corner, and for years afterward he experienced flashbacks, constant agitation, and a harrowing, relentless feeling of being vulnerable to attack. Frederick responded reasonably well to treatment with a combination of antidepressant and antianxiety drugs, which took the edge off his fear, reduced his irritability, and gave him, for the first time in a decade, the sense that he might be able to manage his posttraumatic stress disorder. But the medications alone would not be enough. He talked to me about his religious beliefs and the fact that prayer sometimes afforded him relief of his PTSD symptoms, so I encouraged

Frederick to practice prayer more regularly. Now, whenever he's beset by fear, he relies upon one seven-word prayer as well as a visualization practice focusing on religious imagery. Frederick is making steady progress, I believe, because of the uniquely salutary effect of his medicine along with his spiritual practice.

Everyone has his or her own definition of spiritual growth, so I wish to be as inclusive as possible here. For some it is strictly a matter of religious devotion and observance according to their church, synagogue, mosque, or temple. For others it is rooted in a very personal interpretation of religious principles and a self-styled practice of prayer. For others still, faith is based on a connection to the Divine which they pursue without any regard for religious doctrine. And some people see in their relationships and in nature the basis for a profound spirituality that involves no particular practice.

It's fair to say, however, that personal growth—your ongoing development as a human being, your creative expression, your cultivation of relationships rooted in compassion and mutual caring—is essential to your spiritual evolution, regardless of whether you are a Christian, Catholic, Jew, Muslim, Buddhist, or atheist. Virtually every religious or wisdom tradition embraces this dictum.

I'll describe specific applications of spiritual beliefs, practices, or prayer in the next several sections, which cover the use of serenity skills for particular forms of anxiety.

SERENITY SKILLS FOR GENERALIZED ANXIETY

"There are two words I don't want to hear from people—'CALM DOWN,'" says Anita, the woman who first recognized her generalized anxiety when her daughter began driving a car. "I tell them, if I could calm down, believe me, I'd calm down. My second least favorite phrase is 'Take control of yourself.' Dear, if I could do that—trust me—I would."

The beauty of serenity skills is that they provide the means for you to accomplish both—calming down and taking control. If you have generalized anxiety disorder (GAD) you're probably like Anita: It's not that you haven't tried to calm yourself down, it's that your efforts simply haven't worked. Certain relaxation techniques are tried-and-true methods to relax mind and body when you're anxious, for anxiety is a state of arousal: Your autonomic nervous system is in overdrive, your heart rate and blood pressure may be elevated, you sweat easily if not profusely, and muscle groups in different parts of your body tighten, causing chronic muscle tension. You can downshift this physiologic overdrive by practicing relaxation, and when your body is less tense, your mind begins to gets the message "Maybe you're not in danger!" That's why relaxation not only eases physical tensions, it can allay negative thoughts and anxious emotions.

All of the relaxation or serenity skills can help with GAD, but among the practices most widely used and tested have been progressive muscle relaxation, guided imagery, and mindfulness. (For a basic mindfulness exercise, see page 188.)

Progressive Muscle Relaxation for GAD

A good adjunct to other treatments is *progressive muscle relaxation* (PMR), especially when your anxiety causes you to experience muscular tensions and its symptoms: migraine and tension headaches, back pain, inflammatory conditions, abdominal discomfort, pelvic pain syndromes, fibromyalgia, fatigue, and general aches and pains. These problems, which are both an expression of your anxiety and an ongoing contributor to it, are widespread among GAD patients.

PMR is a systematic technique for achieving deep relaxation by gradually tensing and then releasing muscle groups throughout the body in the following sequence: eyes, jaw, neck, shoulders, arms, back, chest, abdomen, pelvis and buttocks, legs and feet. It was first developed over sixty years ago by Dr. Edmund Jacobson, a distinguished physician and psychologist, and its use and popularity have only grown.

Although PMR focuses on relieving muscular tension, its value is not limited to the physical realm. By breaking the vicious cycle of anxiety–muscle tension–anxiety, it produces an encompassing feeling of deep relaxation. When you practice PMR, you are doing more than engaging in a specific exercise for relieving muscle tension; your focus is so completely on the mind-body task at hand that you also stop thinking altogether. In the context of a relaxation exercise, not thinking is a blessing.

I recommend to patients with GAD that they practice PMR in a quiet place every day at a regular time. However, you can also creatively integrate PMR into your other therapeutic practices, particularly that of exposure. Specifically, when you "expose" yourself to real-life circumstances that elicit anxiety, you can simultaneously practice relaxation to alleviate and manage your distress. PMR is one of the relaxation techniques that can work alongside exposure.

Here are your guidelines for practicing PMR:

Progressive Muscle Relaxation

1. Pay attention to your breathing. Allow your stomach to rise as you inhale and to fall back down as you exhale. Take several deep breaths before you begin.
2. Now concentrate on your forehead. Consciously tighten the muscles of your forehead while counting slowly from one to five. Hold your forehead muscles as tight as you can for the duration

of this count. Then let go of your tense forehead muscles while taking a slow, deep breath. Notice your stomach rise as you inhale and fall back down as you exhale. Now do this again: Tighten your forehead muscles for a count of five; release those muscles as you take a slow, deep breath.

3. For the remainder of the PMR exercise, repeat this process: Move down the body, tightening the muscles in a particular body area for a count of one to five, then *releasing that tension as you take a slow, deep breath*. Repeat this process—tightening and releasing as you breathe—twice for each body area.

4. Now move gradually and practice PMR in these body areas:

   · Tighten and release the muscles around your eyes.
   · Tighten and release your jaw.
   · Tighten and release your neck.
   · Tighten your right shoulder, bringing it upward as high as you can. Let go of the tension.
   · Tighten your right upper arm, from the shoulder to the elbow; let go of the tension.
   · Tighten and release your right forearm.
   · Tighten your right hand into a fist; release.
   · Take a moment now to notice if your right and left arms feel differently now. Is your right arm more relaxed?
   · Repeat this process on your left side, tightening and releasing your left shoulder, upper arm, forearm, and hand in the same manner you did on your right side.
   · Tighten and release your back, all the way from the top of your spine down to your tailbone.
   · Tighten and release your chest.
   · Tighten and release your abdomen.
   · Tighten and release your pelvis and buttocks.
   · Tighten and release your right upper leg.
   · Tighten and release your right lower leg.
   · Tighten your right foot by pointing your toes upward; let go of the tension.
   · Take a moment now to notice if your right and left legs and

feet feel differently now. Is your right leg and foot more relaxed?

· Tighten and release your left upper leg.
· Tighten and release your left lower leg.
· Tighten your left foot by pointing your toes upward; let go of the tension.
· As you complete your progressive muscle relaxation practice do a mental check on your entire body, from your head down to your toes. If you notice remaining areas of tension, tense those muscles for a count of one to five, then let go of these muscles as you take slow, deep breaths.

In writing about their work with PMR and anxiety, psychologists Richard Carr and Paul Lehrer of the University of Medicine and Dentistry of New Jersey relate stories of anxious patients who coupled PMR with exposure. One such patient, Elliot, a sixty-six-year-old man who had just retired, had a history of asthma and emphysema, and after a particularly severe asthma attack that landed him in the hospital, he lapsed into a clinical depression. While Elliot was depressed, Carr's evaluation revealed that he had severe generalized anxiety combined with phobic avoidance. He was terrified that exercise would trigger another severe asthma attack, then his terror broadened to the extent that he was afraid to climb stairs or go outside when it was warm out. Elliot battled anxiety every morning as he got ready to climb out of bed, believing that his early morning congestion was another sign of an impending asthma attack.

Carr had Elliot regularly use a "peak meter," which would help him determine whether he was actually having an asthma attack or just an anxiety attack. (Most of the time it was anxiety.) Then Carr had Elliot gradually and incrementally increase his daily physical activities, the very ones that terrified him—a type of exposure. At the same time, Elliot began training in PMR, relaxing his shoulders and upper body while breathing slowly and deeply. Elliot would get up early in the morning to practice PMR so he could lessen his anxiety while awakening.

Dr. Carr then taught Elliot how to use PMR during exercise (walking, riding his stationary bike, etc.), which involved tightening and relaxing muscle groups not involved in the exercise activity. It was a gradual buildup, but two months into this practice, Elliot was markedly less anxious in the morning and had returned to his exercise bike. He was climbing stairs with no anxiety—and no asthma attacks—and his mood was considerably brighter. Having gained control over his generalized anxiety and avoidance, Elliot cut down significantly on the asthma medication he had taken largely out of fear.

Try using PMR whenever you find yourself in stressful circumstances that would normally provoke an anxiety episode. Alternatively, you can follow Elliot's example by doing graded exposure. Create your own hierarchy of anxiety-producing situations and then, starting with the least distressing circumstance, allow yourself to enter these real-life experiences while you practice PMR, tensing and relaxing areas of the body that are most tense while remembering all the time to breathe— moving your diaphragm freely up and down. See whether this practice helps you accustom yourself to the real-life challenges that normally cause you so much distress.

Imagine Peace: Visualization for GAD

The power of imagery to influence our thoughts, feelings, and physiology is only beginning to be understood. You may already know about guided imagery, or visualization, in which you conjure relaxing images in order to ease anxiety, or you imagine your body's healing system going into action to alleviate a symptom or cure a disease. You may be surprised to learn, then, that imagery is one of the leading causes of anxiety.

How so? Consider what happens when you worry about, say, your child's well-being. You imagine a scene in which he or she is in danger, and that image catapults your mind and body into full alert. What happens when you worry about a life-threatening illness? You imagine the scene in your doctor's office when he gives you the dreadful news, and that image propels you into a state of terror. But if imagery is a trigger of anxiety, it can also be a remedy. Just as you can unwittingly allow disturbing images to trigger your fight-or-flight response, you can consciously summon positive images to elicit your relaxation response. It's important to remember that images can regulate your moods and your bodily state whether you know it or not. You can consciously stop allowing negative images to crowd your mind and instead cultivate images that make you more tranquil, clear-headed, and compassionate toward yourself.

Start with the basic visualization exercise on page 170; it's been used clinically and shown to be effective in helping people to ease the effects of chronic stress. But there are as many variations in visualization practice as there are individual minds to conjure images for healing. Below is the script (in adapted form) of a guided imagery exercise from a leading practitioner, Dr. Martin Rossman, head of the Academy of Guided Imagery in Mill Valley, California. Dr. Rossman's exercise "Going Deeper Within," or what he calls "staircase" imagery, takes basic imagery practice to another level. Before you start, do abdominal breathing and progressive muscle relaxation to clear your body of tensions and your mind of clutter. Then read the script to yourself, have someone read it to you, make a tape you can listen to, or order Dr. Rossman's tape of the exercise (call 800-276-2070).

*Going Deeper Within: Staircase Imagery**

To deepen this comfortable state of relaxation and concentration, imagine yourself at the top of a stairway that has ten steps leading down from where you stand . . . let it be any kind of stairway . . . one you've seen before or one you make up . . .

When you are ready, begin to descend the staircase one step at a time, counting backward from ten to one as you go, one number per step . . . allowing yourself to feel more deeply, more comfortably relaxed with each step you descend . . . let this imaginary staircase help you reach an even deeper, more comfortable level of body and mind with each step down . . . ten . . . nine . . . deeper and more comfortably relaxed . . . eight . . . each step takes you deeper . . . seven . . . and six . . . easily and naturally . . . five . . . halfway down . . . with nothing to worry . . . nothing to bother . . . four . . . deeper . . . more comfortably relaxed . . . three . . . no need to worry about exactly how deeply or how comfortably you go . . . two . . . and one . . . at the bottom of the stairs . . . very comfortable and deeply relaxed in body and mind.

To further deepen your relaxation, imagine yourself now in a very beautiful, peaceful place. This might be somewhere you've visited before or somewhere you just make up in your imagination. Just let the image of the place come to you. It really doesn't matter what kind of place you imagine as long as it's beautiful, quiet, peaceful, and serene. Let this be a special inner place for you . . . where you feel secure and at one with your surroundings. Maybe you've had a place like this in your life . . . somewhere you go to be quiet and reflective. It could be a real place, like a meadow or a beach . . . or an imaginary place like floating on a soft cloud.

Notice what you see there . . . what sounds you hear . . . even the smells or aromas that you sense there. Notice especially what it feels like to be there, and immerse yourself in the beauty, the feelings of peacefulness . . . of being secure and at ease . . .

As you explore this special inner place, find a spot that feels partic-

---

* Exercise adapted from M. Rossman, *Healing Yourself* (New York: Pocket Books, 1989).

ularly good to be in . . . a spot where you feel especially calm . . . centered . . . and at ease. Let this be your "power spot"—a place in which you draw from the deep sense of peacefulness you feel here . . . a place of healing . . . and of rest . . . and a place where you can explore and use the power of your imagination to best effect.

When you are ready, prepare yourself to come back to your waking state . . . to return to waking, but bringing back with you the sense of peacefulness and healing you have experienced here. All you need do is recall the imaginary staircase you descended. Imagine yourself at the bottom of the stairs . . . with ten steps up. As you ascend the stairs, you become more wide-awake, alert, and aware of your surroundings.

Worry Time: Yes, It's a Serenity Skill

Imagine being told by a therapist "I require you to worry every day at 11:00 A.M. for twenty minutes." As an inveterate worrier, you might fall off your chair. You certainly wouldn't think of this prescription as a serenity skill. But, as it happens, this worry time exercise is among the more effective serenity strategies employed by cognitive-behavioral therapists for anxious patients.

There's a catch, of course. You're required to worry for twenty minutes each day during a specific period of time, but you're also required not to worry the rest of the day. The idea is to sequester your worrying to one time frame so it doesn't infect your whole day. Worry time recognizes that worrying serves a purpose for you, which is why you may be willing to put off your fretting as long as you know you'll have your opportunity to worry.

How, you may ask, does your worrying serve a purpose? Doesn't it just make you suffer? Psychologists have found that many chronic worriers use worry as a hedge against their deepest fears. Perhaps you worry because you feel it prepares you for calamity—as though digging into feelings of dread and apprehension lets you know what it would be like should the worst materialize. It may be a bargain you make with God or fate: "I'll feel horrible now, before tragedy hits, and maybe my suffering will hold off the worst. Then I'll get to feel waves of relief if it doesn't happen." Or perhaps you engage in totally magical thinking, as if your worrying will actually protect you from catastrophe.

Ask yourself if your worrying involves any such *secondary gain,* the term psychologists use to characterize thoughts or behaviors that cause conscious suffering but may actually carry unconscious benefits. Usually these benefits come at too great a cost to your well-being—as is the case with chronic, disproportionate worry. If so, try the worry time exercise. Here are the key pointers:

1. Limit your worrying to fifteen to thirty minutes each day, once a day.
2. Try to pick a time of day when you can be alone by yourself to worry, and stick with that time.
3. Really let yourself get into your worrying. Try to cover any issues or problems you purposely stopped yourself from worrying about during the previous twenty-four hours.
4. At any other time during the day when you start to worry, say to yourself, "STOP. Save it for worry time."
5. Make every effort to stick with this strategy. When you tell yourself to STOP, then stop. When you let yourself worry, then worry.

When you stick with worry time, you will find your days becoming freer of worry. Instead of telling your worrying mind "Stop that, you're bad!" you're saying "This is not your time, but you'll have your chance." In a sense, your worrying mind is like that of a distressed child who doesn't need to be shamed but rather taught how to self-regulate.

SOCIAL SERENITY: EASING YOUR SOCIAL PHOBIAS

Serenity skills can be a helpful adjunct to your program for healing social anxiety. Less is known about the benefits of breathing meditations, mindfulness, and other relaxation techniques for social anxiety than for say, generalized anxiety. Although I don't recommend these techniques as a primary treatment for social anxiety, breathing and relaxation exercises can be helpful for both performance anxiety and generalized social anxiety. You can use the following four techniques for treating your symptoms of SAD.

Abdominal Breathing for Social Anxiety

When you're anxious, you stop breathing. Not entirely, of course, but your natural breathing reflex is inhibited. Unknowingly, your diaphragm freezes, failing to move downward as you inhale, which means that you don't let your lungs fully expand and fill with air. Imagine blowing a balloon down onto a table, so there isn't enough room for it to fully enlarge. That's what happens to your lungs if the diaphragm below doesn't move: The lower portions of each lobe never fill up and get saturated with oxygen. When you pay attention to your physical breathing sensations, you realize that you are only breathing into your chest, not into your belly. Unfortunately, the problem feeds on itself, because when you don't get enough oxygen, the brain receives a "danger" signal, which perpetuates your mind–body state of anxiety. Your breathing quickens and becomes even more shallow, and, as I'll explain shortly, in extreme cases can lead to a full-blown panic attack in which you start to hyperventilate. With many forms of anxiety other than panic, however, the same cycle of shallow breathing and ratcheting anxiety also occurs, though it may not reach the point of se-

183

vere hyperventilation. Shallow breathing is common in people with social anxiety, including both performance and generalized social anxiety.

Here are your guidelines for abdominal breathing, which breaks the
cycle of shallow breathing and escalating anxiety.

Abdominal Breathing

1. Take a normal breath. Don't change your breathing; simply observe your breathing as you inhale and exhale.
2. Take a slow, deep breath, letting the air come through your nose
   and move deeply into your lower belly. Witness how your lower
   abdomen expands as you take this deep breath. Perhaps you will
   notice that it takes a bit of effort to allow your belly to move out-
   ward as your lower lungs fill with air . . . this may not be how you
   usually breathe. Just allow the belly to expand, then breathe out
   through your mouth.
3. Let your exhalation be long, slow, and complete.
4. Now take a "normal" breath, one more like your usual breathing.
   Then take a long, deep abdominal breath in which your belly expands. Alternate normal and belly breaths several times. Notice
   the contrast between the sensations from your normal way of
   breathing and those from the conscious abdominal breaths. Does
   your normal breathing now seem constricted? Does the abdominal breath induce any sensations of relaxation?
5. Now practice the deep abdominal breathing alone. If your mind
   wanders, simply refocus on your breathing. You might sigh as
   you take long, slow exhalations. Keep going for several minutes.
6. Keep practicing deep belly breathing for another ten minutes or
   so, but now imagine that the air traveling in through your nose or
   mouth carries with it a sense of peace and calm. As you exhale,
   imagine that the air traveling out carries out your tension and
   anxiety. You might say silently to yourself "breathing in peace and
   calm" and "breathing out tension and anxiety." You might also use
   this two-word phrase on the in- and out-breath: *soft belly.*

7. Continue to focus on your deep breathing, letting in peace and calm, letting go of tension and anxiety. You may spend about fifteen to twenty minutes on abdominal breathing.

MINI RELAXATIONS

You may also consider using mini relaxation methods, which are short versions of the abdominal breathing exercise. You can do these so-called minis anywhere, anytime. Herbert Benson, M.D., of Harvard Medical School, the developer of the relaxation response, recommends mini relaxations to mitigate your fight-or-flight stress responses and reduce anxiety whenever they arise during the day.

With the mini relaxation exercise, you instantly shift from shallow chest breathing to deep abdominal breathing—the essence of any good breathing technique. You can practice minis in the midst of social interplay—at a party, at a meeting, even on a date—without other people knowing. You don't have to excuse yourself and head for the bathroom. For this reason, mini relaxations are superb coping tools for those of you with any kind of social anxiety. If you have performance anxiety, you may find special value in doing minis before—or even during—a performance, whether you're a dancer, musician, actor, comedian, or public speaker. Consider this wide range of circumstances in which you can use the mini relaxation exercise as an instant stress buster:

· Before or during a performance or speech
· When preparing to make an important phone call
· When you first walk into a crowded room
· At parties or any other large gatherings of people
· At business meetings when you're expected to speak
· During difficult interactions with employers, coworkers, or clients
· While eating at restaurants or cafeterias

· While urinating in a public restroom
· Before and during a job interview

Here are four different versions of the mini relaxation exercise. I recommend that you try all four, and see which one, or ones, work best for you in the midst of stressful circumstances that arouse anxiety.

Four Mini Relaxation Exercises*

Each of these four versions of the mini relaxation exercise is a rapid way to elicit the relaxation response and enhance abdominal breathing:

Mini version #1: Take a deep breath and hold it for several seconds. Then, as you very slowly let your breath out, repeat your focus word or phrase or prayer.

Mini version #2: Put your right hand under your navel (belly button). Focus on breathing down into your stomach, not up into your chest. Your hand should rise as you breathe in and fall as you breathe out. Now, as you inhale, say the number ten to yourself. Exhale. With the next breath, say nine, then breathe out. Do this until you reach zero.

Mini version #3: Put your hand just under your navel as you did for Mini #2. As you breathe in, count very slowly up to four. As you exhale, count very slowly to yourself back down to one. So, as you breathe in, you count one, two, three, four; then, as you exhale, four, three, two, one.

---

* Adapted from A. Domar and H. Dreher, *Healing Mind, Healthy Woman* (New York: Delta Books, 1996).

Mini version #4: Breathe in through your nose and then out through your mouth. Do this ten times. Notice how cool the air feels as you inhale, in contrast to how warm it feels when you exhale.

Mindfulness Practice to Ease Your Fears

Turn to mindfulness, both as a meditation and a way of living in the present, to manage your social anxieties. When you suffer with social phobias, you live in a continual state of trepidation about *what could* happen during a social event. (Think of this as the *what could* problem.) You're so afraid of what could occur a month, a week, a day, or a minute from now that you are lost in the present moment. Your mind is filled with images of social humiliation, leaving you with no choice, you feel, but to run or stay away at all costs. By grounding you in the present moment, mindfulness meditation and mindful living are useful forms of escape: Instead of avoiding social interactions because you're so afraid of the *what coulds,* you escape your fears by remaining in the present moment—*what is.* I use the word *escape* with some irony, because we think of escape as evasion. In fact, when you become mindful before and during social intercourse, you're only avoiding your inner world of dread. Moving out of your fearful mind-set, you *move into* the real world, where you can experience the whole spectrum of human emotions—pleasure, joy, anger, sorrow, and, yes, when appropriate, fear. And you can gain a more truthful sense of others and a more grounded sense of yourself.

Remember that mindfulness meditation—a solitary practice—is like a training tool for mindful living. In mindfulness meditation, you close the door behind you, and in quiet contemplation you basically teach yourself how to live in the present moment. With this capacity strengthened, you begin to anchor yourself in the here-and-now with other people. Here is the basic mindfulness meditation exercise:

Mindfulness Meditation

In mindfulness meditation, you reground yourself in the present moment.

1. You start the meditation the same way you do basic meditation (see above): Find a comfortable place to sit and pay attention to your breathing. You don't need to use a focus word or phrase unless you wish to. Your main focus should simply be on your breathing, concentrating on the sensation of air moving in and out of your nose or mouth and on your belly as it moves in and out.

2. You may be aware of thoughts or feelings rising into your consciousness, or images popping up in your mind's eye. Perhaps you are aware of impinging worries, anxieties, fears, fantasies, or other preoccupations involving the past or future. This is an absolutely normal response. It is not a "failure" of your efforts to relax or become mindful; on the contrary, it's an expected part of this process.

3. Simply witness these thoughts, feelings, or images as they enter and exit your mental movie screen. Don't cling to them, and don't push them away. Just be conscious—mindful—of how your mind works, observing, if you will, the ebb and flow of thoughts. Notice how your thoughts change and dissolve in your field of awareness.

4. If and when you notice that you've been carried away in a stream of associations, merely observe them. Then, gently return your awareness to your breath. Allow your breathing to once again become your focus, letting your thoughts recede to the background.

5. When thoughts, feelings, or images arise again, repeat the same process of witnessing and then letting go. Your awareness of your breathing helps anchor you in the present.

6. For the remaining time, keep your breathing in the foreground of your awareness. Notice any sensations in the body, thoughts

in the mind, or sounds in your environment. Be aware of these sensations, or sounds without fighting them or clinging to them. Continue to return to your breathing as the focus of your awareness. Gradually bring your consciousness back to your surroundings.

Practice mindfulness meditation for about fifteen to thirty minutes every day, preferably at the same time. See whether this practice enables you to be more fully aware of the present moment in your daily activities—as you wake up; eat breakfast; travel to work; engage in work activities; enjoy leisure time; participate in relationships with family, friends, and children; and spend time in natural surroundings. Pay more exquisite attention to thoughts, sensations, and experiences, and try (though not strenuously) to develop your facility, gained from mindfulness meditation, for attending to these feelings, images, and preoccupations—then letting go of them.

Relax with People: Body Scan Meditation

A tense mind inevitably means a tense body, and your physical tensions become like a box you can't escape. Progressive muscle relaxation (PMR) is an effective way to relieve those knotty tensions that bind up your energy and keep you stuck in the stress-response cycle. (These tensions also contribute to breathing trouble: Your diaphragm locks in place when your abdomen and chest muscles are tight, so you can't breathe deeply.) Some clinicians who work with people with social anxiety recommend that they practice PMR, and various case reports and other anecdotal evidence suggest that it can be highly beneficial.

A variation on PMR is the body scan meditation, which may be even more valuable for treating social anxiety. Body scan differs from PMR in that you move down your body and reduce muscular tensions but not by purposely tensing and relaxing muscle groups. Instead, you use your mind to first find and focus on these tensions, bringing awareness to each area of the body. You then use your awareness to let go of these tensions. Body scan is like a cross between PMR and guided imagery, because you literally "scan" your body with your mind, visualizing your muscle groups relaxing. Like mini relaxation or mindfulness, the body scan can be practiced *during* a real-life social encounter or experience, which is one reason this approach may be useful for those of you with social phobias. Here are your guidelines for the body scan meditation:

Body Scan Meditation

The body scan meditation is similar in some respects to progressive muscle relaxation (PMR), except that you use only your mind to relax tense muscles instead of performing a series of physical tensing-then-relaxing exercises.

1. Pay attention to your breathing. Allow your stomach to rise as you inhale and to slowly fall back down as you exhale. Take some time to breathe deeply before you begin the body scan.

2. First concentrate on your forehead. As you breathe in, notice the muscles of your forehead. Become aware of any muscle tension in your forehead. As you breathe out, let go of any muscle tension you find there. Continue this practice—awarenesss of forehead tension on the in-breath, letting go of forehead tension on the out-breath—for several slow, deep breaths.

3. For the remainder of the body scan exercise, repeat this process: Concentrate on any muscle tension in a particular body area as you inhale. Now, as you exhale, consciously loosen and release that tension. (Some people find it useful to imagine the breath traveling into that particular body part, then traveling out as they exhale. As the breath leaves the area, they visualize the muscles slackening, as if the departing breath is carrying the tension away

with it.) Make certain to take slow, deep breaths, perhaps noticing how your stomach rises as you inhale and falls as you exhale. Now move down gradually and repeat the process in these body areas:

· Scan your eyes and the muscles around them.
· Scan your mouth and jaw. You may notice that your jaw drops a bit as you exhale, releasing tension in that area.
· Scan your throat and neck.
· Scan your back, all the way from the top of your spine down to your tailbone.
· Scan your shoulders.
· Scan your upper arms, from the point where they meet your shoulders down to the elbows.
· Scan your lower arms, from the elbows down to and including your hands and fingers.
· Scan your chest.
· Scan your stomach.
· Scan your pelvis and buttocks.
· Scan your upper legs.
· Scan your lower legs, ankles, and feet.
· As you complete your body scan relaxation, do a mental check on your entire body, from your head down to your toes. If you notice remaining areas of muscular tension, focus your awareness on them as you breathe in. Let go of these muscle tensions as you breathe out.

Remember, as you follow these guidelines, become aware of muscular tensions as you inhale; let go of these tensions as you exhale. Pay special attention to softening tension in your belly, which may be tight in social situations. (The cultural pressure to appear thin may have something to do with our epidemic of tight bellies.) When your stomach muscles are tight, you can't relax your stomach when you inhale—part of the "stuck diaphragm" syndrome that prevents deep breathing.

Many psychotherapists who specialize in anxiety use relaxation techniques along with exposure. The theory behind exposure is that by deliberately exposing yourself to feared social situations, you learn that your worst-case scenarios rarely (if ever) come to pass, and your anxieties gradually abate. You also learn that you can tolerate the anxiety that does come up, especially when you start this practice. These therapists also believe that it helps their socially anxious patients to have ways to manage their anxiety as they deliberately place themselves in feared social situations. Relaxation techniques fill this bill, and the body scan is one method you can use *during* exposure. For instance, if you are terrified of speaking at a work meeting, as you wait your turn, you can do the body scan without anyone else knowing it. Breathing techniques (e.g., mini relaxations) are also good for this purpose, but the body scan may go deeper by relieving tension in the whole body.

A Spiritual Approach to Social Anxiety: Loving Kindness Meditation

When you suffer with social anxiety disorder (SAD), your assumptions about yourself and others are colored by fear, negativity, and mistrust. You don't trust yourself to perform well, to speak clearly, to be heard. At the same time, you don't trust yourself to handle the anxiety of making mistakes or of being received with less than welcome arms. You believe you would be emotionally overwhelmed, and indeed you might be. You also don't trust others to listen, to be accepting or even polite. Unwittingly, you enter social situations with a rather bleak set of beliefs about people. For such mistrust, many teachers of serenity skills, including Eastern meditation practitioners, recommend a *loving kindness meditation*. It is a 2,500-year-old Buddhist practice that uses repeated phrases and images to evoke feelings of caring and acceptance first toward yourself, then toward others and the world. It is a fairly simple meditation with potentially profound effects on your mind, body, worldview, and spirit.

In the loving kindness meditation, you invite a sense of kindness into your mind and heart. Just as in a mindfulness meditation you return again and again to your breath, in a loving kindness meditation you return again and again to your feeling of acceptance and compassion—of yourself, others, and the world as it is. Start by focusing kindness and caring on yourself, then widen the scope of your loving awareness to include others—first loved ones, then friends, coworkers, members of your community, and, ultimately, strangers and people everywhere, especially those who may be suffering.

Whether your social fears involve people you know, authority figures, work colleagues, blind dates, new friends, or complete strangers, a profound kindness toward and unconditional acceptance of them can help repair the self/other breach that afflicts you. If this resonates with you, try a regular practice of the loving kindness meditation. In his book *A Path with Heart,* Jack Kornfield, a prominent teacher of Buddhism, offers his simple version of the meditation.* He recommends that you start by sitting in a comfortable position, letting go of tensions in mind and body, leaving behind your preoccupations. Then, inwardly recite the following phrases:

> *May I be filled with loving-kindness.*
> *May I be well.*
> *May I be peaceful and at ease.*
> *May I be happy . . .*

Allow the feelings to arise with these words. Adjust the words and images if you wish, finding phrases that open your heart to kindness

---

* See J. Kornfield, *A Path with Heart* (New York: Bantam Doubleday Dell, 1993).

and compassion. Repeat these phrases, letting the feelings permeate mind and body. Continue this practice for a few weeks until you sense an authentic loving kindness *toward yourself.*

When you feel ready, start with this meditation practice, using the same phrases, but gradually expand the focus of your loving kindness to include others. Choose someone in your life who has genuinely cared for you. Imagine the person and carefully recite the phrases *May he/she be filled with loving kindness,* and so forth. You can also include other loved ones in your meditation, visualizing them and reciting the same phrases, evoking loving kindness for them as well. Finally, you may extend your loving kindness to all suffering beings in the world.

Consider moving this private practice of loving kindness meditation out into the world by doing it anywhere. You can use it in business meetings, conference halls, restaurants, stadiums, buses, airplanes, or a thousand other circumstances, saying the words silently to yourself. As you practice this meditation among others, you will feel a deeper connection with them. Loving kindness mediation has the potential to bridge the gap between yourself and others that fuels social anxiety (and other forms of anxiety), to supplant your fearful worldview with a boundless compassion.

TAKE A DEEP BREATH: MANAGING PANIC

Because people with panic respond, at least in part, to their physical experience of an attack, serenity skills are particularly helpful, especially breathing exercises. If your panic attacks include hyperventilating, you'll want to learn *rebreathing* techniques. My colleague Reid Wilson has also developed two excellent breathing exercises that help calm the overexcited nervous system that accompanies panic disorder.

You may also turn to the other serenity skills, since any approach that cultivates the tranquility of mind and body will reduce your panic symptoms.

Rebreathing for Hyperventilation

Rebreathing is an excellent way to interrupt the hyperventilation that many people experience during a panic attack. Hyperventilation occurs during overly rapid breathing, as you overload your body with oxygen and deplete your levels of carbon dioxide. Many people hyperventilate without realizing it. Even during a panic attack, they're more aware of the multiple symptoms that hyperventilation produces than of the fact that these symptoms are generated by their own rapid, shallow breathing. If you're familiar with any of the following symptoms, hyperventilation may be the culprit:

Symptoms Associated with Hyperventilation

Heart palpitations or an uncomfortable awareness of the heart
A racing heart, also known as *tachycardia*
Heartburn
Tension and anxiety
Fatigue and/or weakness
Poor sleep and/or nightmares
Sweating
Dizziness
Poor concentration
Blurred vision
Numbness or tingling in the mouth, hands, and feet
Difficulty swallowing
Stomach pain and/or nausea
The sense of a lump in the throat
A choking feeling
Muscle pains or spasms; shaking

Shortness of breath
Chest pain

During good, deep, abdominal breathing, your body maintains the right balance of oxygen and carbon dioxide. This balance is thrown off by hyperventilation, in which too much oxygen is inhaled while too much carbon dioxide is expelled. You can correct this imbalance with rebreathing: Cup your hands over your mouth and breathe into your hands. The carbon dioxide you've expelled will remain trapped within your cupped hands, so that you can immediately breathe it right back into your system. If you prefer, use a paper bag instead of your hands.

Many behavioral therapists will induce hyperventilation in a session so that their patients can practice rebreathing techniques under supervision. That way, your panic won't prevent you from effectively performing the rebreathing. Once you master the technique, you may be able to practice it at home.

Mindfulness to Ease Panic

As we've seen, mindfulness involves meditation and other techniques designed to help us become calm witnesses of the ebb and flow of our thoughts and emotions. Mindfulness doesn't mean that we're not engaged in our lives or that we have no feelings; rather that we've cultivated an inner observer who stands back peacefully, no matter what stormy emotions grip us or what outer turmoil is taking place.

Jon Kabat-Zinn and his colleagues at the University of Massachusetts Medical School undertook a study on the effects of mindfulness training on people referred to his stress clinic for anxiety and panic attacks. While their study wasn't confined to people with panic, the results do offer hope for people with this condition. Kabat-Zinn and his colleagues taught twenty-three patients various mindfulness techniques. "We found anxiety and depression dropped markedly in virtually every person in the study," writes Kabat-Zinn. "So did the frequency and severity of their panic attacks." More encouraging still, after a three-month follow-up, patients had maintained their improvement. "Most individuals were virtually free of panic attacks by the end of the follow-up period," Kabat-Zinn reports in his book *Full Catastrophe Living,* offering the following explanation of why mindfulness and meditation are so useful in overcoming anxiety:

> With regular practice, you learn to get in touch with and draw upon your own deep capacity for physiological relaxation and calmness, even at times when there are problems that have to be faced and resolved. In doing so, you also learn that it is possible to trust a stable inner core within yourself that is reliable, dependable, unwavering. Gradually the tension in your body and the worry and anxiety in your mind become less intrusive and lose some of their force. . . . [You come] to see . . . that you are not your thoughts and feelings and that you do not have to believe them or react to them or be driven or tyrannized by them. . . . When you look at thoughts as just thought, purposefully not reacting to their content and to their emotional charge . . . you are less likely to get sucked into them quite as much or as often. . . . [Seeing them] as "just thoughts" and no longer as "reality" or "the truth" . . . breaks the insidious chain by which one anxious thought leads to another and to another until you become lost in a self-created world of fear and insecurity.

Natural Breathing and Deep Breathing

An extremely useful support for both mindfulness techniques and rational response work is breathing techniques. My colleague Reid Wilson is a strong advocate of using breathing to elicit a calming response. He points out that the advantages of better breathing are twofold: In addition to its usefulness in interrupting a panic attack, deep breathing also exerts a long-term calming effect on your system.

Following Reid's advice, I support the value of learning two types of breathing: natural breathing and deep abdominal breathing, the one I have detailed above. Here, adapted from his book *Don't Panic,* is how Reid Wilson teaches natural and deep breathing to his patients with panic:

1. Lie down on your back in a comfortable place, with your legs extended and your hands down by your sides. You can do this exercise on a bed, a couch, or the floor.

2. Allow yourself to breathe. Don't force your breath; just be aware of it. Notice which part of your body rises and falls as you breathe, and place a hand there. If your hand is on your chest, you're not taking full advantage of the natural power of your lungs. If your hand is on your abdomen, you're breathing well.

3. If your hand is on your chest, put your other hand on your stomach and focus on sending your breath there. Your goal is to have your abdomen rise and fall, gently, while your chest does not move. If you're having trouble shifting your breathing down to your abdomen, push your stomach out each time you breathe in, and let it fall back each time your breathe out.

    This is natural breathing: gentle, slow, and steady breaths that reach all the way down into your abdomen. Ideally, you breathe this way throughout the day, but many people often breathe rapidly and shallowly from the chest. An excellent way to calm anxiety and release tension is to shift consciously into deep, slow breathing. Just place a hand on your abdomen and feel your breath move down deep into your body. You might also try breathing in and then out on a slow count of four, then six, then eight. The slower and deeper your breaths are, the more relaxed you'll feel. Let your breath flow gently; it's better not to force it. Just feel the air falling deep into your body and rising gently out.

4. Now that you've mastered breathing naturally, you're ready to go on to deep breathing. Put one hand on your chest and the other

on your abdomen. Take a slow, deep breath, feeling the breath fill your lower lungs first, before it rises into the upper lungs. When you breathe out, feel your upper lungs empty first, followed by your lower lungs. You can tell which part of your lungs is filling or emptying by which hand is rising or falling.

Most people find both natural and deep breathing a bit awkward at first. But if you practice these techniques several times a day, they'll come to seem completely automatic—and you'll be amazed at the difference in your mood. It's good to practice each technique for a few moments several times each day. You might find it helpful to associate them with a routine activity, such as passing through a door, for example, or hearing a watch beep to announce the hour.

SERENITY SKILLS FOR HEALING TRAUMA

PTSD affects mind and body, so serenity skills can contribute powerfully to your healing process. Relaxation, breathing exercises, mini relaxations, guided imagery, meditation, and mindfulness can all becalm your agitated nervous system, and they are methods that can help lift the emotional fog that results from traumatic stress.

Solid research data suggest that a package of serenity skills known as *anxiety management* can successfully alleviate PTSD symptoms. Under the direction of my colleague, Professor Edna Foa, researchers at the University of Pennsylvania have treated rape survivors with a version of anxiety management called *stress inoculation training,* or SIT. The SIT program consists of education about PTSD, breathing and relaxation training, thought-stopping techniques, guided self-dialogue, and cognitive restructuring. In one study, patients got either SIT, exposure therapy (both imaginary and real-life), supportive counseling, or no psychological treatment. After six weeks, the researchers found that patients receiving any form of treatment showed significant improvements in their PTSD symptoms, whereas those in the control group did not. Both "stress inoculation" *and* exposure therapy were highly effective, producing better results than did supportive counseling. The combination of both treatments also worked well, suggesting that integrating psychotherapy (especially exposure) with serenity skills may be an effective way to heal your PTSD symptoms.

Psychiatrist James Gordon, director of the Center for Mind-Body Medicine in Washington, D.C., and chairman of the White House Commission for Complementary and Alternative Medicine Policy, has pioneered the use of mind-body skills for treating trauma, especially that of victims of war and terrorism. Working closely with international relief groups, he's led teams of clinicians to the war-torn regions of Bosnia, Kosovo, and Macedonia, training local mental health professionals, teachers, and community leaders in mind-body methods and psychological self-care. His goal is to reach the largest number of victims, whose lives and families have been torn asunder by wanton violence, with healing modalities that include relaxation, meditation, guided imagery, art therapy, exercise, nutrition, and supportive family interventions, all delivered in a group setting.

Gordon and his team have completed a study evaluating the results of their mind-body program, as delivered by teachers they have trained on-site, for young people who'd spent sixteen months in the midst of war in Kosovo. Prior to entering the mind-body program, 90 percent of these children and teenagers had frank symptoms of PTSD. Gordon's preliminary, soon to be published data show that after finishing the program, the percentage of young people still qualifying for a diagnosis of PTSD had declined to 25 percent—a 65 percent drop.

How can you integrate mind-body methods into your own healing program for PTSD, and into your life? First, all the techniques outlined in this chapter can be useful in treating PTSD, but certain methods may be especially useful. Consider these suggestions:

Abdominal Breathing for Traumatic Stress

You can rely on both the abdominal breathing exercise and the short "mini relaxations" to break the anxiety cycle whenever you are stressed, hyped up, startled, jumpy, irritable, angry, experiencing a flashback, or frightened by an event or interaction that triggers the memory of your trauma. Carolyn, the sexual abuse survivor I wrote about in Chapter 2, was instructed by her therapist to practice mini relaxations in which she shifted from shallow chest breathing to slow abdominal breaths that prolonged her exhalation. At first Carolyn did the "minis" twice a week, then she used them whenever she needed. Whenever she was stressed, especially by resonances of her trauma (for instance, when she'd meet alone with with her faculty advisor), she would hyperventilate, and the mini relaxations were a quick cure.

You can also use abdominal mini relaxations as an adjunct to real-life exposure, when you put yourself in the eye of the psychic storm by going to places or interacting with people who trigger traumatic memories. Real-life exposure trains you to tolerate and ultimately transcend your emotional and physical distress, and by practicing deep breathing you teach yourself, in a concrete physical way, that you can achieve this goal. It's another example of how serenity skills can be integrated successfully with psychotherapy techniques to treat forms of anxiety, in this case PTSD.

Releasing Trauma's Tensions: Body Scan Meditation

Because trauma is imprinted on the body, you may have chronic muscular tensions that, metaphorically or actually, "hold" your traumatic memories. It's currently beyond the ken of psychiatrists and neurophysiologists to fully understand this phenomenon, but clinicians and patients alike report that memories and emotions can be "liberated" by practices that loosen bodily tensions.

In his book *Full Catastrophe Living,* Jon Kabat-Zinn observes that people who suffer early trauma often resorted, as children, to repression and denial as the only coping mechanisms available, since they were essentially dependent and defenseless. But, he notes, "the retaining and walling off of such a traumatic psychological experience must in some way induce enormous stress in the body . . ."

In his book, Kabat-Zinn reports the remarkable case of a fifty-four-year-old woman, Mary, who in practicing body scan reported feeling "blocked" in the head and neck. Kabat-Zinn encouraged her to deepen her body scan practice, and as she tried to relax her pelvic region she had a flashback of sexual abuse by her father. A flood of memories ensued, and Mary discovered, after fifty years of virtual amnesia, that she'd been abused between the ages of four and nine. Among the memories that came forth was a startling one: At age nine, she was alone with her father when he died of a heart attack. When her mother entered the room she beat Mary around the head and neck with a broom, because she hadn't immediately called for help.

Mary had been in psychotherapy for five years, and none of these memories had come up. The body scan meditation can be a potent way to bridge the mind-body gap, to loosen the grip of repression and denial, to reconnect with thoughts and feelings long buried. Mary continued religiously with the body scan meditation and increased her psychotherapy sessions to deal with the flood of memories. In time, she experienced dramatic changes: improvement in physical symptoms and a remarkable flowering of her personality. As Kabat-Zinn points out, Mary's experience with this meditation "is not meant to imply that everybody who practices the body scan will have flashback experiences of repressed material. Such experiences are rare. People find the body scan beneficial because it reconnects their conscious mind to the feeling states of their body." Be certain, however, to undertake this sort of practice while supervised by a qualified professional.

Out of the Past: Mindfulness for Posttraumatic Stress

Mindfulness meditation and the principles of mindful living can be important elements in your treatment for PTSD. A regular practice of mindfulness meditation reduces stress, eases anxiety, and grounds you in the present, which can be especially helpful when you are subject to thoughts, memories, or flashbacks that intrude from the past.

You can also rely on mindfulness in everyday life to help you accept reality as it is, recognizing the things you cannot change in both the past and present. Marsha Linehan, M.D., who developed *dialectical behavior therapy* (DBT), teaches mindfulness and related skills to many who have experienced trauma and suffer from PTSD-like symptoms. Many of her mindfulness teachings directly address the kind of suffering you may experience with PTSD.

For instance, whenever you experience emotional or physical distress related to posttraumatic stress, you can use mindfulness to cope. When beset by flashbacks, old feelings, and fears about the future that are rooted in traumas from the past, mindfulness practice helps you to remember that you only have to survive "just this moment." To cultivate this skill, it helps not only to do the mindfulness meditation practice I described above, but also to bring mindful awareness into your daily life as you go about your normal business.

Try practicing a mindful awareness of your thoughts, physical sensations, and experiences as you move through the day. Appreciate every facet of feeling and sensation, slowing down your awareness to take in each moment, each kernel of experience, while you make tea or coffee, wash the dishes, clean the house, take a hot bath, write a report, listen to music, take a walk, run on a treadmill, or make love. Mindfulness as a way of life, not just a serenity skill, roots you in the present, where the stress of past traumas dissipates, its effect on mind and body softened by a compassionate awareness, curiosity about the world, and a capacity for pleasure right now.

SERENITY SKILLS FOR OCD

In the last chapter I explained how exposure and "response prevention" were the keys to healing OCD, which is your diagnosis if you're beset by relentlessly fearful thoughts and use ritual behaviors to try to quash those obsessions. Exposure empowers you to face your fears and, finally, to transcend them. But it requires you to tolerate your anxiety rather than run from it through escapist, repetitive behaviors. Here's where serenity skills can work hand in glove with exposure: Use relaxation, focusing, deep breathing, and mindfulness to accept—and, ultimately, to let go of—the anxious feelings that arise as you stop years of ritual behaviors.

This can be a tricky endeavor, though. Some cognitive-behavioral therapists believe that practicing relaxation during exposure can be a cop-out—another way to quash anxiety when the goal is to *experience* anxiety and to learn that it will subside on its own without any special effort. The point is well taken, but it depends on how you practice relaxation. Namely, you can use abdominal breathing to enhance awareness of your body and emotions rather than to avoid awareness. The same is true of mindfulness practice, which brings you into the moment, providing you with a tool to both accept and let go of painful or panicky emotions.

Using serenity skills for anxiety or depression is sometimes considered "soft" by scientifically oriented doctors and psychiatrists. I don't think that's a fair assessment. While there are fewer data for relaxation techniques in the treatment of anxiety than there are for medications or cognitive-behavioral therapy, relaxation is often included in successful "package" treatments—healing programs that include several elements. Many package programs help people with chronic anxiety, and although we can't always quantify how much serenity skills contribute, the clinicians who use these methods attest to their efficacy. It's true at Duke, where our therapists find these approaches invaluable in many cases.

Serenity skills unquestionably downshift your fight-or-flight stress response, and when you're hounded by anxious thoughts and feelings, your body needs to relax while you are awake! If despite a good night's sleep, your heart pounds, your head aches, and your musculature is as tight as a mummy's throughout the day, it's vital that you release those tensions. You can't think, feel, or even breathe when you're that tense, and you need to think, feel, and breathe in order to overcome anxiety. Learn these serenity skills, take their lessons to heart, and practice them on a regular basis.

6

SOLUTION 4: MEDICATIONS

Over the past two decades, our understanding of the biology of anxiety disorders has advanced in leaps and bounds. These advancements have helped spawn the new generation of antianxiety medications that is frankly revolutionizing the treatment of chronic anxiety.

While the anxiety disorders each have their own neurobiology, they also have common features. In the brain, two systems are activated: one in the brain stem, called the *locus ceruleus;* the other in the midbrain, the walnut-shaped *hypothalamus,* which sends hormonal "danger" messages to the pituitary gland that are relayed, in turn, to the adrenal glands. Both brain pathways jump-start your sympathetic nervous system, which governs your acute stress response. In anxiety states, these fear switches get stuck in the "on" position: Your brain sends danger signals racing between segments of the brain and throughout the body, even in the absence of clear and present danger.

In recent years, neurobiologists searching for deeper answers to the problem of anxiety have set their sights on the passage of molecular information from one neuron to another in the juncture known as the *synapse.* The messages relayed from a single brain cell to its neighboring cell—the basic currency of emotional "information" in the brain—are carried by molecules called *neurotransmitters*. As I noted in Chapter 1, brain scientists have identified three neurotransmitters as playing a crucial role in anxiety: serotonin, norepinephrine, and GABA (gamma-aminobutyric acid).

We know that norepinephrine can activate fight-or-flight behavior, while serotonin and GABA can both quiet the stress response. Normally, each of these three molecules, which are synthesized and released by brain cells into the synapse so they can be "taken up" by neighboring brain cells, make their connections by attaching to receptors shaped specifically for them, just as the interior shape of a lock is designed to receive one key. When you suffer with chronic anxiety, one, two, or perhaps all three of these neurotransmitters are not making their connections properly, either because they are deficient or overactive, their receptors are impaired, or the interactive "dance" that takes place in the synapse is badly choreographed.

Thus, a basic problem in both depression and anxiety is the failure of brain cells to communicate appropriately with other brain cells via the language of neurotransmitters. It's this "failure to communicate" that can be remedied by psychiatric medications.

To understand how these medicines correct neurotransmitter imbalances, it helps to visualize how neurotransmitters pass molecular "information" from cell to cell. Every neuron generates electrical impulses that lead to the release of neurotransmitter molecules, which move into the infinitesimally small space between it and its neighboring neuron. The neurotransmitter remains in the synapse until it hooks onto the corresponding receptor attached to its neighbor neuron's surface. Once this hookup occurs, the biochemical information has been passed to the neuron—information that alters the cell's function. These lightning-quick transactions, and the cellular changes they generate, are the biochemical basis of our thoughts, feelings, and memories. When brain-cell communications that determine our moods are properly regulated and balanced, so are our moods. When these communications are disordered, our moods are, too.

THE MAIN CLASSES OF ANTIANXIETY MEDICATION

Our newly sophisticated understanding of these imbalances in neurotransmitters, especially serotonin and GABA, has contributed greatly to recent advances in pharmacotherapy (drug treatment) for anxiety disorders. Here's how.

GABA and the Benzodiazepines

Many anxiety disorders are linked to a dysfunction of the neurotransmitter GABA. (This has been most well established for GAD and social phobia.) GABA has its own receptor, part of a receptor complex on brain cells that also "receive" the benzodiazepine drugs—antianxiety agents such as Valium, Xanax, and Klonopin. It's an intricate story, but benziodizepenes stimulate GABA receptors in ways that revitalize the GABA system. Since GABA calms our fight-or-flight responses, and people with anxiety disorders have heightened fight-or-flight activity, the benzodiazepines have potent tranquilizing properties. Each medicine has a somewhat different effect, however, so it's our job as psychiatrists or psychopharmacologists to select the right antianxiety agent for you, based on your particular disorder and unique set of symptoms. See Table 6.1 for a complete list of the benzodiazepine medications. A new development is the emergence of other GABA-acting drugs, such as the anticonvulsants gabapentin (Neurontin) and pregabalin, which are helping many anxiety sufferers.

Serotonin and the SSRIs

The neurotransmitter serotonin, which is depleted or poorly transmitted from one brain cell to another in people with depression, has its footprints on every type of anxiety. We find evidence of serotonin malfunction in each of the five major forms. The problem may differ from one form of anxiety to another, but either there isn't enough serotonin, the connections between serotonin and its receptors are poor, some serotonin receptors are oversensitive, or ample amounts of serotonin do not remain in the synapse long enough for these connections to be made. Similar serotonin-related impairments are apparent in depression, as well, and that's why various classes of antidepressants turn out to be highly effective for treating anxiety. Indeed, in the past decade we've seen the serotonin reuptake inhibitor (SSRI) drugs, including Prozac, surpass the benzodiazepines as first-line treatments for anxiety. (Although benzodiazepines remain very useful, they work best for certain anxiety patients and can be combined with SSRIs to benefit some sufferers.)

The primary SSRI medications are Prozac, Paxil, Zoloft, Celexa, Lexapro, and Luvox. (See Table 6.1 for details.) There are many reasons for the rise of SSRIs as antianxiety medicines, but here's the bottom line: They have a broader spectrum of action than most other drugs, and are safer and better tolerated than older antianxiety agents. And for most patients, they are simply more effective, and they don't have the sedating side effects of benzodiazepines (e.g., Valium, Ativan) or their potential to cause psychological dependence or abuse (e.g., Xanax). However, they do produce some side effects, as I shortly describe.

How do SSRIs work? When serotonin molecules are released by a brain cell into the synapse, they remain there to act on the neighboring receptor until taken back up, or inactivated, by the neuron from

TABLE 6.1: PSYCHIATRIC MEDICATIONS FOR ANXIETY DISORDERS

DRUG CLASS	BRAND NAME	GENERIC NAME	TARGET ANXIETY DISORDER	HOW IT'S THOUGHT TO WORK	BENEFITS	DRAWBACKS
Anticonvulsants	Neurontin	Gabapentin	Social Anxiety Disorder (SAD)	Affects GABA	Usually effective within 2 to 4 weeks	Sedation
Azapirones	BuSpar	Buspirone	Generalized Anxiety Disorder (GAD)	Enhances the activity of serotonin	Effective for some people; less sedative than benzodiazepines	Works slowly, and inconsistently
Benzodiazepines	Ativan Centrax Dalmane Klonopin Halcion Librium Paxipam Restoril Serax Tranxene Valium Xanax	Lorazepam Prazepam Flurazepam Clonazepam Triazolam Chlordiazepoxide Halazepam Temazepam Oxazepam Clorazepate Diazepam Alprazolam	GAD, SAD, Panic Disorder	Enhances the function of GABA	Fast-acting—some people feel better the first day	Potentially habit-forming; can cause drowsiness; can produce withdrawal symptoms. Discontinuation should be done slowly; may cause depression

DRUG CLASS	BRAND NAME	GENERIC NAME	TARGET ANXIETY DISORDER	HOW IT'S THOUGHT TO WORK	BENEFITS	DRAWBACKS
Beta-Blockers	Inderal Tenormin	Propranolol Atenolol	SAD (performance type only)	Reduces physical effects of adrenaline	Fast-acting; not habit-forming	Should not be used with certain pre-existing medical conditions, such as: asthma, congestive heart failure, diabetes, vascular disease, and hyperthyroidism
Monoamine Oxidase Inhibitors (MAOIs)	Eldepryl Marplan Nardil Parnate	Selegiline Isocarboxazid Phenelzine Tranylcypromine	Panic Disorder, SAD, PTSD	Blocks the effect of an important brain enzyme, preventing the breakdown of serotonin and noradrenaline	Effective for many people, especially for patients not responding to other medications; 2 to 6 weeks until improvement occurs	Strict dietary restrictions and potentially fatal drug interactions; changes in blood pressure, moderate weight gain; reduced sexual response; insomnia. Selegiline is the least effective MAOI
Selective Serotonin Reuptake Inhibitors (SSRIs)	Celexa Luvox Paxil Prozac	Citalopram Fluvoxamine Paroxetine Fluoxetine	Panic Disorder, OCD, SAD, GAD, PTSD	Affects the concentration of the neurotransmitter	Effective, with fewer side effects than older	Some people experience nausea, nervousness and diminished sex

DRUG CLASS	BRAND NAME	GENERIC NAME	TARGET ANXIETY DISORDER	HOW IT'S THOUGHT TO WORK	BENEFITS	DRAWBACKS
	Zoloft Lexapro	Sertraline Escitalopram		serotonin, a chemical in the brain thought to be linked to anxiety disorders	medications; 2 to 6 weeks until improvement occurs	drive. Some potential for interactions with other drugs increased with rapid discontinuation
Tricyclic Antidepressants (TCAs)	Adapin Anafranil Aventyl Elavil Janimine Ludiomil Norpramin Pamelor Pertofrane Sinequan Surmontil Tofranil Vivactil	Doxepin Clomipramine Nortriptyline Amitriptyline Imipramine Maprotiline Desipramine Nortriptyline Desipramine Doxepin Trimipramine Imipramine Protriptyline	Panic Disorder, PTSD, OCD (Anafranil only)	Regulates serotonin and/or noradrenaline in the brain	Effective for many people; may take 2 to 6 weeks until improvement occurs	Dry mouth; constipation; blurry vision; difficulty urinating; dizziness; low blood pressure; moderate weight gain; sexual side effects; altered heart conduction.
Other Antidepressants	Desyrel Effexor-XR Serzone Remeron	Trazodone Venlafaxine Nefazodone Mirtazapine	Panic Disorer, SAD, GAD, PTSD	Affects the concentration of the neurotransmitters	Effective, with fewer side effects than other medications;	Some people experience nausea, nervousness, weight loss,

DRUG CLASS	BRAND NAME	GENERIC NAME	TARGET ANXIETY DISORDER	HOW IT'S THOUGHT TO WORK	BENEFITS	DRAWBACKS
				serotonin and norepinephrine, chemicals in the brain thought to be linked to anxiety disorders	4 to 6 weeks until improvement occurs	sedation, and diminished sex drive. Liver damage is a rare but serious complication of Serzone; hypertension with Effexor-XR; and weight gain with Remeron

KEY: GAD = Generalized Anxiety Disorder
OCD = Obsessive–Compulsive Disorder
PTSD = Posttraumatic Stress Disorder
SAD = Social Anxiety Disorder

Disclaimer:

This information is for educational purposes only. Speak with your doctor if you have questions about a medication or are experiencing side effects from your medication.

*Table adapted from Anxiety Disorders Association of America website, www.adaa.org, with permission.

whence they came. This "reuptake" process is performed by molecules ("transporters") that act as vehicular couriers: They literally escort the serotonin neurotransmitters back into the neuron. In depression and some anxiety disorders, there may be a dearth of serotonin or an overeager process of reuptake (or poorly responsive serotonin receptors), but the end result is that not enough serotonin makes its way to neighboring neurons. As their name clearly indicates, SSRIs block this reuptake process. Think of them as a checkpoint monitor blocking the reuptake "vehicles" from transporting serotonin molecules back to their home cells. The result? More serotonin remains available in the synapse, which means more serotonin connections are made from neuron to neuron. These connections are central to our capacity for stable moods, whether we tend toward depression, anxiety, or both.

The actions of SSRIs are more complex than I've outlined, and probably more complex than we psychiatrists and neuroscientists can currently fathom. But the clinical studies are certain about one thing: These medications work. For any given SSRI used for a particular anxiety disorder, the success rate usually ranges between 60 and 80 percent. If one SSRI fails to work or causes significant side effects, we usually switch to a different one. Often, patients who don't respond well to one SSRI have much better results with another.

Certain agents carry an official FDA-determined indication for particular disorders, say, Paxil for social anxiety or Zoloft and Paxil for PTSD. But we have enough clinical evidence and experience to know that probably all SSRIs are effective for all the major anxiety disorders, even though they have not been approved by the FDA for each specific disorder. That's why you should take advantage of the knowledge and clinical experience of your psychiatrist or psychopharmacologist. As you work with him or her to develop your ideal drug treatment, you'll realize that your prime goal is to identify medication(s) that are effective but cause the fewest aggravating side effects, the most common of which are sexual dysfunction, loss of sexual interest, nausea, and, less often, a sense of emotional flatness.

Other Medications for Anxiety

While the SSRIs and benzodiazepines are today's leading antianxiety agents, other types of psychiatric medicines help some patients. The class of antidepressants that reigned before the "SSRI era" was the *tricyclic antidepressants,* and, for some patients with anxiety disorders, particularly PTSD, OCD, and panic, these medications can still be useful. The same holds true for the *MAO inhibitors,* though their role is even more limited today because of their potential side effects and interactions with other drugs. *Beta-blockers, anticonvulsants, antipsychotics,* and *mood stabilizers* help patients with certain types of anxiety disorders. These less frequently used agents may be helpful for patients in special circumstances, including some who don't respond to benzodiazepines and SSRIs or who can't tolerate them. But this is relatively unusual, since the SSRIs have fewer and more acceptable side effects than tricyclic antidepressants, MAO inhibitors, and other agents.

Newer antidepressants, which share some properties of the SSRIs but exploit other mechanisms as well, are Remeron, Serzone, Desyrel, and Effexor-XR, all four of which have demonstrated great promise in the treatment of anxiety disorders. Effexor-XR is the lead member of a class known as serotonin-norepinephrine reuptake inhibitors (SNRIs), which has shown particular promise as a treatment for generalized anxiety and most other anxiety disorders as well. One reason why Effexor-XR is so effective and versatile is that it adjusts critical imbalances in both the serotonin and norepinephrine neurotransmitter systems. In fact,

Effexor-XR became the first antidepressant drug to be approved by the FDA for treating generalized anxiety disorder—GAD.

In the remainder of this chapter you will find information and guidelines on the use of specific agents for specific forms of anxiety. Determine which medications have the best track record for your type(s) of anxiety—the ones that are most effective with the fewest side effects. Use this information to guide your discussions with your psychiatrist, psychopharmacologist, or physician as you make informed decisions about your own mental health care.

AGENTS OF HEALING:
MEDICATIONS FOR GENERAL ANXIETY (GAD)

While everyone's treatment strategy for general anxiety may differ, medication can play one of three roles: (1) as your primary and most important healing treatment; (2) as an integral part of a broader treatment program that may also include therapy, relaxation techniques, social support, and lifestyle changes; or (3) as a temporary "bridge" that provides relatively rapid relief from your painful symptoms, enabling you to undergo a gradual transformation through psychotherapy and the other nondrug approaches and thus may facilitate long-term healing of your GAD.

All three approaches are valid. It's simply a matter of determining, in consultation with your psychiatrist or physician, which is best for you. Using medication as a "bridge" to relieve your general anxiety symptoms so you can function and feel better while trying to change long-term patterns allows you to wean off the medicine in a time frame that seems best to you and your doctor.

You might ask, "If GAD is a brain disorder, how can I get well without medication?" The answer is that nondrug approaches—especially psychotherapy—can help to balance your brain biochemistry, but it's a slower process that requires time, patience, and commitment. Hence the "bridge" concept: By balancing your brain chemistry with medication or herbal treatment, you're able to think more clearly, grapple effectively with your condition and its causes, and explore your emotions without having to fight your way through the fog of anxiety. Worry not only saps your energy, it also makes it harder to transform the deep-seated thoughts and feelings that cause you to worry in the first place. Medication can free you from this vicious cycle.

Thomas had such severe GAD symptoms that he was unable to function for days on end. Friends and family members made matters worse by telling him to "snap out of it." "It's like telling someone with a broken leg to snap out of it," says Thomas. His metaphor is apt, because the underlying dysfunction in GAD is absolutely physical. You wouldn't tell someone with a broken leg to tough it out and walk home; you'd drive him to the emergency room so he could get proper medical care. The same holds true for GAD: If you need medical treatment, no one should pass judgment on you, least of all yourself.

The First Line of Defense: SSRIs

Which medications work best for GAD? The SSRI and SNRI antidepressants are first-line treatments for GAD, while the benzodiazepines and other drugs are also useful as first- or second-line treatments for some patients. When I initially diagnose a patient, I am most likely to prescribe one of the two antidepressants that have been approved by the Food and Drug Administration (FDA) for generalized anxiety: Paxil (the generic name is paroxetine), an SSRI, and Effexor-XR (venlafaxine), known as an SNRI (serotonin-norepinephrine reuptake inhibitor). Typically, you would notice improvement with these agents (and virtually all other antidepressants used for anxiety) from three to six weeks after beginning treatment.

One unique antianxiety agent, BuSpar (buspirone), which appears to influence serotonin but is not an SSRI (it's known as an azapirone), has also been approved by the FDA for GAD symptoms, though not for GAD per se. While BuSpar can be effective, it lacks the breadth of reach, biologically and psychologically speaking, that is characteristic of the best antidepressants.

Other antidepressants, though not specifically approved for GAD, are frequently used as first- or second-line treatments. All of the SSRIs, including Paxil, can be highly effective for GAD: Prozac (fluoxetine), Zoloft (sertraline), Luvox (fluvoxamine), Celexa (citalopram), and Lexapro (escitalopram). (For patients who suffer sexual dysfunction while taking antidepressants, Luvox may offer some advantage, since it appears to cause slightly fewer of these side effects. However, Luvox can cause more gastrointestinal side effects.)

Two new-generation antidepressants that alter serotonin balance (and other neurotransmitters) but are not SSRIs are Desyrel (trazodone) and Serzone (nefazodone). Both medications have been shown to be effective treatments for GAD in early clinical studies. But Desyrel causes more sedation or "hangover" effects than Serzone, so the latter may be a better backup choice. With Serzone, there has been some recent concern about rare, but serious, liver damage. If you don't respond well to Paxil or Effexor-XR, either because they are ineffective or cause intolerable side effects, I suggest that you discuss with your doctor the possibility of a trial with another SSRI or a benzodiazepine, since they, too, can be effective for GAD.

Paxil, Effexor-XR and SSRIs: The First Port of Call

The research supporting the use of Paxil and Effexor-XR for generalized anxiety is considerable. Both have consistently been shown to be safe, well-tolerated, and effective. Effexor-XR, in particular, has a strong track record: it has consistently proved its effectiveness in a study of over two thousand patients. My colleagues and I randomly assigned over 400 GAD patients to receive either Effexor-XR, BuSpar, or a placebo. We assessed 365 patients over two months, and Effexor-XR was significantly better than both BuSpar and placebo on a self-rating measure of generalized anxiety. A recent study tracked the progress of 250 GAD patients who were taking Effexor-XR or placebo. Seventy percent of the patients receiving Effexor-XR achieved major improvements in their symptoms, an effect that lasted six months. It was the first study to show the long-term effectiveness of any medication for GAD. All of these studies evaluated Effexor-XR (extended-release), which enables you to take your dosage once a day. Recent studies have also supported the value of Zoloft (sertraline) and Lexapro (escitalopram) in generalized anxiety.

Still Useful After All These Years: Benzodiazepines

For decades prior to the ascension of SSRIs and SNRIs to a first-line role in the treatment of GAD, the benzodiazepines, and also the tricyclic antidepressants, were the mainstays of medical treatment. The benzodiazepines still play an important role for many patients. What are their advantages? These medications, including Klonopin (clonazepam), Xanax (alprazolam), Valium (diazepam), and Ativan (lorazepam), among others, take effect rapidly and are very effective at reducing the somatic (bodily) symptoms of chronic anxiety. They are also less likely to cause some of the attendant side effects of antidepressants, including sexual side effects.

What are their disadvantages? Some benzodiazepines are sedating, a problem we see less often with SSRIs and SNRIs. And several benzodiazepines, especially Xanax, can cause withdrawal symptoms when patients stop taking them and thus require a long-term "tapering" strategy. Finally, one of the central advantages of using the new antidepressants for GAD is that they also alleviate depression, and many GAD patients—upward of half—are also depressed. Although benzodiazepines can help some depressive symptoms, their effects are inconsistent, and they sometimes aggravate depression.

While most benzodiazepines can relieve symptoms of generalized anxiety, the two most often used today are probably Xanax and Klonopin. Klonopin is easier to withdraw from than Xanax, though as with all benzodiazepines, it also requires tapering when patients come to the point of stopping their medication.

When is it appropriate to use benzodiazepines? When you require rapid relief from symptoms or when first-line antidepressants (especially SSRIs) are ineffective or cause unacceptable side effects. Most of you with generalized anxiety benefit from ongoing treatment with medications—for months or years—and many doctors believe it's inappropriate for people to take benzodiazepines continuously. But I have found that long-term treatment, when administered to properly selected patients and carefully managed, is both safe and effective. I have patients who have taken Klonopin for years, and they remain in remission with few untoward side effects. And in some cases, it's possible to lower the dose over time without losing the benefits. For some people with severe GAD who are also depressed, I may combine an SSRI or SNRI with a benzodiazepine. I recall many patients who have thrived on these combinations after years of unmitigated suffering.

Modestly Useful After All These Years: Tricyclic Antidepressants

The tricyclic antidepressants were the class of agents that reigned in the "pre-SSRI" era. Today, their place in the treatment of anxiety is limited, but we turn to them when our patients don't respond well to the newer agents.

Several tricyclic antidepressants, most notably Tofranil (imipramine), have good track records for relieving the symptoms of worry, irritability, and "comorbid" depression among GAD patients. But the tricyclics remain backup selections for the same reason that they have largely been replaced by SSRIs as the medications of choice for depression: They can cause more troubling side effects, including dry mouth, constipation, dizziness, weight gain, sedation, sexual side effects, and potentially serious cardiac effects. Sometimes, where chronic pain is also present, the tricyclics are especially useful.

Transformation of GAD: Margaret's Story

The vast majority of GAD patients who come to our clinic and receive medication respond well. They can experience remissions of their worst symptoms of chronic worry, tension, irritability, and insomnia. These remissions can be dramatic. Margaret was forty-seven when we first met, and she'd been struggling with GAD since she was a teenager. Margaret worried obsessively about her job and whether her husband or kids would suddenly die. She was so hounded by worry, deep into her nights, that for the year before she sought treatment she only got two to four hours of sleep a night.

Margaret was a successful business executive who, when first hired by her employer seven years earlier, had given a misleading response about her educational background on her application. Now she lived in constant fear of being found out. In our sessions together, she spoke about the influence of her past on her current anxieties. Her mother had suffered from manic depression: "She was either ecstatically happy or withdrawn and distant," she said. "As a child I never felt like I was on solid ground with my mother." Her mother committed suicide when Margaret was twenty-five years old, leaving her with emotional scars and the feeling that she was never fully anchored and safe in the world.

It's impossible to say whether Margaret's GAD was genetically determined or solely the result of her childhood and adult traumas, although it may have been both genetic and psychological in origin. Yet I had no doubt, and neither did Margaret, that her chronic anxiety had taken on a life of its own.

Margaret had been in traditional "talk therapy" for years, and she was certain it helped her plumb the depths of her feelings about her mother and make connections between her past and present fears. But it didn't stop her from worrying. She also tried practicing relaxation with the help of an audiotape. "After a while," she recalled, "the relaxation tape only made me more tense."

Both Margaret and I believed that, in her noble attempts to combat anxiety, she'd been swimming upstream against her remorseless, biologically based disorder. One answer, we both felt, could perhaps be found in a medication to correct her neurotransmitter imbalances. I asked if she would participate in a controlled, double-blind study of Effexor-XR for anxiety, and she agreed. ("Double-blind" means that neither the doctors, researchers, nor patients know which patients are getting an active drug or a placebo.) Margaret would receive either Effexor-XR or a sugar pill, and if after three months we discovered that she'd been taking placebos, I would prescribe Effexor-XR (or another effective antianxiety drug) to be certain that she got proper treatment. I am immensely grateful to patients like Margaret who are willing to temporarily postpone their recovery process in order to help us help other anxiety sufferers.

At first, Margaret was convinced she'd been swallowing sugar pills. For several weeks, she continued to ruminate about her family and job, waking up at 1:00 A.M. and lying in bed till 4:00 A.M. "A month later, I was ready to drop out of the study," recalls Margaret. "I didn't feel any different." Then, as part of our study design, we gave her an additional pill, and neither she nor I knew whether it was just another placebo or a dose escalation of Effexor-XR. "After I got the next pill, my husband and I went on a month-long vacation. Next thing I knew I had stopped worrying. I wasn't getting up at 1:00 A.M. every night. I thought, 'Maybe it's just that I'm on vacation.' But then I went back to work, and it was like magic. I still wasn't worrying!"

After the study was completed, we learned that Margaret was indeed taking Effexor-XR. I then prescribed a 75-mg. dose, which is modest but had been proved effective in her case. I always prefer to start out with the lowest dose and move up progressively to the maximal dose that a patient can tolerate and that produces a good antianxiety effect. Margaret's recovery and growth continued apace. She experienced an impressive reduction in worrying about "getting caught" at her job, her husband's health, and her children's safety.

"Now I go to sleep before my husband and get up at 7:00 A.M.," she said. Margaret was sleeping eight hours a night. The medication had corrected a set of problems that she traced back to early childhood. "When I was a kid I didn't sleep because I was afraid I would die," she said. "I thought your eyes had to be shut to die, and the secret of eternal life was keeping your eyes open. That continued in a different way when I was older. Now, for the first time in my life, I sleep through the night."

OUT OF ISOLATION:
MEDICATIONS FOR SOCIAL ANXIETY

"You see yourself as really intelligent, and you don't have any major physical flaws that should make you feel embarrassed or self-conscious in public. You're well educated and motivated. But none of that seems to matter. Because you want to do your best, you want to excel in your career, and you just feel like you cannot. It's a horrible sensation, just humiliating."

So said Jeffrey, professor of meteorology at a Midwest institution, about his social anxiety disorder. When Jeffrey was first hired, he didn't give many talks, but as he rose in the academic ranks he was required to lecture more, speak at faculty meetings, and give talks at major conferences. He's an expert in global warming, and as the topic got more attention, Jeffrey was given high-profile speaking opportunities. All this terrified him, because whenever he was the center of attention, he became wracked by anxiety and would sweat profusely. As with many SAD sufferers, Jeffrey was painfully self-conscious about his sweating, the visible sign of his social terror. "No matter how cold it was in the dead of winter, I wore short sleeves, just in case I had to speak publicly. I even put underarm deodorant on my forehead."

After becoming a full professor at his university, Jeffrey's public profile became higher, and his social anxiety worsened. "It got to the point where my wife and I never went out to restaurants with other people because I was uncomfortable in that situation," he said remorsefully. "It changed our lifestyle completely." At its worst, Jeffrey's social anxiety forced him to reevaluate his whole life. "After a couple of years at the university, my symptoms were having such significant impact that I thought seriously about finding a different career."

Jeffrey consulted his personal physician, who thought he suffered from a bad case of performance jitters. The doctor prescribed Inderal, a beta-blocker that can be an effective treatment for performance anxiety, but it did little to alleviate his symptoms. He also tried anticholinergic medicine to control his sweating, but that failed, too. Then Jeffrey read about our anxiety and stress disorders program, and he contacted me. He described his symptoms, and I told him he had social anxiety disorder, which included but went beyond performance anxiety. "Even before you told me there were treatments that might be effective, it was such a relief," Jeffrey told me recently. "The fact that it wasn't just me, that it could be diagnosed, that someone understood, was a huge weight lifted off my shoulders."

Jeffrey came to me over a decade ago, when the new generation antidepressants were not yet first-line treatments for anxiety disorders. At the time, the benzodiazepines were medications of choice for social phobia, so I prescribed a course of Klonopin (clonazepam). Within a few weeks, we had increased the dose up to 2.5 milligrams in divided doses. I also spent several sessions with Jeffrey explaining social anxiety—its causes and symptoms—so he could finally get a rational handle on his condition. I let him know that his entire range of emotions—dread, shame, humiliation, even despair—were normal among people with SAD. I explained the psychological and biological roots of social anxiety, and I offered him a way to move beyond his suffering.

Jeffrey had a rapid and dramatic response to medical treatment. He describes how his symptoms disappeared in successive stages: The physical symptoms of tension and sweating went away first, then over the course of months, the psychological terror abated. "The more successes I had, whether it was lecturing or leading a meeting, the more comfortable I felt, and the more my self-confidence began to rise," he recalls. "The effect was unbelievable." Over time, Jeffrey was gradually able to cut down his dosage of Klonopin from 2.5 milligrams to .5 milligram—one half of one tablet per day.

I first saw Jeffrey a decade ago, and, in the years since, his career in meteorology has taken off. He gives major talks to hundreds and, on occasion, thousands of people. "The recovery has been so complete that I no longer get the slightest bit of anxiety," he said. "In the last ten years I have been to almost forty countries to give speeches. A few years ago I spoke at a major conference in Los Angeles. I stood on the stage of the ballroom and talked for forty minutes to two thousand people."

While medication for social anxiety does not always produce such striking results, the majority of patients enjoy relief from their symptoms that ranges from significant to remarkable, as in Jeffrey's case. We now have an array of pharmacologic choices to treat SAD, from the SSRI antidepressants and benzodiazepines to MAO inhibitors and beta-blockers. Frequently, you can use medication as a bridge to wellness, since it grants you the ability to sustain some social interaction. Medical treatment can therefore grant you emotional equilibrium. For some, this alone is sufficient; for others, optimal results occur when medication is complemented with rational response and exposure, serenity skills, and lifestyle changes.

The Serotonin-Active Drugs

SSRIs are the current first-line medication for general social anxiety. One of them, Paxil (paroxetine), has been approved by the FDA for the treatment of social anxiety, based on positive trials of Paxil versus placebo. (Three major multicenter trials showed that about 70 percent of patients responded well to Paxil.) Interestingly, the rise of Paxil as an effective therapy has spurred increasing public awareness of social anxiety disorder, in part as a result of information and public awareness campaigns. The other SSRIs, particularly Zoloft (sertraline), Luvox (fluvoxamine), Prozac (fluoxetine), and Lexapro (escitalopram) have also been shown to be effective. At this point, we have no strong evidence that one SSRI is better than another for social anxiety.

The majority of my social anxiety patients respond well to these SSRIs. Their value for people with SAD probably relates to their direct effects on serotonin, but it may also be attributed to indirect effects on dopamine activity. In our experience, SSRIs reduce most symptoms of social anxiety, including some of the physical symptoms—the sweating, trembling, or heart palpitations—that can cause so much distress, as well as the psychological symptoms—the intense worry and anticipatory anxiety. Some patients, even if they still sweat or shake after treatment, simply aren't psychologically bothered any more by these physical manifestations.

As yet there are no published data from controlled trials of Effexor-XR (venlafaxine, an SNRI) for treating social anxiety, but results from completed studies indicate that it works well. In one small Italian study, investigators showed that Effexor was quite effective for a group of social anxiety patients who had not responded to previous treatment with SSRIs.

The Benzodiazepines

As you gleaned from Jeffrey's story, benzodiazepines (in his case, Klonopin [clonazepam]) can have a fairly rapid and often dramatic effect on reducing the symptoms of SAD. In the early 1990s, my colleagues and I conducted a ten-week study of seventy-five patients with social anxiety, half of whom received Klonopin, while the other half received a placebo. Fully 78 percent of the SAD patients taking Klonopin experienced major improvements, in comparison with 20 percent of those on placebo. Two other benzodiazepines have proved beneficial for SAD—Xanax (alprazolam) and a medication used in South America, bromazepam.

A benzodiazepine such as Klonopin can be very helpful for some people suffering with social anxiety. The benzodiazepines relieve anxiety more rapidly than the SSRIs, but they have some side effects that give rise to concern, including sedation, dizziness, and withdrawal symptoms when they are discontinued. (Although some withdrawal is also associated with most SSRI/SNRI drugs.) Also, they are not as effective as the SSRI/SNRI drugs in relieving the depression and other psychological symptoms so common among people with social anxiety.

No Cheese, Please: Nardil and other MAOIs

Nardil (phenelzine) is an MAO inhibitor, an older class of antidepressants that work by blocking the effects of an enzyme (monoamine oxidase) that breaks down neurotransmitters, including serotonin, thereby reducing their availability in the brain. Nardil and other MAO inhibitors can increase the activity of specific neurotransmitters that enhance mood or lessen anxiety. Nardil most likely works for social anxiety because it effectively promotes the activity of both dopamine and serotonin in the brain.

Nardil has a quite striking impact on social anxiety disorder. Research during the 1980s and 1990s consistently demonstrated a 70 percent response rate. But Nardil can cause troublesome side effects. Patients may gain weight, suffer from insomnia, experience sexual dysfunction, and changes in blood pressure. When taking an MAO inhibitor, you must also stick with certain dietary restrictions (including most cheeses!), and these drugs are hard to manage because of their potentially dangerous interactions with a host of other medications. Thus, Nardil and MAO inhibitors are down the list of psychopharmacologic choices for social anxiety. That said, in my clinical experience, Nardil can work when other medications (e.g., SSRIs and the benzodiazepines) have failed, and it's worth considering when other medical strategies simply haven't worked.

Neurontin and Antiseizure Medications

Among the more interesting new agents for SAD are the antiseizure medications (also known as anticonvulsants), the most widely used of which is Neurontin (gabapentin), a drug prescribed not only for seizures but for chronic pain syndromes. Neurontin jump-starts the actions in the brain of the anxiety-modulating neurotransmitter GABA. Another antiseizure drug, pregabalin, an analogue of GABA, is still being investigated for social anxiety and therefore not available in the United States outside of a clinical trial.

I was co-investigator on a randomized trial of Neurontin for patients with social phobia, in which the active drug was compared with placebo. The patients treated with Neurontin were significantly more likely than patients getting placebos to respond to treatment. By one measure, 38 percent of patients receiving Neurontin had a meaningful reduction in symptoms in comparison with 17 percent of patients in the placebo group. Some patients receiving Neurontin experienced side effects—mild to moderate dizziness, dry mouth, sleepiness, and mild nausea—but overall the adverse effects were not serious.

Currently, Neurontin is worth considering if you have not responded to SSRIs, SNRIs, or benzodiazepines, or if you've had serious side effects from them. Together with your physician, consider these factors as you make a risk-versus-benefit decision about trying Neurontin.

Beta-Blockers for Performance Anxiety

Performance anxiety, it turns out, has its own neurophysiology, which overlaps but also differs from that of generalized social anxiety disorder. When your anxiety is limited to the experience of performing in front of an audience, you have physical symptoms such as sweating, palpitations, shaking, and tremor, the latter being a particularly bedeviling problem when you play a musical instrument, say, a violin. You dread these physical symptoms, how they interfere with your performance, and the sheer embarrassment when they occur.

If you have performance anxiety, your physical symptoms are caused by an upsurge of stress hormones released by your sympathetic nervous system. The medications known as beta-blockers jam the cellular receptors for the adrenergic stress hormones, preventing the whole array of jittery physical symptoms. (They're called beta-blockers because they block so-called "beta-adrenergic" receptors.) Early success with these agents, most notably Inderal (propranolol) and Tenormin (atenolol), has led to their use not only for performance anxiety but also for generalized social anxiety.

But we've learned that beta-blockers may not be effective for people with generalized social anxiety, probably because the physiology of these two conditions differ. If you believe that your symptoms are consistent with those of performance anxiety, talk to your psychiatrist or doctor about beta-blockers. If, on the other hand, you feel that you have more generalized social anxiety, including but not limited to public performances, consider the new-generation antidepressants such as Paxil, Zoloft, Lexapro and Effexor-XR.

MEDICAL RELIEF FOR PANIC

One of my patients was Joseph, a social worker and teacher who'd been suffering from severe panic attacks since he was in college. By the time he came to me, Joe was unable to cross a bridge, stand in line at the grocery store, or enter an elevator. "It got to the point where I didn't really want to get out of the house much," he recalls. "And flying had just been terrifying. I couldn't catch my breath. The whole world became my own tight space, like the whole world was impinging upon me and everybody was looking at me."

Part of the agony for Joe was the feeling that he couldn't tell anybody what was happening to him. "I felt like people would think I was crazy," he says. When he finally came to me, he felt that he'd reached the point where he couldn't function, "Not as a social worker, not as a husband, and not as a member of society. These attacks were just getting the best of me every day."

I recommended to Joe a course of Prozac (fluoxetine), the SSRI that has proved to be remarkably effective in the treatment of panic. Within a week, Joe noticed an enormous difference. Although he still felt anxious, the medication eliminated nearly 95 percent of his anxiety attacks . However, Joe was uncomfortable with the side effects from

Prozac, especially his feeling that his emotions had been dampened. While taking Prozac, Joe felt that he slept too much, gained weight, and experienced some loss of sexual function. These problems prompted a change in strategy: I switched him to Zoloft, which alleviated his panic attacks with far fewer side effects.

Today, Joe feels that he has finally been liberated from the panic attacks that once constricted his life to an unmanageable extent. "I finally don't dread going to the hospital for visiting clients," he says. "I don't get anxious in grocery stores or going over bridges. I actually fly a lot more often—overseas, to Jamaica. Before, I never would have even considered flying over the water, not since I'd been in college."

Beyond gaining a wider life, Joe feels more at peace with himself. "People would notice that I'm a lot happier," he says. "I enjoy jokes and laughter and whistling. It's like I've been released from a demon. And the experience has actually helped me in my social work practice, because people will share with me occasionally that they're having panic attacks, and I can tell them that there is help available."

Choosing the Right Medication for Panic

With the advent of SSRIs for panic, I usually commence medical treatment by prescribing one of these agents. If an initial trial with an SSRI is ineffective or causes too many side effects, I generally encourage patients to switch to a different SSRI before moving to an entirely different class of agents. If a second-line SSRI is not effective, I generally prescribe a benzodiazepine, preferably Klonopin (clonazepam) or, in some cases, Xanax (alprazolam). My third choice would be to prescribe a tricyclic antidepressant. Except in extraordinary circumstances, I would not prescribe benzodiazepines on an "as needed" basis for people with panic. Rather, I would recommend that they take the medication every day but limit themselves to the prescribed dose, regardless of the daily number of panic attacks. A combination of SSRIs and a benzodiazepine may also help patients with particularly severe and recalcitrant panic attacks.

Lydia's Story: Bouncing Back from Panic and Phobias

Lydia was driving home from a seaside weekend with her husband and daughter when she felt unable to breathe. Her husband noticed Lydia's labored breathing. "I don't know what's happening," Lydia replied. "I feel like I'm going to faint." They were only ten miles from home, but Lydia had to pull her car over to the side of the road. She jumped out and sat on a curb, hoping to regain her breath and get hold of herself. "What's wrong? Do you want to go to the hospital?" asked her husband. "I don't know what's wrong, and I don't know what to do," she gasped.

It was Lydia's first panic attack, and her reply to her husband's question would be prescient: "I don't know what's wrong, and I don't know what to do" summed up her next decade of confusion and struggle. The next day she had another attack, this time with heart palpitations and trembling, and she was so frightened that she took herself to an ER. It would be just the beginning of Lydia's worsening condition. Her panic attacks became so relentless, occurring on a daily basis, that she quit her job at an insurance company. Lydia and her husband, Norm, never traveled far because she so was so scared of having a panic attack on an airplane. To avoid flying, she once drove for three days from North Carolina to Chicago to see her ailing mother.

For years, no health professional ever suggested to Lydia that she had panic disorder, though she was referred to psychiatrists who treated her with sundry psychiatric medications, all of which, Lydia said, made her feel like a zombie. She also went from doctor to doctor in search of a medical explanation and cure for her disturbing symptoms.

Lydia came to see me in 1988, a decade after her first panic attack, a decade that was virtually lost to her. She worked only intermittently, rarely slept more than a few hours a night, and had been hospitalized several times. She had never been properly diagnosed, and the medications she'd been prescribed were largely ineffective and caused too many side effects. I explained to her that she had panic disorder, a diagnosis she'd never heard before. I told her that with the right kind of medication or therapy, she'd be able to control her attacks and get her life back.

My words themselves seemed to have a therapeutic effect on Lydia. "That was the turning point," she later told me. "To know that there was hope of being able to live without panic."

We settled on the benzodiazepine Klonopin, which immediately reduced the frequency and intensity of her panic attacks. "The vicious cycle of fear and panic attacks had to be broken," said Lydia. "I needed something to stop that cycle long enough to feel what 'normal' meant. The Klonopin did that."

Within a few months, Lydia's panic attacks stopped altogether. She knew that under conditions of stress she'd be vulnerable, so she continued taking Klonopin, though she has gradually lowered her dose to a modest maintenance level. When I first met her, Lydia was unable to work. Once she began to recover, she summoned up the courage to apply for a desk job for a major airline, and a few years later a colleague told her about an opening for a flight attendant. "I thought, 'I'm just going to see if I can do this,'" she said.

Lydia took the six-week flight attendant training program and was accepted for the opening. Despite her earlier fear of flying and her decade of panic attacks, she has been a successful flight attendant for the past nine years—and she hasn't had a single panic attack on an airplane.

Yet Lydia has experienced a return of strong anxiety in the aftermath of 9/11. As flight attendants, she and her colleagues have been faced daily with constant reminders of their vulnerability: the tightened security measures, cancelled flights, and constant vigilance for potential terrorists. Soon after the attacks, with her stress levels rising along with the fear that her panic attacks would return, she consulted with me again. I added another medication to her regimen—Celexa, an SSRI antidepressant. This new drug, along with her high level of self-awareness and ability to communicate her fears, has helped Lydia adjust to the threats of our post-9/11 world, which are no more apparent than in the skies above our big cities. Despite her history of severe panic, Lydia is functioning and feeling well, and she still works as a flight attendant.

Lydia's story illustrates that panic can be managed successfully with medication as a primary treatment approach. It also shows that events in our world can intensify our fears; that medications can be managed creatively to address those fears, and that some people—Lydia being a prime example—can become strong and resilient in ways they and their doctors would never have predicted.

HELP IS ON THE WAY:
MEDICATIONS FOR PTSD

Antidepressants are now the most widely used and best studied medications for PTSD. In the 1980s, the primary psychiatric medicines tested in uncontrolled studies were the tricyclic antidepressants, MAO inhibitors (primarily Nardil), and beta-blockers. Our team at Duke was among the first to conduct a controlled clinical trial of medication for PTSD, and we showed that the tricyclic antidepressant amitriptyline was more effective than placebo in veterans of combat.

But in the years since, we've seen the rise of the SSRI antidepressants as treatments of choice for PTSD. As I've shown, the SSRIs are as effective as the older medications, if not more so, with fewer adverse effects We now have sufficient evidence that the SSRIs can reduce all three types of PTSD symptoms: intrusive memories, flashbacks, and thoughts; hyperarousal, including irritability and startle reactions; and avoidance and numbing. Since SSRIs are also effective antidepressants and work for the entire spectrum of anxiety, the person with PTSD who is also depressed or has other forms of anxiety can frequently get all the help he or she needs, pharmacologically, from one agent.

That said, other medications can also be useful for PTSD, usually in combination with SSRIs. (Some exceptions may be the antidepressants Serzone, Remeron, and Effexor, which may be useful as a sole medication for PTSD. These drugs are not SSRIs but have balancing effects on both the serotonin and noradrenaline neurotransmitter systems.) Other agents can be added if SSRIs alone do not sufficiently relieve a sufferer's symptoms or if he or she has other psychiatric disorders (e.g., manic depression, psychosis) that require multileveled medical treatment. Other classes of drugs for PTSD include the anticonvulsants, the new antipsychotic medicines, and the benzodiazepine antianxiety agents.

Zoloft and the SSRIs

In December 1999, the FDA approved Zoloft (sertraline) as the first and only pharmacologic agent specifically indicated for PTSD, a milestone in the development of effective treatment for PTSD sufferers.

Our team at Duke has led several clinical trials of Zoloft for PTSD, including a recent multicenter trial with over two hundred patients, roughly half of whom received Zoloft while the other half got placebos. (We used flexible daily doses of Zoloft ranging from 50 to 200 milligrams.) At the end of twelve weeks, patients taking Zoloft responded with clinical improvements far beyond those taking placebos on four different measuring scales. Overall, 60 percent qualified as responders, in comparison with 38 percent of the placebo patients. We later found that patients who continued taking Zoloft for up to thirty-six weeks experienced important benefits. The control group who received placebos were six times more likely to relapse than patients who remained on Zoloft. This finding led us to conclude that patients with PTSD do well to maintain therapy for at least one year, if not longer.

The other SSRIs—Prozac (fluoxetine), Paxil (paroxetine) and Luvox (fluvoxamine)—are also effective in the treatment of PTSD. [As yet we don't have sufficient data on Celexa (citalopram) to add it to the list.] My colleague Kathryn Connor and our team at Duke have led a controlled trial of Prozac with fifty-three civilians who suffered from PTSD, since most pharmacotherapy trials in the past have focused on combat veterans. These were patients who had survived rape, incest, traumatic bereavement, violent crime, serious accidents, or physical abuse. On several measures of PTSD symptoms, the patients taking Prozac did strikingly better than those taking placebos.

Since the SSRIs are so relatively effective, with fewer side effects than many other drugs used for PTSD, our approach is this: If one agent does not work or causes side effects that harm quality of life, it's best to try another SSRI before moving to a different class of drugs. Despite the fact that these medicines share a mechanism of action, they are not exactly the same, and everyone's biochemistry is sufficiently unique that if you do not respond to one SSRI, you may well respond to another.

Multidrug Strategies: When SSRIs Are Not Enough

When SSRIs don't work sufficiently or at all, it makes sense to shift strategies. Remeron (mirtazapine) or Effexor-XR (venlafaxine-XR) are reasonable alternatives. Serzone (nefazodone) is another option for PTSD, particularly for patients troubled by the sexual side effects of SSRIs, since Serzone appears less likely to cause this problem. (One problem that limits the use of Serzone is the rare occurrence of serious liver damage.) I may consider shifting to a tricyclic antidepressant or an MAO inhibitor, but I usually reserve this option, since these agents have many potential adverse effects. More frequently, I add other drugs to an SSRI regimen for patients with posttraumatic stress.

For PTSD patients who respond only partially to SSRIs, we sometimes add a benzodiazepine (e.g., Klonopin, Xanax) or another type of antianxiety agent [e.g., Neurontin (gabapentin)], particularly for those with persistent panic or phobic symptoms. BuSpar (buspirone) is sometimes helpful if excessive use of alcohol complicates the picture. For patients who continue to have unstable mood, insomnia, angry outbursts, or difficulty controlling their impulses, we might add an anticonvulsant (Depakote, Neurontin, Topamax, or Lamictal). I might include one of the new antipsychotic medications, such as Risperdal, Zyprexa, or Seroquel, especially when patients exhibit any psychotic symptoms. For patients who remain jumpy, irritable, or nervous, adding BuSpar to their SSRI can be helpful. And for persistent insomnia, I consider Remeron, Serzone, or Desyrel in addition to their SSRI.

One note of caution: Using benzodiazepines alone for PTSD can be associated with some risks. A few studies have suggested that Xanax or

Klonopin are ineffective medications in PTSD. It is even possible that these may interfere with the process of resolving the trauma and healing its effects. Another concern is that benzodiazepines can sometimes induce depression, and many PTSD patients are also depressed. In addition, these drugs can sometimes lift inhibitions, which is not a good idea if you have trouble with impulse control or are prone to violent outbursts. Their use in PTSD is limited mainly to select cases in which they are added to SSRI antidepressants to help with severe anxiety reactions.

Tamara's Story: Finding Your Native Resilience

Tamara, whose nightly sleep was jolted by nightmares about her violent stepfather, is the creative director for a children's television network. Her sleeplessness caused her to become increasingly exhausted at her work, a serious problem since her job requires high-octane energy. Tamara had been stalled in other areas of her life, too. She had been in a loving relationship with Benjamin for many years, but they seemed to be going nowhere. "I didn't want to get married or have kids," she said recently. "I felt like I was . . . I've used this word before, *diseased*. I didn't want my husband to have a wife with awful, wicked nightmares, who wakes up covered in sweat every night. What if my children were like this? I thought I had this terrible affliction I would pass on."

Tamara spent several years in standard "talk therapy," which helped her understand how her early abuse had caused her current symptoms and problems. But her therapy had not cured the nightly onslaught of frightful dreams, her dread of the stepfather who had victimized her family, or her reluctance to move forward in her relationship and start a family.

When Tamara was five, her parents divorced, and she moved in with her mother. She and her two younger siblings, Mark and Karen, saw their biological father once a month, but in time they saw him more rarely, as he struggled with alcoholism and depression. He was absent for most of their lives. A year after the divorce, Tamara's mother married a man who dominated the family as a strict authoritarian with unbending religious views. Her stepfather's dictatorial rule spilled over into violence, as he regularly beat Mark and Karen. "I was subjected to that a few times," she says. "But as the oldest, I had this pressure to be really, really good. Still, I got a lot of verbal abuse."

But Tamara was more traumatized by witnessing the brutality inflicted upon her younger brother and sister. Her stepfather's beatings of her two siblings persisted for nine straight years, and Tamara described this physical abuse as "borderline torture." The regularity and horror of these events and her helplessness to protect her beloved siblings caused her intense lifelong anguish and "a form of survivor's guilt."

One morning when Tamara was sixteen, she was heading to school dressed in her cheerleader garb for a championship football game. She was dating the star of the team, and it was a red-letter day for her. Tamara doesn't recall the pretext—it might have been the short length of the cheerleader skirt she wore—but her stepfather slapped her across the face with such force that it left a bright red mark. "It was bad enough that he hit me so hard," she said. "But it was so important to me then to keep up my image of the perfect life. I was devastated going to school like that . . . less than perfect."

It was also the final straw for Tamara. When she got to school that day, the nine years of tyranny welled up inside, then boiled over. "I told the teacher I needed to go to the infirmary, and walked out of class," she recalls. "I don't know if you can classify it as a nervous breakdown, but when I got there I remember crying for six hours, literally. It got so bad I started hiccuping and gagging. I pleaded with the attendants to go get my younger sister out of class, which they did. I took Karen aside and said, 'That's it, we're leaving home.' And she was like, 'Oh, yeah!'"

Tamara proceeded to orchestrate a late-night escape with Mark, then ten, and Karen, seven, from their mother's and stepfather's house. She arranged ahead of time to go to their biological father's house, where they would live from then on. While the father had his own share of problems, he was certainly more caring, and he wasn't an abuser. While the "escape" was successful, there was a period of struggle during which Tamara's mother and stepfather waged a battle to get them back, to no avail. The children refused to return, and their biological father stood by them. They had freed themselves from the terror, but not before Tamara's mother unleashed a torrent of invective, calling her "an evil child" who "will never amount to anything."

Yet Tamara stuck to her guns. In the years since, she has sustained a bond of love and unfailing mutual support with Mark and Karen, who've had their own share of symptoms, no doubt variations of PTSD. Though Tamara demonstrated remarkable courage by extricating herself and her siblings from their violent household, her own psychic wounds did not readily heal. When she came to Duke for treatment, two decades after the night she spirited Mark and Karen out of the house, her nightmares and depression were only getting worse. Tamara entered one of our studies of Prozac for PTSD, and she experienced rapid results.

In just three weeks, her nightmares and flashbacks began to recede. Two full months after starting Prozac, during which time her dosage was gradually increased to 40 milligrams, Tamara says that she "felt like a completely different person." The nightmares were few and far between, her sleep pattern normalized, her relationship with Ben became

241

calmer and more intimate, and she felt physically revitalized. Before treatment, Tamara says she had twenty trauma-related nightmares every month. Now, she has only one a month, if that.

The cascade of positive changes continued. She had not seen her mother or stepfather for fifteen years, and recently she invited them for a weekend at her home. To call it a reconciliation would be an over-statement, but Tamara was gratified by the simple fact that she could spend time with them without lapsing into terror and self-loathing.

Her most meaningful change? She now feels ready to marry Ben and have children. "I used to think I'd be a horrible mother," reflects Tamara. "But I no longer think I have an 'affliction'—something so wrong with me that I can't be a mom. Now, I can hardly wait. I'll run the marathon this autumn, then Ben and I will get going."

MEDICATIONS FOR OBSESSIVE-COMPULSIVE DISORDER

A major advance in the medical treatment of obsessive-compulsive dis-order occurred when studies showed that the tricyclic antidepressant Anafranil (clomipramine) was a truly effective healing agent—the first prescription medication with a reasonably good track record in treat-ing people afflicted by obsessive anxieties and compulsive rituals. This leap forward occurred as psychiatrists recognized the role of serotonin imbalances in OCD, and Anafranil is an exceptionally good serotonin reuptake inhibitor.

But Anafranil is not a *selective* serotonin reuptake inhibitor (SSRI), like Prozac and its chemical brethren. That one modifier becomes im-portant to the story of medical advances against OCD. While Anafranil was highly effective at reducing symptoms in the majority of OCD patients, it caused side effects that are typical of the tricyclic class of antidepressants: weight gain, dry mouth, constipation, and some sedation. It was a price worth paying for many OCD patients without other options, but it was still steep.

Now, with the advent of the SSRI class, people with OCD can benefit from roughly the same degree of effectiveness but without as many difficult side effects. Prozac, Paxil, Zoloft, and Luvox are all approved by the FDA for the treatment of OCD, because they've all been shown to work. Two newer SSRIs, Celexa and Lexapro, are not yet approved, but both appear to be effective as well.

While you stand a good chance of responding well to an SSRI or to Anafranil, some people with OCD are only partial responders. In our clinic, we see a fair number of patients whose symptoms persist while they are on SSRIs, so we must become creative in our medical approaches. In most cases, this does not mean abandoning SSRIs. It does mean adding newer agents to SSRIs in combination treatments that improve the outcome for our patients.

Depending on the nature of your symptoms, we might add: (1) a mood stabilizer, such as Lithium or Depakote; (2) an antianxiety medication, such as the benzodiazepine Klonopin, or BuSpar; (3) an anticonvulsant such as Neurontin; or (4) an antipsychotic such as Zyprexa, Seroquel, or Risperdal.

An altogether different strategy has been to combine Anafranil and Luvox, both of which work powerfully on the serotonin system. Luvox appears to influence the body's breakdown of Anafranil, in such a way that higher levels of Anafranil's active metabolites are achieved. Since the two drugs potentiate each other, the combination may be useful in patients who have tenacious symptoms and who don't respond particularly well to SSRIs alone.

One of my patients, Bonnie, was an inveterate checker who also struggled with repetitive gestures that bordered on tics. Bonnie checked the stove twenty times before leaving the house; she turned the locks on her apartment door ten times; and she felt compelled to touch the fridge door to make sure it was closed many times a day. She also had some more unusual rituals, like licking the binder of a book before she put it down, rolling her tongue in her mouth, and repetitively touching her face in particular patterns.

As with so many OCD patients, Bonnie's symptoms only worsened with time. "It was beginning to drive me crazy," she remarked. "You're in bed, you're nice and comfortable and warm, and you have to get up and check the door. Yet you know it's irrational. 'Why do I have to do this again?' you wonder. I just wanted to be normal."

After a few months on a combination of Zoloft and Klonopin, Bonnie became normal again. Almost all of her ritual compulsions stopped, with the exception of some face-touching gestures. The lock checking, stove checking, fridge touching, and the licking of books had ceased. Her companion, Ken, was thrilled; their relationship strengthened as Bonnie's time and energy were liberated and as her spirits were lifted.

The new medication strategies for OCD are not perfect, but they are leaps and bounds beyond what we had to help patients as recently as fifteen years ago. Patients like Bonnie have experienced genuine healing, and others have combined medication with psychotherapy and self-care skills in integrated programs that finally yield results.

We now have a pharmacopeia for treating every form of anxiety that is vastly more sophisticated, molecularly targeted, and effective than anything we might have imagined twenty years ago. If you don't respond to one medical strategy, many more options exist, and for the great majority of our patients, we find a suitable regimen that frees them from the relentless grip of fear. But medication to correct biochemical imbalances is often not enough; you may need other healing solutions to address imbalances not only in your brain chemistry but in your emotional state, work life, relationships, and lifestyle habits. If you feel that's true for you, think of medication as a bridge to recovery, one you traverse in order to gain the strength and perspective to change how you habitually think and feel.

7

SOLUTION 5:

DIET, EXERCISE, AND HERBS

I have seen how changing negative beliefs, exposure therapy, serenity skills, and medication can be blended together in various combinations to help my patients lift themselves from the helplessness of chronic anxiety. When your potential has been hindered by anxiety for decades and the dark cloud of dread begins to disperse, you open to a newfound freedom, a vigorous appetite for life and its possibilities. At this stage, one final brick can be placed in your foundation: a commitment to self-care and a healthy lifestyle.

All too frequently, anxiety crushes not only your spirit and your potential, but your ability to take care of your mind and body. Many anxiety sufferers neglect their bodies, eating to relieve tension rather than to nourish themselves, snacking on fatty or sugary foods, avoiding exercise, or drinking too much coffee or alcohol. Each of these behaviors, many of them short-sighted attempts to relieve anxiety, only *intensifies* anxiety: Excess fat and sugar, as well as the weight gain that often results, can contribute to unstable moods. Coffee and alcohol can exacerbate anxiety, and a sedentary lifestyle is bad not only for physical health, but also for psychological health.

When you modify your lifestyle by improving your diet, eating less fat and sugar, initiating a daily exercise routine, and cutting down significantly on coffee and alcohol, you instantly eliminate a whole series of anxiety triggers. Moreover, when you add nutrients that are good for brain health (the vitamins, minerals, and phytochemicals in fruits, vegetables, and grains, and the omega-3 fatty acids in fish, nuts, and seeds) and engage in physical exercise—a proven antidepressant—you demonstrate as much tender loving care toward your mind as toward your body. We are also learning that "complementary medicine" has something to offer people with anxiety, including herbal medicines whose activity in the brain appears to curb anxiety.

Self-care is both an expression and a condition of self-esteem. When you start eating healthfully and exercising regularly, you are affirming for yourself that "I'm worthwhile and my health matters." That's why dietary change and exercise must be included in any genuinely comprehensive approach to treating your anxiety disorder. While different forms of anxiety may call for specific lifestyle changes, certain basic guidelines apply to the entire spectrum of anxiety disorders. In the following sections, I will present general guidelines for an antianxiety diet and exercise program, and I will explore whether and when you might turn to herbal medicines to treat your anxiety. The herbal approach is controversial, and I will review the evidence to help you cut through the conflicting claims so that you can make informed decisions about using herbs to treat your anxiety.

DIETARY CHANGES TO REDUCE ANXIETY

Despite seemingly contradictory reports, experts in both internal medicine and nutrition still largely agree on guidelines for a health-promoting diet: It should be low in saturated animal fats (red meats and full-fat dairy), low in refined carbohydrates (mainly sugary foods and starchy foods such as white bread), and high in fruits, vegetables, and whole grains, which are complex carbohydrates. Some fats are clearly healthy, namely the essential fatty acids (also known as omega-3 fats) in fish, flaxseed, and many types of nuts. Other healthier sources of fat are mono-unsaturated oils, including olive and canola oil, staples of the so-called Mediterranean diet. The healthiest sources of protein are fish; beans, including soybeans and soy products; nuts; and legumes. The vast majority of population and clinical studies suggest that this dietary prescription is heart healthy, prevents cancer, and limits premature aging. We now have some evidence that this same diet is good for your brain and, hence, for your moods, emotional states, and cognitive abilities.

Much of the confusion about diet stems from weight loss controversies. The dietary guidelines above can help you lose weight, but so can other types of diets, including the much-ballyhooed high-protein diet, which is high in fat and low in most types of carbohydrates. Although most nutritionists agree that the low sugar intake in these diets is health-promoting, there is much serious concern about the high intake of saturated fats—red meats, butter, and full-fat dairy products. The bottom line is that you can lose weight on some diets, including the high-animal-protein, high-fat variety, but they aren't necessarily good for your long-term health. Indeed, epidemiological research is consistent in this regard: Diets high in saturated fats increase your risks of heart disease and cancer.

Once you can ingest, if you will, this consistent and coherent message, fashioning an "antianxiety diet" for yourself should not be a confusing or difficult matter. At the beginning, sticking within these clear guidelines might not be so easy, not because the diet is confusing but because you're probably accustomed (if not addicted) to eating too much sugar and saturated fat. But this healthy diet carries so many benefits, and allows for so many pleasurable eating choices, that your commitment pays off immeasurably in the medium- and long-term. In other words, you can lose weight, improve your energy, and probably reduce your anxiety levels all at the same time.

For example, there is a variety of evidence suggesting that a depletion of omega-3 fatty acids in the brain and body are associated with mood disorders. This depletion appears to be common in people who eat lots of animal foods high in saturated fats and few servings of fish and nuts. In a 1999 paper, Jerry Cott of the National Institute of Mental Health and Adrian Fugh-Berman of George Washington University Medical School cited evidence that supplementing with omega-3 fatty acids can stabilize mood, and there is increasing interest in omega-3 fats, whether dietary or supplemental, for treating psychiatric disorders, including depression and anxiety. It remains to be seen whether omega-3s will have specific therapeutic value in anxiety disorders, but they are clearly good for your heart, brain, major depression, and overall health.

The diet I recommend may also be helpful for other reasons. It is rich in B vitamins, which are important for the healthy functioning of the brain and the adrenal system, and for maintaining a balanced mood and cognition. A low-sugar diet also helps prevent the wild fluctuations in blood sugar that can cause hypoglycemia. When you ingest too much sugar, your body may overproduce insulin, the hormone that allows blood glucose to be taken up by cells. Once the insulin goes into full gear, your blood sugar levels crash, so that within an hour of a high-sugar meal you may experience the classic symptoms of hypoglycemia (low blood sugar): light-headedness, trembling, a feeling of weakness, and, yes, anxiety. The symptoms of severe hypoglycemia are not that far removed from those of a panic attack. One way to prevent hypoglycemia is to eat a steady diet that is relatively low in the refined white sugars found in candies, cakes, ice creams, and other baked goods and snacks.

The dietary guidelines I present are not complicated. They don't involve calorie counting, fat-gram counting, or rigid menu planning. They involve four simple but essential principles: (1) Choose healthy fats and cut "bad" saturated fats; (2) make sound protein choices; (3) cut refined sugars; and (4) eat more whole foods—fruits, vegetables, and grains. Stick by these four principles, and your diet will not only help you lose excess weight and prevent life-threatening diseases, it may also reduce anxiety. Here are the only important details you need to follow these four principles.

1. *Choose healthy fats.* Reduce "bad" saturated fats (red meat and whole-fat dairy, including butter, cheeses, and milk) and polyunsaturated vegetable oils (corn, safflower, etc.) while increasing "good" fats (omega-3 fatty acids in flaxseed and fish oils, and nuts and seeds) and monounsaturated oils (olive and canola oils).

2. *Make sound protein choices.* Make sure you get sufficient protein from these healthy sources: fish, especially salmon, mackerel, and halibut, which are all rich in omega-3 essential fats; nuts and seeds; legumes; and soy products, including soy, miso, and tempeh. If you eat poultry as a protein source, try to obtain organic free-range chicken and turkey (which are free of potentially damaging steroid hormones), and remove the skin, which contains much saturated fat. Rely on low-fat or preferably nonfat dairy: milk, cheeses, and yogurts. Include one of these protein sources with every meal.

3. *Cut refined sugars.* Cut down significantly on refined white sugars, including baked goods (cookies, cakes) and all other processed sweets, desserts, and candies.
4. *Eat more whole foods—fruits, vegetables, and grains.* Increase your intake of fresh fruits to two servings a day and fresh vegetables to five or six servings a day. Natural fruit sugars, or fructose, don't cause the same wild fluctuations in blood glucose as refined sugars. Both fruits and vegetables are replete with hundreds of phytonutrients that we need for the prevention of disease. Eat more whole grains (wheat breads, whole-grain cereals, and grain dishes, including wheat berries, oats, brown rice, millet, quinoa, etc.) rather than refined wheat products such as white pastas, white rice, and white bread.

I also strongly recommend these three additional guidelines, also related to nutrition, to help limit your anxiety levels.

· Eliminate coffee, replace it with decaf, or keep your intake to one or two cups a day, maximum. Excess coffee intake can clearly increase the severity of any form of anxiety. Cutting down on coffee can yield significant—and often surprising—dividends in reducing your restlessness, irritability, sleeplessness, and fearfulness. If you have panic disorder, consider cutting back entirely, since even one cup might contribute to panic—at least for some sufferers. Caffeine can certainly exacerbate or even cause insomnia, which by itself contributes mightily to anxiety. Watch out, too, for the caffeine in teas, sodas, and chocolate by cutting back these sources as well.
· Don't indulge in more than three or four alcoholic beverages a week.
· Take a multivitamin/multimineral supplement with the full spectrum of B vitamins, which play an important role in sharp cognition, memory, and balanced moods.

EXERCISE FOR BALANCED MOODS

We have long known that physical exercise has a remarkably strong antidepressant effect, but less has been reported on the potential of exercise to mitigate anxiety. While there is less research on the effects of exercise on anxiety than on depression, there are enough data to suggest that exercise is highly beneficial and should take its place in any complete program for people with anxiety.

According to a recent paper by sports medicine expert Scott Paluska of the Rex Sports Medicine Institute in Cary, North Carolina, anxiety symptoms and panic improve with regular exercise, and the beneficial effects appear to equal those of meditation, relaxation, and other serenity skills. Imagine, then, the potential calming effects you'll experience by combining exercise with a regular practice of serenity skills.

In a 1997 German study that found that patients with panic or agoraphobia avoided aerobic exercise, researchers theorized that their avoidance contributed to a vicious cycle: Their reduced aerobic fitness probably worsened their panic disorder. When it comes to exercise, panic disorder is something of a special case. When they exercise, people with panic can sometimes have an attack that is triggered, it seems, by their own increased physiological arousal. But these individuals can work toward increasing their physical activity very gradually, and begin to accept that their strongly beating heart and increased blood flow do not signal impending doom, so that they ultimately benefit marvelously from the antianxiety effects of exercise. That's why some people with panic disorder should combine rational response work with exercise, getting help when necessary from a cognitive therapist.

How might exercise reduce anxiety levels? A variety of mechanisms are probably at play for most people, including:

· Improved mood, which is probably related to an increased pro-
  duction of the natural pain-reducing and mood-moderating brain
  chemicals, known as *endorphins.* For instance, the so-called runner's
  high involves a rise in endorphin levels that stimulate a sense of
  well-being.
· Relaxation of tight muscles, which is both a symptom and a cause
  of anxiety in people who hold their stress in patterns of muscular
  tension in the body. (This is true of vast numbers of people with
  generalized anxiety and other forms of the disorder.)
· Improved blood circulation and reduced blood pressure.
· Elimination of chemicals in the body that may cause sluggishness,
  fatigue, and irritability.
· Better regulation of blood sugar levels, which helps to prevent
  hypoglycemia.
· More efficient metabolism of excess stress hormones, including
  adrenaline, which otherwise contribute to anxiety states.
· Release of pent-up frustration, anger, and other negative emotions.

We should all now recognize that exercise is good not only for our
hearts, bones, muscles, and immune systems; it also benefits our self-
esteem and emotional well-being.

What Kind of Exercise Program Should I Pursue?

There is no one clear-cut prescription for an antianxiety exercise program. But most experts in exercise physiology and mental health agree
that an aerobic program is ideal. Aerobic exercise is any physical activity that requires oxygen and raises your heart rate into what is known
as "the target zone." (Here's the well-known formula for aerobic exercise: You must get your heart rate up into the zone, which is $(220 -$
your age $\times$ .75), for at least ten minutes. Most of the time, fifteen to
twenty minutes of brisk walking, jogging, stationary biking, vigorous
dancing, swimming, or biking can elevate your heart rate into the aer-

obic zone, which increases cardiovascular fitness and reduces skeletal muscle tension. The evidence suggests that regular aerobic exercise may be particularly good at reducing stress, depression, and anxiety.

But don't be intimidated by the recommendation that you do aerobic exercise. First, exercise that does not achieve aerobic levels still has physical and mental health benefits. Second, you can gradually build up to aerobic exercise if you've been sedentary for a long time or have physical limitations due to injuries, handicaps, or aging. Anaerobic exercise, which involves short bursts of high-intensity activity, and does not require oxygen, still burns stored glucose and builds muscle. Also, when you do anaerobic exercise for a long enough period of time with sustained intensity, it becomes aerobic. Examples of anaerobic exercise are weight lifting, calisthenics, and short-distance sprinting or swimming.

Your exercise program will require commitment, but recognize that even moderate exercise carries great benefits. You don't need to do heavy weight lifting, long aerobic classes, two-hour sessions on the NordicTrack or StairMaster, or long-distance running. Even one half-hour of regular walking four or five times a week has a cardiovascular and, for many, a psychological payoff.

Here are some choices you may consider for an antianxiety, mood-enhancing, psychophysically calming exercise program.

- Spend at least twenty to thirty minutes five times a week walking, jogging, dancing vigorously, playing sports, or using a treadmill or StairMaster. These aerobic activities are ideal but not mandatory.
- If you have a physical condition that limits vigorous exercise, engage in regular walks or swimming, the least stressful exercises that still provide significant cardiovascular benefits and can help balance mood. If need be, work gradually up to aerobic levels by at first walking or swimming for just a few minutes a day, taking weeks or even months to increase your time spent to fifteen to thirty minutes.

· If you have panic disorder and vigorous exercise frightens you, start with a simple walking program of twenty minutes, four to five times a day, and work your way up to forty-five minutes. Try increasing your speed a little bit at a time, until your recognize that you can experience an increase in heart rate without having a panic attack.
· Consider a program of twenty to thirty minutes five times a week in which you alternate aerobic activity (walking, jogging, swimming, or dancing) with anaerobic activity (weight-lifting or strength-training machines, short-distance running or swimming, sit-ups, pull-ups, or push-ups). The combination may be ideal for heart health, bone health, and muscle tone, as well as psychological well-being.

The best advice I can offer regarding your exercise is this: Give yourself a chance to develop a routine that is truly pleasurable. If you've been sedentary for years, your biggest problem with committing to an exercise program is your deep-set belief that it will be onerous. But if you tailor your program to your own needs and enjoyments, engaging in types of activities you find fun and in levels of activity you can handle, you'll reap immediate benefits in terms of a better mood. Stretch yourself if you can, but the "no pain, no gain" philosophy only applies if you have a fixed goal like rapid weight loss or strength training. Create a realistic weekly exercise routine you can sustain, one that boosts your energy and lifts your spirits, and you'll soon reap its antianxiety benefits.

A GENTLE HEALING: HERBAL MEDICINES

Herbal medicine for anxiety? Few psychiatrists and psychologists are aware of the research backing the use of certain herbal medicines in the treatment of anxiety disorders. Indeed, the public is largely more aware of antianxiety herbs, but there is a good deal of misinformation out there. Herbs with the most research supporting their antianxiety

255

potential are kava and St.-John's-wort. Several other herbs, including valerian (a proven mild but effective sleep agent), passionflower, Melissa, and camomile, are also touted for their antianxiety effects. However, there is little hard scientific evidence to support the use of any of these herbals for treating full-blown anxiety disorders.

Kava: Nature's Benzodiazepine?

The most well-studied herb for anxiety is kava, sometimes called "kava kava." Often touted as the "great green hope," kava has been used as a relaxant and euphoric by South Pacific islanders for about three thousand years. Until recently, it was a top-selling herbal medicine in the United States.

But is there proof that kava works for anxiety? As with other herbal medicines, Europe has been far ahead of the United States in its research and clinical use. Three placebo-controlled clinical trials and two head-to-head studies comparing kava with benzodiazepines have all produced positive results. In the treatment of anxiety disorders, kava was significantly superior to placebo and roughly equivalent to a benzodiazepine. Such results have prompted the widespread use of kava in Europe: Roughly 350,000 prescriptions are written in Germany each year. Kava appears to have relatively few side effects and few negative interactions with other drugs, though some precautions, which I'll set forth, are indicated. A recent advisory from the FDA suggests that liver damage may be a rare but worrisome adverse effect (see below for guidelines on how to guard against this problem). Two recent double-blind studies of kava by our group have failed to show any benefit for generalized anxiety (GAD), but an English study suggests possible benefit as a stress reliever for people with mild symptoms of stress burnout.

Therefore, without clear-cut evidence that kava is effective in the long-term treatment of anxiety disorders, at this time we recommend it only for short-term treatment of states of stress. And we only suggest a trial run if you have no history of liver problems, are not pregnant, and do not drink alcohol regularly.

That said, clinical experience suggests that kava is sometimes effective for people with mild to moderate anxiety. It also has a reputation as a tranquilizer as well as an anticonvulsant and muscle relaxant. While it's easy to oversell the value of such a remedy, we need more research to confirm its utility against all forms of anxiety and to compare it with SSRIs and benzodiazepines. We still don't know which forms of anxiety respond best to kava.

When should you use kava rather than a conventional psychiatric medicine? Before or after you try those remedies? The efficacy of SSRIs and benzodiazepines has been well documented, and I would not recommend kava (or other herbal agents) first. Some herbal remedies can be considered when conventional psychiatric medicines either don't work or have adverse side effects. However, for patients with moderate to severe symptoms, I would try several mainstream antianxiety medications before recommending a trial of herbal remedies.

See Table 7.1 for key facts about kava, including its uses, contraindications, side effects, and dosages. In the following sections, I'll tell you about kava's use in treating generalized anxiety (GAD) and social anxiety. There is less research on kava for the other forms of anxiety, although it may ultimately be proved useful for panic, PTSD, and perhaps OCD.

Kava for Generalized Anxiety

Kava is the most well-substantiated herbal medicine for people with generalized anxiety, or GAD. The evidence is based on three placebo-

TABLE 7.1: ESSENTIAL FACTS ABOUT KAVA

MAIN USE	Anxiolytic (antianxiety treatment), stress relief
OTHER REPORTED USES	Muscle relaxant, sedative/tranquilizer and sleep aid, antidepressant, urinary antiseptic, pain reliever
WHEN NOT TO USE THIS HERB	During pregnancy, when trying to conceive, or breastfeeding; use with caution if under eighteen or with alcohol. If taking any other medicines, whether prescription or over-the-counter, use only under a doctor's supervision. Do NOT use kava if you have any liver disease.
POTENTIAL INTERACTIONS	Benzodiazepines, antidepressants, antipsychotics, CNS depressants (sedative/hypnotics)
SIDE EFFECTS	Stomach discomfort, headache, a sense of being "washed out" or exhausted, "flaccidity" (or looseness), possible serious liver damage (rare)
WHEN TO EXPECT RESULTS	Within hours for tension, sleep, muscle relaxation
COMMON PREPARATION FORMS	Pill, capsules, liquid, tea, tincture, spray
AVERAGE EFFECTIVE DAILY DOSAGE	70 to 280 mg. of kavalactones (most brands contain concentrated kava root standardized to anywhere from 30 to 70 percent kavalactones; a capsule containing 240 mg. of concentrated kava root, standardized to 30 percent, would provide 70 mg. of kavalactones), usually taken in divided doses one to two times a day

controlled trials from Germany. While this research plainly shows that kava reduces anxiety, the studies are not uniformly sound, because the criteria for measuring GAD aren't always clear. Nevertheless, the studies proved that kava was significantly better than a placebo in reducing anxiety.

In one of the double-blind studies twenty-nine women who got 100 milligrams of kava extract three times a day were compared to another twenty-nine women who received placebos. After one month, the women getting kava experienced a significant reduction in symptoms of anxiety and somatic complaints, including headache, chest pain, heart palpitations, dizziness, and gastric irritation. (The researchers also reported that the women getting kava, standardized to contain 70 percent kavalactones, suffered no adverse side effects.) However, on the negative side, our two studies on kava for GAD have not shown benefits.

So when should you consider taking kava for your generalized anxiety? Basically, if you have mild symptoms of GAD, or if you've tried several different antianxiety medications and they are either ineffective or cause difficult or serious side effects. I have also had patients who simply preferred taking an herb to taking psychiatric medications. In such cases, I informed them of the limitations of kava and other herbal antianxiety medicines: They are less potent than psychiatric drugs, have less research to back up their efficacy, and are less likely to help people with more severe symptoms of GAD.

On the positive side, I have clearly observed benefits in a number of my GAD patients who have taken kava. They become less burdened by excessive worries, or, in other words, they're able to stop "sweating the small stuff." They tend to sleep better, and the herb is effective in relaxing the muscular tensions so common in people with GAD.

Until recently, there appeared to be almost no downside to kava, but we now have concerns about kava's potential to cause serious liver damage. These reports are being carefully reviewed by the FDA. At present, we cannot definitively conclude that kava alone caused the damage in most cases, because many of the users already had liver disease, or they were taking drugs toxic to the liver or drinking alcohol excessively. Some also took excessive doses of kava. Still, I advise caution when using kava for GAD, insomnia, or any other anxiety disorder. Don't take kava if you have liver disease, drink alcohol regularly, or take medications (e.g., Tylenol or anticholesterol "statin" drugs) that affect the liver. And don't exceed the dosage recommendations above.

Kava for Social Anxiety

Although some European studies of kava have proved the herb to be beneficial for people with anxiety disorders, we don't know how people with social phobia did specifically, so we can't make any definitive statements about recommending kava for social anxiety. Some of my patients with social anxiety, especially those with mild symptoms, have found kava helpful. The current cloud over the possibility that kava could be harmful to the liver needs to be cleared up before we can recommend the herb for a condition that responds fairly well to other approaches.

St.-John's-wort: Nature's Prozac?

I recently served as principal investigator of a large multicenter clinical trial of St.-John's-wort for major depression, the first of its kind in the United States. This trial, supported by the federal government's National Center for Complementary and Alternative Medicine (NCCAM), took place at Duke University Medical Center and twelve other medical centers. We randomly assigned 340 patients with moderately severe depression to one of three groups that were taking St.-John's-wort, Zoloft (sertraline), or placebos. Our final results failed to show that St.-John's-wort was more beneficial than sugar pills. At the same time, on our primary depression measure, patients taking Zoloft also did not benefit more than placebo patients—a disappointing outcome, but one we occasionally see in trials of prescription drugs known to be effective.

Still, it was a disappointing result for St.-John's-wort, considering that previous European trials had suggested real benefits. It appears, however, that the patients in the European trials were more mildly depressed than those in our multicenter study. We still need more research to determine whether or not St.-John's-wort is of value to any specific subgroups of depressed patients.

Our results also raise questions about using St.-John's-wort to treat anxiety. In my clinical experience, I have found that St.-John's-wort helps some anxious individuals who don't respond to kava, even though no clinical trials have proved its effectiveness for anxiety.

St.-John's-wort is believed to have a balancing effect on more neurotransmitter systems than does kava, which primarily influences receptor activity for GABA. By contrast, St.-John's-wort appears to have a mood-stabilizing influence on serotonin and dopamine systems as well as on GABA and other neurotransmitters. While its activity may be similar to that of the SSRIs, it probably has more than one active constituent—including hypericin and hyperforin, among others—with multiple actions in the brain. The herb's array of effects in different regions of the brain explains why St.-John's-wort may ultimately prove to be a more versatile and effective herbal antianxiety agent.

My guidelines for the use of St.-John's-wort are similar to those I provided above for kava: when someone has relatively mild symptoms of anxiety or, has not responded to several trials of conventional anti-anxiety medications or has benefited from these medications but paid too high a price in side effects. St.-John's-wort has far fewer and less troublesome side effects than virtually all the leading antianxiety drugs, including the SSRIs and benzodiazepines.

See Table 7.2 for key facts about St.-John's-wort, including its uses, contraindications, side effects, and dosages.

TABLE 7.2: ESSENTIAL FACTS ABOUT ST.-JOHN'S-WORT

MAIN USE	Antidepressant
OTHER REPORTED USES	Anxiolytic (antianxiety), anti–obsessive-compulsive property, hypnotic (sleep aid), seasonal affective disorder (SAD), antimicrobial, anti–inflammatory (wound healing)
WHEN NOT TO USE THIS HERB	During pregnancy, when trying to conceive, or breastfeeding; when taking therapeutic UV light treatments, while using cocaine, stimulants, cyclosporine, indinavir, digoxin, or diet aids such as phentermine. Do NOT take St.-John's-wort for a week before surgery. If taking any medications, including cancer chemotherapy, consult your physician.
POTENTIAL INTERACTIONS	MAOI and serotonergic antidepressants (e.g., SSRIs, Remeron, Effexor, Serzone, tricyclics), digoxin, cyclosporine, Coumadin, indinavir

	Reduces effect of oral contraceptives. Some cancer chemotherapy drugs, especially Camptosar (irinotecan) or Taxol, may be weakened. Consult your oncologist.
SIDE EFFECTS	Mild nausea; headache, sleepiness, dry mouth, constipation, itchiness, restlessness, dizziness, mania (in those at risk for bipolar disorder), sunburn (from increased sensitivity to sunlight).
WHEN TO EXPECT RESULTS	After two to eight weeks of use.
COMMON PREPARA-TION FORMS	Tablets, capsules, liquid, tea, tincture, ointment (topical only), and oil (topical only, particularly aromatherapy).
AVERAGE EFFECTIVE DAILY DOSAGE	600 to 1,800 mg., standardized to 0.3 percent hypericin (1.8 to 5.4 mg. hypericin), usually divided into two to three doses per day.

St.-John's-wort for General Anxiety

Though little research has specifically evaluated the efficacy of St.-John's-wort in treating generalized anxiety, it does have potential in the treatment of anxiety. Regarding the herb's effectiveness in treating mild to moderate depression, studies have produced conflicting results. As we've seen, the final results from our NIMH-funded multicenter clinical trial of St.-John's-wort for depression failed to show greater benefits than a placebo for patients with moderately severe depression. Yet the many positive European studies lead us to believe that the jury on St.-John's-wort for depression is still out.

The questions raised about using the herb to treat depression do not preclude the possibility that St.-John's-wort may be useful in treating anxiety. However, I have only found one trial that has specifically investigated its use for anxiety. In this 1985 German study, 100 patients with high scores on an anxiety scale were randomized into two groups: 50 received a pill combining St.-John's-wort with valerian; the other 50 received Valium (diazepam). After two weeks of treatment, 78 percent of the patients receiving the herbal medication experienced a significant reduction in anxiety, whereas only 54 percent of those who received Valium showed a similar benefit. This trial has a few problems: First, two weeks is a short time frame to expect such a clear-cut response to St.-John's-wort, and, second, it's impossible to tell how much the valerian, or some unique aspect of the combination, contributed to the positive results.

We need much more research on using St.-John's-wort for treating all forms of anxiety disorders, including generalized anxiety. The herb's mechanisms of action, and my clinical experience with some of my GAD patients, suggest that St.-John's-wort can relieve symptoms of worry, apprehension, irritability, insomnia, and physical tensions. I certainly have observed patients who have experienced clear-cut relief from their anxious suffering.

One of those patients was Anita, the social director of a hotel whose severe worrying began when her daughter got her driver's permit. She was gripped by an obsessive fear that something terrible would happen to her daughter, and that fear spread to other parts of her life.

While I thought Anita would respond to antianxiety medications, I felt she was a good candidate for an herbal approach, because, after a lengthy discussion about her choices, Anita expressed hesitation about the potential side effects of prescription medications. She was willing to try St.-John's-wort, she said, because she was not taking any other medicines that might interact with it. We began a trial run of St.-John's-wort. My clinical experience with the herb suggested that it could help patients who, like Anita, suffered from mild to moderate GAD. And I knew that if St.-John's-wort did not work for Anita, we could move directly to one of the more established antianxiety agents.

Within three weeks of starting St.-John's-wort, Anita noticed a change. "I really felt better," she said. "I'd been worrying about my kids for years, and it had only gotten worse. Suddenly I was headed in the right direction. The negative vibes just weren't with me all the time." She still had anxious thoughts, but they stopped flooding her consciousness and ruining her ability to focus, get work done, and have fun. "Before, dread took over every other feeling. Now, I can cope with everyday life. If I don't talk to my kids every day, I'm fine and they're fine."

St.-John's-wort doesn't work for all patients, and, like kava, it may not prove beneficial for patients with the most severe symptoms. But you might consider a trial run of St.-John's-wort if: (1) you believe you have mild generalized anxiety, meaning that it does not last long or impair your ability to function (talk to your physician or psychiatrist to confirm your opinion that your GAD is not severe); (2) you have not had sustained success with conventional antianxiety medications, because they didn't work, stopped working, or caused serious side effects. Follow the recommendations for dosage and the guidelines regarding drug interactions on pages 262–263.

I suspect that in the long run St.-John's-wort may prove as effective for treating GAD as other herbal remedies, including kava. Its actions in the brain are in some ways more comparable to those of the SSRIs than to the benzodiazepines, and we now recognize that SSRIs are more useful first-line treatments for GAD. With St.-John's-wort, be aware of drug interactions (e.g., with the anti-HIV drug indinavir, the immunosuppressant cyclosporine, the heart drug digoxin, and some anticancer drugs) and the side effect of photosensitivity. Monitor its effectiveness and try another option if St.-John's-wort does not substantially relieve your GAD symptoms after a few weeks.

St.-John's-wort for Other Types of Anxiety

We need more research of St.-John's-wort for other forms of anxiety. Recently, however, a small study of the herbal medicine for OCD revealed some promise. Leslie Taylor, M.D., and Kenneth Kobak, Ph.D., of the Dean Foundation in Middleton, Wisconsin, treated twelve OCD patients with St.-John's-wort, and used established tests for OCD and doctors' ratings to measure their symptoms over the course of three months. As a group, the patients experienced significant improvement—similar to that found in clinical trials of other established treatments. Forty-two percent were "much" or "very much" improved, 50 percent were "minimally improved," and one patient (8 percent) showed no change. It's far from hard-core proof, but it suggests that the herbal medicine may indeed benefit people with OCD. Taylor and Kobak are now embarked on a double-blind, placebo-controlled trial of St.-John's-wort in forty patients with social anxiety disorder.

I have had some limited clinical experience using this herbal medicine for social anxiety, panic, and OCD, and it appears to offer modest benefits to some patients with these conditions. In theory, St.-John's-wort would be more effective than kava for social anxiety, because of its more wide-ranging effects on neurotransmitter systems, especially serotonin. (As you'll recall, kava is more like a benzodiazepine, and its primary influence is probably on GABA.) But we need clinical studies to help guide any use of St.-John's-wort for social anxiety.

One of my panic-beset patients, Melody, had a good experience with St.-John's-wort, which I prescribed to her after a sudden and overwhelming panic attack on a vacation in upstate New York. Overcome by an apparently claustrophobic response to being in a large, crowded hotel room, Melody began to shake and sweat until she was soaking wet and disoriented. A psychiatrist prescribed BuSpar, an antianxiety drug that he thought might help combat her anxiety. Feeling better, Melody eventually stopped the BuSpar, but then her anxiety returned with a vengeance. When she came to me, she was uncomfortable with the idea of being medicated, but she was also desperate for relief.

At that time, I had already observed good results for some anxiety patients who were using herbal remedies, so I suggested that she try kava. But kava proved to be no help, so I suggested to Melody a course of St.-John's-wort. Within three weeks, Melody felt like a different person. "The negativity just left me," she says. "I really felt better. They don't go away—you never forget that feeling of dread—but it didn't take over every other feeling. It's still there, I still live with it, but I can push it to the side and function." Such cases don't prove the efficacy of St.-John's-wort in treating panic, but they offer a credible basis for further study.

Valerian and Passionflower

In his book titled *Valerian: The Genus Valeriana,* Peter J. Houghton writes about the folk and historical uses of this herbal medicine, which has sedating properties and, by some accounts, antianxiety actions.

Houghton notes that valerian extracts were extensively used during both world wars for treating the condition known at one time as "shell shock." Of course, we recognize today that shell shock refers to symptoms of PTSD, especially the startle reactions of some combat veterans. These historical reports of the use of valerian during the wars appear credible, and the use of the herb for this purpose was apparently quite widespread.

Today, valerian is primarily used as a mild sedative, though claims have been made for its potential in the treatment of PTSD and other forms of anxiety. Yet no clinical trials clarify valerian's potential as a specific antianxiety agent, though several studies support its use for treating insomnia. Interestingly, a recent English study of students showed that 1,200 milligrams per day of valerian helped lessen the rise in blood pressure and feelings of stress in a pressure situation.

The active compounds responsible for its sedating effects are the *valepotriates* and *valerenic acid*. The herb has been shown to improve sleep quality in normal subjects, and in two randomized trials it helped people with insomnia. One trial demonstrated that valerian was significantly more effective than a placebo, with 44 percent reporting "perfect sleep" and another 45 percent reporting "improved sleep." Valerian seems less likely to cause the morning grogginess people may experience after taking benzodiazepines or other sedatives at night to treat insomnia.

Based on these findings, you might try valerian if your anxiety causes insomnia, but I wouldn't recommend it for treating the other symptoms of general anxiety, PTSD, or other forms of anxiety, since there is no research support for these indications. Valerian extract standardized to contain at least 0.5 percent essential oils or valerenic acid is best, and the recommended dosage is 150 to 300 milligrams before going to bed.

Passionflower *(Passiflora incarnata)* has a long history as a folk remedy for anxiety, but until recently there was no scientific support. Recently, however, Iranian researchers published a small but intriguing study of thirty-six patients who met strict criteria for GAD. Half received a passionflower tincture (liquid extract) and a placebo pill, while the other half received a benzodiazepine, Serax (oxazepam) and placebo drops. After one month, both groups showed significant improvements in measures of anxiety, but there was no difference between the two treated groups. In other words, the passionflower extract was as effective for generalized anxiety as a potent benzodiazepine. We don't know whether either treatment would have been better than a placebo, and this isn't enough evidence for me to recommend passionflower as a primary treatment for your anxiety or insomnia. But if your general anxiety is mild, you don't wish to take kava or St.-John's-wort, or they haven't worked, you may consider a trial run of passionflower.

While I have put herbal remedies for anxiety to the test in clinical trials, and I've used them in my clinical practice, their usefulness remains uncertain, especially in light of the recent study questioning the effectiveness of St.-John's-wort for treating depression and the concerns about the safety of kava. I have also studied homeopathic remedies and found them to be mildly effective for some people with depression and anxiety, and consider them to be further down the list of possible choices.

Here's a simple rule of thumb when it comes to herbal and homeopathic treatments for anxiety: Compared with psychiatric medicines, they have fewer side effects but also less potent beneficial effects. Another rule of thumb: You should not take herbal antianxiety agents at the same time as conventional psychiatric medications without medical or psychiatric supervision, because of the risk of untoward drug interactions. We may discover exceptions to this rule, but for now, you should err on the side of caution. Lastly, it's wise not to assume that because these treatments are "natural" that they are automatically "safe."

Dietary modification, physical exercise, and herbal remedies are among the lifestyle and complementary strategies that can contribute greatly to your ability to manage anxiety. You may experience their benefits rapidly, but their biggest contribution is long term. Namely, you can achieve a quicker result with psychiatric medications than, say, dietary change, but you don't need to choose between medicines and lifestyle modification; you can thrive with both. For instance, if you pursue psychotherapy and/or medication, you may experience marked relief from your anxiety symptoms in a matter of weeks. When your anxiety levels abate, you'll find it easier to make the lifestyle changes, particularly those involving diet, because anxiety drives unhealthy eating. (Anxiety and especially depression may also blunt the motivation to exercise, too.) Suddenly, lifestyle changes that once seemed impossible seem doable.

Once you begin to eat more healthfully, cut down on coffee and alcohol, and establish a pleasurable exercise routine, you replace the *vicious cycle* of unhealthy behaviors and increasing anxiety with a *healing cycle* of healthy behaviors and an increasing calm, self-esteem, and *joie de vivre*.

8

RESILIENCE:

LIFE BEYOND ANXIETY

Myths, movies, plays, and novels can capture the emotional contours and behavioral nuances of a mental health condition as well as, or better than, any psychiatric manual. I think of *The Wizard of Oz,* the childhood classic that has attained mythic stature as a book and a movie, because its characters exemplify all of the major anxiety disorders.

The young heroine, Dorothy, having been hounded by a witchlike matron intent on taking away her little dog, then knocked unconscious by a flying object in the middle of a terrifying tornado, ends up (in the nightmare portions of her Oz fantasy) with a mild case of posttraumatic stress disorder. The Tin Man shakes and rattles at any prospect of danger, and he's phobic about water and rust. But most of all, the Cowardly Lion suffers from a laundry list of anxiety symptoms: He's an inveterate worrier who's scared of everyone and everything, including his own tail. He's phobic about other lions, tigers, bears, wizards, witches, and just about any creature with four appendages. "I haven't slept in weeks," he tells Dorothy when they first meet. "And I can't count sheep because I'm too afraid of 'em." The Lion trembles at the mere prospect of addressing the Wizard (a sign of social phobia), and when actually confronted by the great man's giant visage, he has a panic attack that causes him to faint dead on the floor. He uses superstitious ritual (as in obsessive-compulsive disorder, another anxiety syndrome) to ward off evil spirits, as when he stammers, "I do believe in spooks. I do believe in spooks. I do I do I do!" while repetitively rubbing his tail. Perhaps the storybook's representation of the less anxious ideal is the Scarecrow, whose fear of fire is understandable and who has a healthy fearlessness in the face of the Wicked Witch, her henchmen, and the flying monkeys. Along with Dorothy, the Scarecrow is never really cowed by the Wizard's frightening façade.

Regarding anxiety, positive and even sophisticated lessons shine through in the *Oz* classic. First, the quaking Cowardly Lion is no less lovable than the overtly courageous and imperturbable Scarecrow, or even the heroine, Dorothy. As you get caught in the story's spell, you find the Lion so identifiable and sympathetic in his wish for courage, and, finally, in his ability to find his inner fortitude, that you absorb a liberating message: Chronic anxiety is a real problem but not a badge of shame. The Lion's metamorphosis suggests that you can overcome anxiety, as long as you follow through with an intention to change. (The Yellow Brick Road is not a bad metaphor for taking a healing journey.) But you must get help—from friends who join you on the path, and from mental health professionals, who, in the real world, I suppose, take the place of wizards.

The other theme, brought home toward the end of the movie when the Wizard bestows symbolic gifts upon the four seekers, is that the healthy traits you've been searching for, the ones you thought were utterly lacking in your genes or personality, are right there within you, lying in wait. In the case of the Lion, beneath his dread is a latent fear-lessness, one that shows in the movie's climax, when the foursome fi-nally subdue the Wicked Witch. This is true of many people with chronic anxiety, too, though of course it takes more than a trinket from an ersatz wizard to tap into that native courage.

To some, the idea of latent courage and the capacity to change deep-set patterns is foolishly idealistic. But in my clinical work and, most surprisingly, in my research endeavors, I've found strong evidence that people beset by anxiety can become emotionally stronger and more able to handle life's vicissitudes.

GAINING GRACE UNDER PRESSURE

After completing one of my medication studies of patients with PTSD, my colleague Dr. Kathryn Connor and I recognized that our patients not only were experiencing relief from their symptoms but also were coping much more effectively with everyday stress. In short, they were becoming more *resilient*. When once upon a time stressful situations caused them relentless worry, panic, numbness, or ritual behaviors, they now handled daily hassles with far more grace under pressure. The con-cept of resilience has been studied, but I was fascinated by its relatively sudden appearance, after medical and/or psychological treatment, in people who had previously displayed so little bounce-back ability.

Recall from the last chapter the story of Lydia, who suffered from such severe panic that she quit her job and was hospitalized on several occasions. When her mother was gravely ill in Chicago she drove there from North Carolina because she was so scared of flying. For a full decade she was never properly diagnosed by a physician or psychiatrist, and the medications she did receive were unhelpful. Once she came to our program at Duke, where we gave her the correct diagnosis, the best available medication, reassurance, and self-help skills, Lydia was on an open road to recovery. The dramatic aspect of Lydia's recovery is best illustrated by her current vocation: She's a flight attendant for one of the major airlines. That's resilience.

Jason, a professor of urban affairs, was so frightened of appearing in front of others that he couldn't even attend faculty meetings. His social phobia intensified until he was paralyzed in his career development. When he lapsed into severe depression, he knew he needed help. With medication, cognitive therapy, self-awareness, and support, Jason experienced a rather astonishing turnabout. Within months, he began to function as he had prior to the onset of his anxiety. But in time—over a few years of continuing treatment—something even more dramatic occurred. Jason began to function as he *never* had in the past. His work flourished as he became virtually free of any social trepidation. Jason now gives testimony to the federal government on matters related to his academic work, and he's receiving research grants to the tune of millions of dollars. Jason's story is yet another illustration that even people with severe anxiety can develop resilience.

Isaiah, whose story I told in Chapter 2, was an executive at a software company who was terrified of presenting himself to others. "I'd do anything to sidestep presentations," said Isaiah. "My work was valued by all the higher-ups, so they offered me a promotion. But I knew I'd have to be much more visible at meetings. So I turned them down." He was only one of countless patients I've had whose social anxiety was so severe that they would rather sabotage their own success than be more out front. Isaiah joined our program's cognitive-behavioral therapy group, and he gradually learned to tolerate his anxious feelings in social circumstances. (The paradox of this approach, as I've emphasized, is that when you learn to tolerate anxiety, it finally begins to dissipate.) Role-play exercises, the warm support of the therapist and fellow group members, and take-home exercises enabled Isaiah to overcome his social anxiety in a few months' time. Recently, he accepted a major promotion, and he's thriving in his company, presenting to large groups with barely a bead of perspiration on his brow. Isaiah says that his recovery has had a positive ripple effect in every dimension of his life, including relationships with friends and family.

I've long observed patients in our clinic with every form of anxiety who, after treatment, develop resilience, one definition of which is *the activation of personal strengths in the face of fear and stress*. But the real impetus to study this phenomenon came when Kathryn Connor and I were completing a study of Prozac for patients with PTSD. In analyzing our data, it became crystal clear that a sizable number of patients not only experienced remission of their PTSD symptoms, but also showed increasing signs of resilience. Those of you with PTSD are often highly vulnerable to having your symptoms worsen under stress, so becoming more resilient means you can handle life's ups and downs without being subject to more irritability, "hot" reactions, insomnia, avoidance, numbness, depression, nightmares, or flashbacks.

PUTTING RESILIENCE TO THE TEST

Our discovery that anxious individuals actually developed resilience as a result of treatment was a new finding with important ramifications. Kathryn Connor and I therefore decided to develop a test to tap resilience. We wanted to pin down whether our patients with PTSD and other anxiety disorders would indeed become more resilient after treatment. At the time, we were both reading Alfred Lansing's spellbinding book, *Endurance: Shackleton's Incredible Voyage,* about Sir Ernest Shackleton's ill-fated 1914 expedition on the ship *Endurance.* After a full year, the ship, which had been heading to the South Atlantic, became trapped in ice in the Antarctic and was finally crushed. Shackleton and his crew stayed afloat on drifting ice packs in one of the most dangerous regions of the world, until some of them finally set sail again in one of the ship's lifeboats across several hundred miles of fierce and inhospitable ocean. The story of how Shackleton and his crew survived is a tale of unsurpassed courage. As Kathryn and I read Lansing's account, we both had the same reaction: If you wanted to know what resilience meant, you only had to read this book, since their circumstances would have driven most people to despair and helplessness. So why did they endure? We made notes on the traits exhibited by the survivors: humor, commitment, decisiveness, communication, and mastery.

We used *Endurance* and other psychological sources to create a scale that captures resilience. We have tested the scale on over 1,000 people, about 650 of which were nonpatients randomly picked from a telephone survey and the remainder, patients in our clinical program. Items included the following key elements of what makes a person resilient:

1. Being able to a adapt to changes.
2. Being able to deal with whatever comes your way.
3. Having confidence from past successes.
4. Seeing humor in the face of difficulty.
5. Feeling that you can become stronger by going through difficulty.

6. Having the capacity to bounce back after illness, injury, or other hardships.
7. Staying focused and thinking clearly under pressure.
8. Being able to handle unpleasant or painful feelings like sadness, fear, and anger.
9. Feeling in control of your life.

Since we designed this "resilience" scale, we've administered it to patients with PTSD and other anxiety disorders before and after medical treatment. We continue to find that patients make short-term gains in resilience, and we plan to use it in many of our studies to further our understanding. Why would treatment with an SSRI build resilience? Perhaps by correcting imbalances in serotonin and other brain chemicals, SSRI drugs are able to build resilience. Some studies suggest that these changes enhance the growth of new tissue in the hippocampus, a part of the brain that is centrally involved in learning and memory. I also strongly suspect that established psychotherapies for anxiety also foster resilience.

We have, in fact, recently completed a study which found that adding psychotherapy to Zoloft produced even greater resilience in PTSD sufferers than did Zoloft alone. The following six aspects of resilience were most strongly associated with protection from PTSD symptoms in the aftermath of a violent trauma. Doing the necessary work to cultivate these attributes may help you to ward off the damage that can otherwise be caused by extreme stress.

1. Being able to handle whatever comes along.
2. Tending to bounce back after stress.
3. Having confidence derived from past successes.
4. Staying focused and thinking clearly when under pressure.
5. Being able to see the humorous side of things when faced with stress.
6. Believing that coping with stress can make a person stronger.

Here, I offer you a version of our resilience test that has been adapted specifically for this book. I recommend that you take it before, during, and after you initiate your treatment program. Assess the extent of your resilience to begin with. And if your resilience level was low at the start, find out whether your healing solutions—whether they involve one or all five levels—have boosted your resilience. We continue to gather evidence that resilience is a true litmus test of whether you've become stronger in the face of fear and uncertainty.

RESILIENCE SELF-TEST

	NOT AT ALL	A LITTLE BIT	SOMEWHAT	QUITE A BIT	NEARLY ALL THE TIME
1. I can bounce back from stress or disappointment.	0	1	2	3	4
2. I can adapt to change.	0	1	2	3	4
3. When up against it, I still have a sense of humor.	0	1	2	3	4
4. I don't give up easily.	0	1	2	3	4
5. I can deal with negative feelings like anger, sadness, and disappointment.	0	1	2	3	4

	NOT AT ALL	A LITTLE BIT	SOMEWHAT	QUITE A BIT	NEARLY ALL THE TIME
6. I feel my life has a purpose, even when times are bad.	0	1	2	3	4

SCORING KEY: 0–6   Very fragile
7–12   Somewhat fragile
13–18   Somewhat resilient
19–24   Very resilient

RESILIENCE AND SPIRITUALITY: IS THERE A LINK?

Kathryn Connor, Li Ching Lee, and I recently completed a community survey of 1,200 individuals, 648 of whom were survivors of violent trauma. We wanted to find out if resilience or other factors, including spiritual beliefs, and emotions such as anger had an influence on their likelihood to develop PTSD or other health problems. As we theorized, the trauma survivors who demonstrated high resilience (as measured by our resilience test) were significantly less likely to suffer from serious physical or mental health problems. Moreover, if they did have PTSD, it was less severe. We also found that higher levels of anger predicted more health problems and a greater likelihood of PTSD.

One key finding surprised and perplexed us: People with stronger spiritual beliefs were *more* likely to suffer physical and mental health conditions, including more severe PTSD.

Does this mean that spiritual beliefs make you more *vulnerable* to stress and trauma? We're not certain, but our finding was not at all consistent with the literature on spirituality and health. A wealth of data suggests that spiritual practice and religious participation *lessen* your risk of physical *and* mental ill health. One possible explanation: People who've experienced trauma that they have yet to resolve through psychological or medical treatment are simply more prone to turn to religion or spirituality to cope with their pain and their symptoms.

If that theory proves true, then our message is coherent: While spiritual and religious practices can contribute to healing PTSD and other forms of anxiety, it's not realistic to view spirituality as a panacea. If you have chronic anxiety, you are best served by medical treatment, therapy, or both to resolve your symptoms. Then your pursuit of spiritual practice—including prayer—is only a boon to your healing process.

My instincts as a doctor tell me that spirituality and religious belief have been enormously comforting to my anxiety patients, often bolstering their ability to recover and to bounce back from tough challenges as they reenter the stream of life with a great deal more confidence. My almost three decades of experience with anxiety patients has convinced me that integrating spirituality or the pursuit of meaning into the healing process can be of value, along with medical or psychological treatments and self-care skills. Of course, spiritual pursuits are not for everyone, and you have every opportunity to get well without bringing this dimension into your healing program.

RESILIENCE AND RISK:
FACING DOWN YOUR FEARS

In our post-9/11, economically uncertain times, in which the stock market rises and tumbles precipitously, wars against terror continue to be waged, and the threat of terrorism at home seems omnipresent, a generalized fear blankets our daily lives, one that unnerves even those of us with high levels of resilience. For those of us already vulnerable to anxiety when stressed, this blanket of fear can be smothering. The everyday stresses of work, finances, and family life are difficult enough to withstand; when the broader world feels decidedly unsafe, our need for resilience—emotional or even spiritual fortitude in the face of fear—becomes even more pressing.

Rachel Yehuda, a psychologist at Mt. Sinai Hospital and the Bronx V.A. Hospital in New York, is an expert in posttraumatic stress who's written clearly about what it takes to cope with stress in a manner that protects us from psychological and physical disorders. She recently presented a "risk and resilience" model that emphasized these points:

· Our initial response to fear is biological, but it is also influenced by our subjective interpretation of events, which depends on our own personal psychological history. We can change how we view the world, which in turn will influence our biology.
· Recovering from trauma involves confronting our own human vulnerability (and sometimes that of others) in a way that promotes learning and resilience.
· When we're prone to chronic anxiety, our body's biological responses (e.g., a hyped-up sympathetic nervous system, neurotransmitter imbalances, etc.) may perpetuate states of fear.
· The normal, healthy path is emotional and biological recovery from stress or trauma, and this path is strengthened when we have good support systems and the willingness to use them.
· Medical and psychological treatments can facilitate our recovery from stress or trauma.

Many of Dr. Yehuda's ideas, recently presented in a paper she wrote for the *New England Journal of Medicine,* are consistent with our own work on resilience. Even those of you who are prone to severe anxiety may build your own resilience. You can do so not only with medication, which to some extent resets your biological response to fear, but also by altering your worldview. Through what lens do you view events in your life and in the world? If you've always worn dark glasses, do you have to keep them on forever? Can you recognize that the most difficult times in your own life and in the broader world won't persist indefinitely?

Every stress or trauma is, to borrow Dr. Yehuda's phrase, a confrontation with human vulnerability. Do you have to be overwhelmed by an awareness of your vulnerability and that of others? Or can you learn from hard experiences, both personal and global, to accept your vulnerability as part of your intrinsic human condition and allow that awareness to fortify rather than weaken yourself?

On some level, we all intuitively recognize that harsh difficulties can make us more resilient, but how can we encourage the development of our hidden strengths? As a psychiatrist, this fundamental question has led me to investigate not only the nature of mental disorders but also the biology and psychology of mental health. Resilience characterizes mental health in the face of fear, and it's my job to help people with anxiety become more resilient. I believe that the five solutions presented in *The Anxiety Book* can all promote resilience, just as we now know that medications can help build this capacity. Based on the whole body of literature on cognitive-behavioral therapy, I'm confident that changing our fearful beliefs, exposure therapy, and serenity skills can contribute powerfully to our personal strengths under pressure.

Thus, the key elements of resilience building included among the five healing solutions are: (1) consciously removing the dark glasses through which we view the world and replacing them not with rose-colored lenses but with clear, transparent ones that reveal our world as a place of manageable risk, just as was described by Winston Churchill's "disillusioned eye" (2) reversing patterns of avoidance of the people, places, objects, or experiences that frighten us, "exposing" ourselves to these realities so that we grasp, once and for all, that they are not the threats we believed them to be; (3) actively engaging our religious or spiritual resources, if we are so inclined; (4) seeking and accepting the support we need from our network of family and friends; and (5) seeking and accepting professional help to treat our anxiety symptoms, which may include (6) medications and/or therapy to help reset our off-kilter biological responses to stress, the ones that underlie and perpetuate our fearfulness.

I believe that our findings on resilience have vital ramifications. If you've been living with unhealthy anxiety for years or decades, you may feel that you're living a partial life. When you view every stress as a threat rather than a challenge, it's not only hard to solve problems, it's hard to get through the day. When fear torments your waking hours, you're not only less effective at work but also less able to experience pleasure in your relationships, creative pursuits, and leisure time. Your chronic anxiety probably started when you were a child, adolescent, or young adult. And your symptoms—whether panic, worry, phobias, social anxiety, obsessions, or PTSD—may have been tormenting you ever since. Chronic anxiety blocks your potential at every turn, reducing your ability to succeed, take creative risks, and grow in your relationships. When you finally treat your condition, especially with the integrated approach I've presented here, you get more than just "relief." You get a second chance for a fully productive, emotionally rich, and fulfilling life.

ENDNOTES

3   Statistics on prevalence of anxiety disorders:
National Institute of Mental Health. The Numbers Count; Mental
Disorders in America. NIMH website: http://www.nimh.nih.gov/
publicat/numbers.cfm. 2002.
Statistics on women, men, and anxiety:
Jans, L, Stoddard, S. (1999) *Chartbook on Women and Disability in the
United States.* An InfoUse Report. Washington, D.C.: U.S. National
Institute on Disability and Rehabilitation Research.

3   More people visit doctors for anxiety than for colds:
Barlow, DH. 1988 Anxiety and its disorders. New York: Guilford.

4   A December 2000 paper on anxiety from the 1950s to the 1990s:
Twenge, JM. The age of anxiety? Birth cohort change in anxiety
and neuroticism, 1952–1993. J Pers Soc Psychol. 2000 Dec;79(6):
1007–21.

11 Paper on rise in anxiety:
Twenge, JM. The age of anxiety? Birth cohort change in anxiety
and neuroticism, 1952–1993. J Pers Soc Psychol. 2000 Dec;79(6):
1007–21.

12 Mark Schuster and colleagues on stress and 9/11:
Schuster, MA, Stein, BD, Jaycox, L, et al. A national survey of stress
reactions after the September 11, 2001, terrorist attacks. N Engl J
Med. 2001 Nov 15;345(20):1507–12.

18 Growing body of evidence on spirituality and health:
Ellison, CG, Levin, JS. The religion-health connection: evidence,
theory, and future directions. Health Educ Behav. 1998 Dec;25(6):
700–20.

19   Recent multicenter trial of St.-John's-wort for depression:
      Hypericum Depression Study Group. Effect on Hypericum perfo-
      ratum (St John's wort) in major depressive disorder: a randomized
      controlled trial. JAMA. 2002 Apr 10;287(14):1807–14.

28   Lifetime prevalence of GAD and related statistics:
      Wittchen, HU, Zhao, S, Kessler, RC, Eaton, WW. DSM-III-R
      generalized anxiety disorder in the National Comorbidity Survey.
      Arch Gen Psychiatry. 1994 May;51(5):355–64.
      National Institute of Mental Health. The Numbers Count; Mental
      Disorders in America. NIMH website: http://www.nimh.nih.gov/
      publicat/numbers.cfm. 2002.

28   Rates of depression and other psychiatric disorders in people with
      GAD:
      Sanderson, WC, DiNardo, PA, Rapee, RM, Barlow, DH. Syn-
      drome comorbidity in patients diagnosed with a DSM-III-R anxi-
      ety disorder. J Abnorm Psychol. 1990 Aug;99(3):308–12.
      Kaufman, J, Charney, D. Comorbidity of mood and anxiety disor-
      ders. Depress Anxiety. 2000; 12 Suppl 1:69–76.

31   Community sample of stressful life events and GAD:
      Newman, SC, Bland, RC. Life events and the 1-year prevalence of
      major depressive episode, generalized anxiety disorder, and panic
      disorder in a community sample. Compr Psychiatry. 1994 Jan-Feb;
      35(1):76–82.
      A National Institute of Mental Health study of stressful life events
      and GAD:
      Newman, SC, Bland, RC. Stressful life events and the onset of a
      generalized anxiety syndrome. Am J Psychiatry. 1987 Sep;144(9):
      1178–83.
      One recent study of female twins . . . and genetic risks of GAD:
      Kendler, KS, Neale, MC, Kessler, RC, Heath, AC, Eaves, LJ. Gen-
      eralized anxiety disorder in women. A population-based twin
      study. Arch Gen Psychiatry 1992 Apr;49(4):267–72.

32   The biology of GAD, an overview:
      Hidalgo, RB, Davidson, JR. Generalized anxiety disorder. An impor-
      tant clinical concern. Med Clin North Am. 2001 May;85(3):691–710.

38   The majority of people with social phobia never get treated:
     Rapee, RM. Descriptive psychopathology of social phobia. In:
     Heimberg, RG, Liebowitz, MR, Hope, DA, Schneier, FR (Eds.),
     Social phobia: Diagnosis, assessment, and treatment (pp.41–66).
     1995. New York: Guilford Press.
     Community sample of 13,000, over half with social phobia:
     Schneier, FR, Johnson, J, Hornig, CD, Liebowitz, MR, Weissman,
     MM. Social phobia. Comorbidity and morbidity in an epidemio-
     logic sample. Arch Gen Psychiatry. 1992 Apr;49(4):282–8.

39   In his intriguing book, Isaac Marks looks to evolutionary theory:
     Marks, IM. Fears, phobias, and rituals: Panic, anxiety, and their dis-
     orders. 1987. Oxford: Oxford University Press.

40   Psychiatrist Murray Stein . . . found strong associations between
     abuse and social anxiety:
     Stein, MB, Walker, JR, Anderson, G, Hazen, AL, Ross, CA, El-
     dridge, G, Forde, DR. Childhood physical and sexual abuse in pa-
     tients with anxiety disorders and in a community sample. Am J
     Psychiatry. 1996 Feb;153(2):275–7.
     Sociologist W. J. Magee found that sexual abuse is factor in . . . so-
     cial phobia:
     Effects of negative life experiences on phobia onset. Soc Psychiatry
     Psychiatr Epidemiol. 1999 Jul;34(7):343–51.

41   Gordon Parker compared the self-reports of patients with social
     phobia to controls:
     Parker, G. Reported parental characteristics of agoraphobics and
     social phobics. Br J Psychiatry. 1979 Dec;135:555–60.
     One Dutch reviewer found patterns of parenting among social
     phobics:
     Arrindell, WA, Emmelkamp, PM, Monsma, A, Brilman, E. The
     role of perceived parental rearing practices in the aetiology of
     phobic disorders: a controlled study. Br J Psychiatry. 1983 Aug;143:
     183–7.
     Generalized social anxiety 10 times more common using close rel-
     atives of social phobics:
     Stein, MB, Chartier, MJ, Hazen, AL, Kozak, MV, Tancer, ME,

Lander, S, Furer, P, Chubaty, D, Walker, JR. A direct-interview family study of generalized social phobia. Am J Psychiatry. 1998 Jan;155(1):90–7.

42   Research from Medical College of Virginia on over 2,000 twins and genetic risks of social phobia:
Kendler, KS, Neale, MC, Kessler, RC, Heath, AC, Eaves, LJ. Generalized anxiety disorder in women. A population-based twin study. Arch Gen Psychiatry. 1992 Apr;49(4):267–72.

Patients with social anxiety have hypersensitive receptors for serotonin:
Nutt, DJ, Bell, CJ, Malizia, AL. Brain mechanisms of social anxiety disorder. J Clin Psychiatry. 1998;59 Suppl 17:4–11.

People with SAD have receptors for dopamine that don't bind sufficiently:
Schneier, FR, Liebowitz, MR, Abi-Dargham, A, Zea-Ponce, Y, Lin, SH, Laruelle, M. Low dopamine D(2) receptor binding potential in social phobia. Am J Psychiatry. 2000 Mar;157(3):457–9.

Nicholas Potts and myself ran MRI scans of the brains of social phobia patients:
Potts, NL, Davidson, JR, Krishnan, KR, Doraiswamy, PM. Magnetic resonance imaging in social phobia. Psychiatry Res. 1994 Apr;52(1):35–42.

48   2.4 million Americans suffer from panic disorder:
National Institute of Mental Health. The Numbers Count; Mental Disorders in America. NIMH website: http://www.nimh.nih.gov/publicat/numbers.cfm. 2002

Lifetime prevalence of 1.3% to 3.8%; age of onset in early 20s:
Eaton, WW, Dryman, A, Weissman, M. 1991. Panic and phobia. In: Robins, LN & Roger, DA (Eds.) *Psychiatric disorders in America.* (pp. 155–179). New York: Free Press.

58   13 million Americans suffer from PTSD; an estimated 70% of Americans experienced trauma; 20% of them develop PTSD:
Statistics on PTSD Alliance website: http://www.ptsdalliance.org/about_what.html

5 percent of men and 10 percent of women:

National Center for PTSD: Epidemiological Facts about PTSD, 2002. URL: http://www.ncptsd.org/facts/general/fs_epidemiological. html

62   PTSD is associated with a strikingly high prevalence of depression, etc.:
Kessler, RC, Sonnega, A, Bromet, E, Hughes, M, Nelson, CB. Posttraumatic stress disorder in the National Comorbidity Survey. Arch Gen Psychiatry. 1995 Dec;52(12):1048–60.

63   Telephone survey of 560 adults in the U.S. within week of 9/11:
Schuster, MA, Stein, BD, Jaycox, L, et al. A national survey of stress reactions after the September 11,2001, terrorist attacks. N Engl J Med. 2001 Nov 15;345(20):1507–12.
A survey of 1,008 Manhattan residents after 9/11 in New England Journal of Medicine:
Galea, S, Ahern, J, Resnick, H, Kilpatrick, D, Bucuvalas, M, Gold, J, Vlahov, D. Psychological sequelae of the September 11 terrorist attacks in New York City. N Engl J Med. 2002 Mar 28;346(13): 982–7.
Survey of 8,300 of New York City's schoolchildren after 9/11 reported in:
Goodnough A. Post-9/11 pain found to linger in young minds. New York Times, May 2, 2002.

65   Footnote on 65% rate of PTSD among men who were raped:
Kessler, RC, Sonnega, A, Bromet, E, Hughes, M, Nelson, CB. Posttraumatic stress disorder in the National Comorbidity Survey. Arch Gen Psychiatry. 1995 Dec;52(12):1048–60.

74   Statistics on OCD prevalence:
National Institute of Mental Health. The Numbers Count; Mental Disorders in America. NIMH website: http://www.nimh.nih.gov/ publicat/numbers.cfm. 2002.

76   Study of OCD patients with significantly more childhood trauma:
Lochner, C, du Toit, PL, Zungu-Dirwayi, N, Marais, A, van Kradenburg, J, Seedat, S, Niehaus, DJ, Stein, DJ. Childhood trauma in obsessive-compulsive disorder, trichotillomania, and controls. Depress Anxiety. 2002;15(2):66–8.

77   Among 65 percent of identical twins in which one has OCD, so
      will the other:
      Steketee, GS. 1993. Treatment of obsessive-compulsive disorder.
      New York: Guilford Press.
77   Brain imaging studies and the portions of the brain involved in
      OCD:
      Micallef, J, Blin, O. Neurobiology and clinical pharmacology of
      obsessive-compulsive disorder. Clin Neuropharmacol. 2001 Jul-
      Aug;24(4):191–207.
84   "Rational response" is based on CBT techniques, drawn from
      work of Aaron Beck and David Burns:
      Beck, AT. 1979. Cognitive Therapy and the Emotional Disorders.
      New York: New American Library.
      Burns, D. 1980. Feeling Good: The New Mood Therapy. New
      York: William Morrow & Co.
100   One recent analysis of 42 clinical trials of CBT for social anxiety:
      Taylor, S. Meta-analysis of cognitive-behavioral treatments for so-
      cial phobia. J Behav Ther Exp Psychiatry. 1996 Mar; 27(1): 1–9.
106   Robert Leahy and Stephen Holland have provided a list of false as-
      sumptions among people with social phobia:
      Leahy, RL, Holland, SJ. Treatment plans and interventions for de-
      pression and anxiety disorders. 2000. New York: Guilford Press.
127   Edna Foa's catalogue of the errors apparent in obsessive thinking:
      Foa, EB and Kozak, MJ. Emotional processing: Theory, research,
      and clinical implications for anxiety disorders. In: Safran, JD and
      Greenberg, LS (Eds.) Emotion, psychotherapy, and change (pp. 21–
      49). 1991. New York: Guilford Press.
162   Combination of exposure and response prevention has highest re-
      sponse rates for OCD:
      Foa, EB and Kozac, MJ. Psychological treatment for obsessive-
      compulsive disorder. In: Mavissakalaian R & Prien RG (Eds.)
      Long-term treatments of anxiety disorders (pp. 285–309). 1997.
      Washington, DC: American Psychiatric Press.
171   The late Dr. David Larson and research on religion or spirituality
      and mental health:

McCullough, ME and Larson, DB. Frontiers of research in religion and mental health. In: Koenig, HG, ed. Handbook of Religion and Mental Health. San Diego: Academic Press. 1998: 95–107.

177   Psychologists Carr and Lehrer relate stories . . . of PMR for anxiety: Lehrer, P and Carr, R. Muscle Relaxation and Breathing Technique. In: Roth WT (Ed.) Treating Anxiety Disorders. 1996. San Francisco: Jossey-Bass.

185   Herbert Benson, M.D., developer of the relaxation response:
Benson, H. The Relaxation Response. 1990. New York: Avon Books.

194   My colleague Reid Wilson's breathing exercises:
Wilson, RR. Don't Panic: Taking Control of Anxiety Attacks. 1996. New York: HarperCollins.

196   Jon Kabat-Zinn . . . understood a study of mindfulness for anxiety and panic:
Kabat-Zinn, J, Massion, AO, Kristeller, J. Effectiveness of a meditation-based stress reduction program in the treatment of anxiety disorders. Am J Psychiatry. 1992 Jul;149(7):936–43.

197   Jon Kabat-Zinn on results of his study:
Kabat-Zinn, J. Full Catastrophe Living. 1990. New York: Delta Books.

199   Researchers at the University of Pennsylvania on studies of stress inoculation and exposure for PTSD:
Hembree, EA, and Foa, FB. Posttraumatic stress disorder: psychological factors and psychosocial interventions. J Clin Psychiatry. 2000;61 Suppl. 7:33–9. Review.

200   James Gordon and his study of mind-body therapy for trauma in Kosovo:
See: www.cmbm.org/international/wowdescription.html

203   Marsha Linehan, M.D., who developed dialectical behavior therapy (DBT):
Lineham, M. Cognitive-behavioral treatment of borderline personality disorder. 1993. New York: Guilford Press.

206   Neurobiologists . . . on the passage of molecular information in the synapse . . . and the basic currency of information in the brain carried by neurotransmitters. For a complete discussion of the neu-

robiology of anxiety and depression, and the psychopharmacology underpinning medical therapies for these conditions, see:

Stahl, SM. Essential Psychopharmacology: Neuroscientific Basis and Practical Applications, 2nd Edition. 2000. Cambridge: Cambridge University Press.

227 Three studies of Paxil (paroxetine) for social anxiety.

Allgulander, C. Paroxetine in social anxiety disorder: a randomized placebo-controlled study. Acta Psychiatr Scand. 1999 Sep;100(3): 193–8.

Baldwin, D, Bobes, J, Stein, DJ, Scharwachter, I, Faure, M. Paroxetine in social phobia/social anxiety disorder. Randomised, double-blind, placebo-controlled study. Paroxetine Study Group. Br J Psychiatry. 1999 Aug;175:120–6.

Stein, MB, Liebowitz, MR, Lydiard, RB, Pitts, CD, Bushnell, W, Gergel, I. Paroxetine treatment of generalized social phobia (social anxiety disorder): a randomized controlled trial. JAMA. 1998 Aug 26;280(8):708–13.

227 Small Italian study of Effexor-XR for social anxiety disorder:

Altamura, AC, Pioli, R, Vitto, M, Mannu, P. Venlafaxine in social phobia: a study in selective serotonin reuptake inhibitor non-responders. Int Clin Psychopharmacol. 1999 Jul;14(4):239–45.

228 My colleagues and I conducted a placebo-controlled clinical trial of Klonopin for social anxiety:

Davidson, JR, Potts, N, Richichi, E, Krishnan, R, Ford, SM, Smith, R, Wilson, WH. Treatment of social phobia with clonazepam and placebo. J Clin Psychopharmacol. 1993 Dec;13(6): 423–8.

Other benzodiazepines have proved beneficial for SAD:

Hidalgo, RB, Barnett, SD, Davidson, JR. Social anxiety disorder in review: two decades of progress. Int J Neuropsychopharmacol. 2001 Sep;4(3):279–98.

237 Our team's multicenter placebo-controlled clinical trial of Zoloft (sertraline) for PTSD:

Davidson, JR, Rothbaum, BO, van der Kolk, BA, Sikes, CR, Farfel, GM. Multicenter, double-blind comparison of sertraline and placebo in the treatment of posttraumatic stress disorder. Arch Gen Psychiatry. 2001 May;58(5):485–92.

237   My colleague Kathryn Connor led study of Prozac for PTSD: Connor, KM, Sutherland, SM, Tupler, LA, Malik, ML, Davidson, JR. Fluoxetine in posttraumatic stress disorder. Randomised, double-blind study. Br J Psychiatry. 1999 Jul;175:17–22.

238   When SSRIs don't work sufficiently, it makes sense to shift strategies. For detailed discussion of alternative and combination pharmacotherapy strategies for PTSD, see the book I wrote with Rachel Yehuda, Ph.D.:
Yehuda, R, Davidson, J. Clinician's Manual on Posttraumatic Stress Disorder. 2000. Science Press Ltd.

242   A major advance . . . occurred when studies showed that Anafranil (clomipramine) was effective for OCD:
Hewlett, WA, Vinogradov, S, Agras, WS. Clonazepam treatment of obsessions and compulsions. J Clin Psychiatry. 1990 Apr;51(4): 158–61.

249   1999 paper that omega-3 supplementation can stabilize mood:
Fugh-Berman, A, Cott, JM. Dietary supplements and natural products as psychotherapeutic agents. Psychosom Med. 1999 Sep-Oct; 61(5):712–28.

252   Scott Paluska of the Rex Sports Medicine Institute on exercise and improvement in anxiety:
Paluska, SA, Schwenk, TL. Physical activity and mental health: current concepts. Sports Med. 2000 Mar;29(3):167–80.

252   1997 German study on exercise avoidance in patients with panic:
Broocks, A, Meyer, TF, Bandelow, B, George, A, Bartmann, U, Ruther, E, Hillmer-Vogel, U. Exercise avoidance and impaired endurance capacity in patients with panic disorder. Neuropsychobiology. 1997;36(4):182–7.

256   Three placebo-controlled and two head-to-head comparison studies of kava for anxiety:
Warnecke, G. [Psychosomatic dysfunctions in the female climacteric. Clinical effectiveness and tolerance of Kava Extract WS 1490]. Fortschr Med. 1991 Feb 10;109(4):119–22.

Kinzler, E, Kromer, J, Lehmann, E. [Effect of a special kava extract in patients with anxiety-, tension-, and excitation states of non-psychotic genesis. Double blind study with placebos over 4 weeks] [No authors listed] [Drug therapy of panic disorders. Kava-specific extract WS 1490 compared to benzodiazepines] Nervenarzt. 1994 Jan;65(1 Suppl):1–4.

Volz, HP, Kieser, M. Kava-kava extract WS 1490 versus placebo in anxiety disorders—a randomized placebo-controlled 25-week outpatient trial. Pharmacopsychiatry. 1997 Jan;30(1):1–5.

Woelk, H, Kapoula, S, Lehrl, S, et al. Treatment of patients suffering from anxiety N double-blind study: Kava special extract versus benzodiazepines. Ztschr Allgmeinmed 1993;69:271–277.

256   Two recently completed studies of Kava for GAD by our research group: Connor, KM, Davidson, JR. A placebo-controlled study of Kava kava in generalized anxiety disorder. Int Clin Psychopharmacol. 2002 Jul;17(4):185–8.

Davidson JR. In press.

259   One of the double-blind studies compared 29 women on kava to another 29 on placebos:
Kinzler, E, Kromer, J, Lehmann, E. [Effect of a special kava extract in patients with anxiety-, tension-, and excitation states of non-psychotic genesis. Double blind study with placebos over 4 weeks]

260   Our multicenter clinical trial of St.-John's-wort for depression:
Hypericum Depression Study Group. Effect of Hypericum perforatum (St John's wort) in major depressive disorder: a randomized controlled trial. JAMA. 2002 Apr 10;287(14):1807–14.

263   The final results from our multicenter NIMH-funded trial of St.-John's-wort:
Hypericum Depression Study Group. Effect of Hypericum perforatum (St John's wort) in major depressive disorder: a randomized controlled trial. JAMA. 2002. Apr 10;287(14):1807–14.

264   German study of 100 anxiety patients on St.-John's-wort and valerian:
Panijel M. Die behandlung mittelschwerer angstzustande. Therapiewoche 1985;41:4659–68.

266   Leslie Taylor and Kenneth Kobak study of St.-John's-wort for OCD:

Taylor, LH, Kobak, KA. An open-label trial of St. John's Wort (Hypericum perforatum) in obsessive-compulsive disorder. J Clin Psychiatry. 2000 Aug;61(8):575–8.

267   Book on valerian by Peter J. Houghton:

Houghton, PJ. Valerian: The Genus Valeriana. 1997. Harwood Academic Publishers.

275   Study by Connor of Prozac for PTSD:

Connor, KM, Sutherland, SM, Tupler, LA, Malik, ML, Davidson, JR. Fluoxetine in posttraumatic stress disorder. Randomised, double-blind study. Br J Psychiatry. 1999 Jul;175:17–22.

276   Alfred Lansing's spellbinding book:

Lansing, A. Endurance: Shackleton's Incredible Voyage. 1994. Adventure Library Press.

279   Kathryn Connor, et al., on community survey of PTSD and resilience factors:

Connor, KM, Li Ching, L, Davidson, JR. (Unpublished data.)

281   Rachel Yehuda has written about what it takes to cope with stress. Drawn in part from:

Yehuda, R. Posttraumatic stress disorder. N Engl J Med. 2002 Jan 10;346(2):108–14.

RESOURCE GUIDE
FOR ANXIETY DISORDERS

AMERICAN PSYCHIATRIC ASSOCIATION
1400 K Street, N.W.
Washington, DC 20005
202-682-6000
www.psych.org

To request written materials:

Call APA fastFAX (APA's toll-free fax-on-demand service) for a menu
of items available free by fax: 1-888-267-5400, or write:

AMERICAN PSYCHOLOGICAL ASSOCIATION
750 First Street, N.E.
Washington, DC 20002-4242
Telephone: 800-374-2721; 202-336-5510
www.apa.org

AMERICAN GROUP PSYCHOTHERAPY ASSOCIATION
25 East 21st Street, 6th Floor
New York, NY 10010
212-477-2677; 877-668-2472
info@agpa.org; http://www.groupsinc.org

ANXIETY DISORDERS ASSOCIATION OF AMERICA, INC.
8730 Georgia Avenue, Suite 600
Silver Spring, MD 20910

240-485-1001
www.adaa.org

INTERNATIONAL SOCIETY FOR TRAUMATIC STRESS STUDIES
60 Revere Drive, Suite 500
Northbrook, IL 60062
847-480-9028
www.istss.org

NATIONAL ASSOCIATION OF COGNITIVE-BEHAVIORAL THERAPISTS
102 Gilson Avenue
Weirton, WV 26062
Toll Free: 1-800-853-1135
Outside USA: 1-304-723-3982
General Information: nacbt@nacbt.org
http://www.nacbt.org (includes referral database)

NATIONAL CENTER FOR PTSD
VA Medical Center (116D)
White River Junction, VT 05009
802-296-5132
www.dartmouth.edu/dms/ptsd

NATIONAL INSTITUTE OF MENTAL HEALTH PUBLIC INQUIRIES
6001 Executive Blvd., Room 8184 MSC 9663
Bethesda, MD 20892-9663
301-443-4513
FACTS ON DEMAND: 301-443-5158
www.nimh.nih.gov

NATIONAL INSTITUTE OF MENTAL HEALTH
Website with information for public: http://www.nimh.nih.gov/
publicat/index.cfm

NATIONAL MENTAL HEALTH ASSOCIATION
2001 N. Beauregard Street, 12th Floor
Alexandria, VA 22311
Phone 703-684-7722
Fax 703-684-5968
Mental Health Resource Center 800-969-NMHA
TTY Line 800-433-5959

U.S. VETERANS ADMINISTRATION
Mental Health and Behavioral Sciences Services
810 Vermont Avenue, N.W., Room 990
Washington, DC 20410

202-273-8431

ONLINE RESOURCES

General

NIMH Anxiety Disorder Page: http://www.nimh.nih.gov/anxiety/anxietymenu.cfm

The Anxiety Panic Internet Resources: http://www.algy.com/anxiety

Anxiety Disorder Treatment and Recovery: http://www.anxietyrecovery.com

The Anxiety Community: http://www.anxietyhelp.com

Panic/Anxiety Disorder on About.Com: http://panicdisorder.about.com

Anxiety Disorders Caregiver Site: http://www.pacificcoast.net/~kstrong

Anxiety Support Groups List: http://groups.yahoo.com/search?query=anxiety

Psych Central—Dr. Grohol's Mental Health Page: http://www.grohol.com

Panic Disorder

Panic Disorder: http://panicanxiety.cjb.net

The Panic Center: http://panicanxiety.cjb.net

Agoraphobia in Australia: http://www.agoraphobiaaustralia.org

Panic Disorder Support Group List: http://groups.yahoo.com/search?query=panic

SUPPORT4PANIC: http://www.support4panic.com

Generalized Anxiety Disorder

The Anxiety Panic Internet Resources: http://www.algy.com/anxiety

GAD Generalized Anxiety Support Chat: http://www.support4hope.com/gad

NIMH GAD Information (HealthyPlace.Com):
www.healthyplace.com/Communities/Anxiety/nimh/gad

National Mental Health Association GAD Information:
http://www.nmha.org/pbedu/anxiety/gad.cfm

Posttraumatic Stress Disorder

National Center for PTSD: http://www.ncptsd.org

Posttraumatic Stress Resources: http://www.long-beach.va.gov/ptsd/stress.html

RapeRecovery.com: http://www.RapeRecovery.com

Gift From Within–PTSD Resources: http://www.giftfromwithin.org

Trauma Information Pages: http://www.trauma-pages.com

PTSD Alliance: http://www.ptsdalliance.org/home2.html

Obsessive-Compulsive Disorder

Obsessive-Compulsive Foundation: http://www.ocfoundation.org

OC and Spectrum Disorders Association: http://www.ocdhelp.org

Social Anxiety Disorder

Social Phobia/Social Anxiety Association: http://www.socialphobia.org

Social Anxiety Support: www.socialanxietysupport.com

Social Anxiety Network: http://www.social-anxiety-network.com

Social Anxiety Support: www.socialanxietysupport.com

The Social Anxiety Institute: http://www.socialanxietyinstitute.org

INDEX

Index

Index

Index

JONATHAN DAVIDSON, M.D., is recognized as one of the country's leading experts on anxiety, traumatic stress, and complementary/alternative medicines. Dr. Davidson is professor of psychiatry and director of the Anxiety and Traumatic Stress Program at Duke University Medical Center. His research includes studies on risk factors, herbal medicine, conventional pharmacology, and treatment outcomes for a wide range of depressive and anxiety disorders, with special emphasis on social phobias and posttraumatic stress disorder. He is a Fellow of the American Psychiatric Association and the American College of Neuropsychopharmacology. Dr. Davidson provides care for patients and their families, lectures internationally and educates health professionals on depression, anxiety, trauma, and complementary/alternative medicines.

HENRY DREHER is a veteran health writer specializing in mind-body medicine, psychology, and integrative medicine. He has authored numerous articles and books, including *Your Defense Against Cancer, The Immune Power Personality* and the upcoming *Mind-Body Unity.*